Theatre Bedside Book

Also by J. C. Trewin

THEATRE HISTORY AND CRITICISM

The Shakespeare Memorial Theatre (with M. C. Day)—The English Theatre—We'll Hear a Play—The Theatre since 1900—A Play Tonight—The Stratford Festival (with T. C. Kemp)—Dramatists of Today—Drama 1945–1950—Mr Macready: A Nineteenth-Century Tragedian and his Theatre—The Night Has Been Unruly—Benson and the Bensonians—The Gay Twenties (illustrated by R. Mander and J. Mitchenson)—The Turbulent Thirties (with Mander & Mitchenson)—The Birmingham Repertory Theatre: 1913–1963—Shakespeare on the English Stage: 1900–1964—The Journal of William Charles Macready (Editor)—The Drama Bedside Book (with H. F. Rubinstein)—Drama in Britain 1951–1965—The Pomping Folk: in the Nineteenth-Century Theatre—Robert Donat: A Biography—Shakespeare's Plays Today (with Arthur Colby Sprague)—Peter Brook: A Biography

THEATRE MONOGRAPHS

Edith Evans—Sybil Thorndike—Paul Scofield—Alec Clunes—John Neville

AUTOBIOGRAPHY AND BELLES-LETTRES

Up from The Lizard—Down to The Lion—London–Bodmin (with H. J. Willmott)—Lamb's Tales (completed: Nonesuch edition)

HISTORY AND TOPOGRAPHY

Printer to the House (with E. M. King)—The Story of Stratford-upon-Avon—The Story of Bath—Portrait of the Shakespeare Country—Portrait of Plymouth

PLAYS AND VERSE

A Sword for a Prince: Plays for a Young Company—Plays of the Year (43 volumes: Editor)—I Call My Name—Down South—Long Ago (verse pamphlets)

ECCENTRICITY

An Evening at the Larches (with Harry Hearson, Ronald Searle)

EDITED

Sean (Eileen O'Casey)—A Year in the Country (Beach Thomas)—Sir Walter Scott: A Prose Anthology—The Critic (Sheridan)—The West Country Book—Footprints of Former Men in Far Cornwall (Hawker)—Theatre Programme

Theatre Bedside Book

An Anthology of the Stage

Edited and introduced by

J. C. Trewin

Imogen What hour is it?
Lady Almost midnight, madam.
Imogen I have read three hours, then . . .
Fold down the leaf where I have left.

SHAKESPEARE, *Cymbeline.*

DAVID & CHARLES

Newton Abbot London North Pomfret (VT) Vancouver

FOR WENDY

'She is, indeed, a wonder.'

Robert Jephson's *Braganza*, Act I.

0 7153 6746 3

Set in 11 on 13pt Times New Roman
and printed in Great Britain
by Latimer Trend & Company Ltd Plymouth
for David & Charles (Holdings) Limited
South Devon House Newton Abbot Devon

Published in the United States of America
by David & Charles Inc North Pomfret
Vermont 05053 USA

Published in Canada
by Douglas David & Charles Limited
3645 McKechnie Drive West Vancouver BC

Contents

(Unless otherwise stated, books and journals mentioned were published in London; the editor has supplied titles for the extracts)

Introduction

Doubtless an anthology of the theatre, like Mrs Monfort's elocution, according to Colley Cibber, should be 'round, distinct, voluble, and various'. It ought to have a reasonable continuity, and its director should know when to drop the curtain. Here, unfashionably, I speak in terms of a proscenium stage—while not forgetting the glory of that spring running on Bankside long before the picture-frame:

> There was heard
> The high, unclouded summer of the word.

I agree that, if an anthologist is too uninhibited, his book may suffer something comparable to the fate of Edmund Falconer's drama, *Oonagh; or, The Lovers of Lisnamona*. This was much too voluble. It straggled on so relentlessly at its première (Her Majesty's, 1866) that, at about two o'clock in the morning, stage hands tugged the carpet from under the actors' feet. They fell prone, and the curtain was rung down.

Falconer-fashion, an anthologist does not find it easy to stop. Still, in this collection spanning about 360 years, the cast at least is unexampled. I have put its players roughly in chronological order. Besides some famous passages—for one could hardly do without Partridge at *Hamlet* or Hazlitt on Siddons—there are others that may be unexpected, and from sources not readily available. If we have planted our king-post in the nineteenth century, this is because that was among the most exciting periods in stage history: the Kembles and Keans and William Charles Macready conquering the immense caverns of Drury Lane and Covent Garden, practically a day's march from the footlights to the back of the pit; later in the century, the Lyceum blaze of Henry Irving; the efflorescence of drama criticism, the artists' preservative, that began with Hazlitt and Hunt; and, always, the 'gypsies', as Pinero's Vice-Chancellor called them, or the 'pomping folk', as they were known in South Cornwall, loyally on their rural circuits: 'Pomping folk from the market square,/The night, the booth, the torches' flare . . .'

Naturally, one honours the theatre's majestic names in their 'acted passion beautiful and swift'; but there are also the toilers of various ranks, from the major provincial houses to the dismal gaffs. They are here now, remembered by Stirling and Coleman and Vandenhoff, and earlier in the endeared garrulity of Tate Wilkinson (late eighteenth century) on his Yorkshire circuit:

> Miss Cleland has a good person, a good understanding, and a great deal of whim; and were she to act Emilia in *Othello*, Mrs Marwood, Lady Touchwood, Nottingham, Mrs Frail, and many characters which require comprehension from the performer, Miss Cleland is very adequate, and might be a valuable acquisition on any stage; but she should carefully avoid to ensnare and captivate the audience with foolishly wishing to strike at either the amiable, the gentle, the tender, or the great. By such mode she loses her value with the public; and her own folly hurts her own peace of mind, which by a false ambition renders her unhappy, and that too by her own means—*Fie, Cleland! fie!*

I am absorbed, too, by the Victorian melodramatists of the Surrey side ('They nearly always end the same upon the Surrey side'), or out in the East End. Consider that 'peculiar drama' at the Standard, *The Midnight Angel; or, Twelve o'Clock and the Spirit of Death*, with its villain who is 'continually shooting somebody'.

So much that could have been used we have had to leave in store. The articles of agreement, say, between the Lord Chamberlain and Killigrew's company at the Theatre Royal, Drury Lane, in December 1675: 'Whereas by Experience Wee find our Cloathes Tarnished and Imberelled by frequent Wearing them out of the Playhouse it is thought fit noe woeman presume to go out of the house with the Play House Cloathes or Properties upon Penalty of theire Weekes pay.' Or John Keats writing to his sister (28 August 1819): 'The Covent Garden Company is execrable. Young is the best among them and he is a ranting, coxcombical, tasteless Actor—A Disgust, a Nausea—and yet the very best after Kean.' Or C. E. Montague at Benson's Stratford seventy years ago: 'No one comes here who does not care for plays or acting . . . You feel a whole audience to be delightedly tasting flavours and valuing qualities in what they hear. When the play ends, outside there is white river mist and dead silence.' Or something on what used to be called 'musical comedy' from the comedian, W. H. Berry, who wrote sternly in the kind of patter he affected on stage: 'When the landlady came in with the toffee and coals—er—sorry, coffee and rolls.' Or the tale of a nervous Lady Sneerwell and Snake who opened a performance of *The School for Scandal* with the odd exchange: 'The snakes, you say, Mr Paragraph, were all inserted?'—'Yes, your Majesty.'

We might, I suppose, have recalled the struggle of the minor theatres against the monopolists of the great 'Patent' houses, theoretically until 1843 the only homes of 'legitimate' drama in London, though there were many ways of circumventing the law. Dutton Cook describes a charming device to aid one of the small houses from which in the 1830s the Lord Chamberlain withheld his licence. No money passed at the theatre, but a customer who paid 4s an ounce for rose lozenges at the confectioner's next door received a free admission to the boxes; half an ounce of peppermint drops (two shillings) included a check for the pit. In 1843 the monopoly and the multiplying absurdities were wiped out. J. R. Planché, in verses for a Haymarket entertainment in 1844, observed the new freedom. The

Drama, about to emigrate, was stopped by Portia in her gown as Doctor of Laws:

> I say you're free to act where'er you please,
> No longer pinioned by the patentees.
> Need our immortal Shakespeare mute remain
> Fixed on the portico of Drury Lane;
> Or the nine Muses mourn the Drama's fall
> Without relief on Covent Garden wall?
> Sheridan now at Islington may shine,
> Marylebone echo Marlowe's mighty line;
> Otway may raise the waters Lambeth yields,
> And Farquhar sparkle in St George's Fields;
> Wycherley flutter a Whitechapel pit,
> And Congreve wake all 'Westminster to *wit*'.

What else could we have included? Possibly Charles Kean's obsession with his scenery and costumes at the Princess's? Thus, in *The Winter's Tale*, 1856 (a child named Ellen Terry was Mamillius) he changed the fourth-act Bohemia to Bithynia which does not border on the sea and 'affords an opportunity of representing the costumes of the inhabitants of Asia Minor at a corresponding period . . . [It acquires] additional interest from close proximity to the Homeric kingdom of Troy.' Just over half a century later, Oscar Asche, in *As You Like It*, at His Majesty's, was representing Arden by two hundred pots of fern, periodically renewed (in places the fern was two feet high); large clumps of bamboos, moss-grown logs, and cartloads of autumn leaves.

Pastoral-comical, historical-pastoral, tragical-historical, tragical-comical-historical-pastoral: there is so much. I think of that 'lamentable tragedie', *Locrine*, one of the vaguest entries in the 'Shakespeare Apocrypha' ('Tell me, Assarachus, are the Cornish chuffes/In such great numbers come to Mercia?'). I prize a cluster of stage directions ('A cave in the forest; thunder and lightning; enter Devil'; 'After their going in, is heard the noise of a sea-fight'). I delight in playbills (Newcastle, 1826: '*The Tragedy of Virginius* . . . Virginius by Mr Macready; [followed by] a Comic Song by Mr Dodd . . .'); and programmes that bristle with times, places, relationships, and do not leave us in some unspecified limbo.

Very well; but this is to make an anthology within an anthology. I stand by the mosaic already chosen, bringing together pieces that have been widely dispersed. Here are the varying iconoclasts, Prynne and Rymer, and the enthusiasts, Pepys and Cibber. Here Tate has a word with Shakespeare, Lamb sits at Godwin's *Antonio*, Boaden reflects on the extraordinary *Pizarro*. Kemble's pronunciation worries Leigh Hunt; Edmund Kean tries Timon, now few people's pleasure; Lewes muses unkindly on John Webster. On through the nineteenth century, its ardours and endurances, its vendettas, its passionate love of a Theatre Theatrical, its mingling of naivete and an intense professionalism. Then to our own century and some of its crests, *The Playboy of the Western World*, *Saint Joan*; Gielgud's Lear and Olivier's Othello finely summoned by, respectively, T. C. Worsley and Robert Speaight; rare Ben Travers's memory of the richest farces of the age before 'Aldwych' was shorthand for the Royal Shakespeare Company; and Ivor Brown's noble farewell to the Irish player (he was O'Casey's Joxer), Sydney Morgan. Peter Bull—I could have quoted him on *Waiting for Godot*—flashes up *The Boy David*; the drama critic of *The Times* deals phonetically ('Weederdee') with an unfortunate *Antony and Cleopatra*; and, on the very eve of the National Theatre opening, Robert Speaight's fascinating prophecy is recovered from the 1930s.

So—and I hope it is distinct and various—we have what Peter Brook, in another context, calls a celebration of the arts of the theatre. Only three fictional pieces appear (with the exception of the extract from *The Angel in the Mist*), and these are for the sake of Partridge, Wopsle, and Pooter, which sounds like a matured firm of family solicitors. We leave the English-speaking theatre only to note Talma at Kemble's farewell dinner, and to allow Charlotte Brontë and Matthew Arnold their celebration of a great French actress. My favourite single line is Nahum Tate's 'Old Kent throws in his hearty Wishes, too' from the last scene of his *Lear* perversion.

Let the procession move down the years from, remarkably, a shipboard *Hamlet* through the astonishments of the English stage and its people:

> Where are the passions they essayed,
> And where the tears they made to flow?
> Where the wild humours they portrayed
> For laughing worlds to see and know?
> Othello's wrath and Juliet's woe?
> Sir Peter's whims and Timon's gall?
> And Millamant and Romeo?
> Into the night go one and all . . .*

No, not entirely. Many of them are here, and the carpet has not been tugged away.

Hampstead, 1974 J.C.T.

* W. E. Henley, *A Ballade of Dead Actors.*

Acknowledgments

I am most grateful to my wife, herself a drama critic, who has been with me to so many theatres; to my sons, Ion and Mark; to Christopher Fry, Harald Melvill, and Herbert van Thal; and, for permission to reprint, to the literary executors of the late James Agate for two extracts, one from *Ego 1*, another from *The Contemporary Theatre 1924*; to Mr Ivor Brown for his valediction to Sydney Morgan; to Mr Peter Bull and his publishers, Peter Davies, for the extract from *I Know the Face, But...*; to Mr Robert Speaight for the extract from *The Angel in the Mist*, and to him and the Editor of *The Tablet* for the review of Sir Laurence Olivier's Othello; to Mr Ben Travers for the passage on Aldwych farce from *Vale of Laughter*; to Mr T. C. Worsley for the review of Sir John Gielgud's King Lear from *The Fugitive Art*; and to Mr James Bishop (Editor) and the *Illustrated London News* for allowing me to use my article, 'The Woman Plays', which appeared, under another title, in *Window on the World*.

J.C.T.

Note: The illustrations, an anthology in themselves, are not necessarily related to the extracts.

T. D. SCOTT. T. SHERRATT.

TO WILLIAM CHARLES MACREADY, ESQ.

In commemoration of his management of the Theatre Royal Covent Garden; in the Seasons 1837–8 and 1838 and 9. When his personation of the Characters, his restoration of the Text, and his illustration by the best intellectual Aids, of the Historical Facts and Poetical Creations of the Plays of Shakspeare; formed an Epoch in Theatrical Annals, alike honorable to his own Genius and elevating in its influence upon the Public taste.

—This Testimonial is presented by the Lovers of the National Drama.

JOHN TALLIS & COMPANY, LONDON & NEW YORK.

B

1

All at Sea

The *Dragon* (Captain William Keeling), an East India Company's ship, was off Sierra Leone in September 1607, with the *Hector* (Captain William Hawkins), and *Consent*, all bound for the East Indies. The entries are from Captain Keeling's journal. My father, also a merchant captain (of a later date), decided that it must have been highly unprofessional, but added a little enviously: 'I never had that kind of crew.'

September 5 1607

I sent the interpreter, according to his desier, abord the Hector whear he brooke fast, and after came abord mee, wher we gaue the tragedie of Hamlett.

September 30 1607

Captain Hawkins dined with me, wher my companions acted Kinge Richard the Second.

March 31 1608

I envited Captain Hawkins to a ffishe dinner, and had Hamlet acted abord me: which I permitt to keepe my people from idleness and unlawful games, or sleepe.

William Keeling

2

Fire on Bankside

The Globe Theatre (the 'wooden O'—probably it was polygonal) was built on Bankside, in Southwark on the south bank of the Thames during 1599. Cuthbert Burbage and his younger brother, Richard, the great Shakespearian actor, used timber from the 'Theatre', the first English playhouse, erected in Shoreditch by their father James (d 1597). On 29 June 1613 the Globe was destroyed during a performance of Shakespeare's *Henry VIII.* Sir Henry Wotton (1568–1639), diplomatist and poet, who wrote to Elizabeth of Bohemia the famous lyric, 'You meaner beauties of the night', described the occasion in a letter to Sir Edmund Bacon. Writing to Sir Ralph Winwood, the scholar John Chamberlain also described the burning: 'It was a great marvaile and fair grace of God, that the people had so little harm, having but two narrow doors to get out.' A new Globe was built in 1614 'in far fairer manner than before', and remained for thirty years. John Taylor (1580–1653), the 'water-poet,' said of it:

> As Gold is better that's in fire tried,
> So is the bankeside Globe that late was burn'd:
> For where before it had a thatched hide,
> Now to a stately Theator is turn'd.
> Which is an Emblem, that great things are won,
> By those that dare through greatest dangers run.

Here is Sir Henry Wotton.

Now, to let matters of state sleep, I will entertain you at the present with what has happened this week at the Bank's side. The King's players had a new play, called *All is True*, representing some principal pieces of the reign of Henry VIII, which was set forth with many extraordinary circumstances of pomp and majesty, even to the matting of the stage; the Knights of the Order with their Georges and garters, the Guards with their embroidered coats, and the like: sufficient in truth within a while to make greatness very familiar, if not ridiculous. Now, King Henry making a masque at the Cardinal Wolsey's house, and certain chambers being shot off at his entry, some of the paper, or other stuff, wherewith one of them was stopped, did light on the thatch, where being thought at first but an idle smoke, and their eyes more attentive to the show, it kindled inwardly, and ran round like a train, consuming within less than an hour the whole house to the very grounds. This was the fatal period of that virtuous fabric, wherein yet nothing did perish but wood and straw, and a few forsaken cloaks; only one man had his breeches set on fire, that would perhaps have broiled him, if he had not by the benefit of a provident wit put it out with bottle ale.

Sir Henry Wotton

3

Ignoble Pleasures

William Prynne, ferocious Puritan pamphleteer (1600–69), denounced popular stage-plays as 'the very Pompes of the Divell which we renounce in Baptisme'; as 'sinfull, heathenish, lewde, ungodly Spectacles, and most pernicious Corruptions'; and as 'intolerable Mischiefes'. 'Play-poets' and Stage-players were 'unlawfull, infamous, and misbeseeming Christians'. These observations, and a great deal more, Prynne put into the full title of his *Histrio-mastix, The Players Scourge* (1633); he also disliked 'dancing, dicing, health-drinking, etc.' For his pains—being assumed to have scandalously libelled Queen Henrietta Maria, who acted in masques—Prynne was sentenced to life imprisonment, a fine of £5,000, and the loss of both ears. In 1637, for a pamphlet against the Bishops, he lost the stumps of his ears and his cheeks were branded. Though in 1640 the Long Parliament released him, he was never happy unless attacking someone when it was most dangerous to do so, and in 1650–3 he found himself imprisoned again, without trial. After all this, he became during the Restoration a Member of Parliament and Keeper of Records in the Tower.

I doubt whether 'Pompes of the Divell' inspired the Cornish expression for actors, 'pomping folk'; but it is a nice phrase. Prynne had attended only four plays in his life, but he had read widely. The following extract is from *Histrio-mastix.*

Pity it is to see how many ingenious youths and girls; how many young (that I say not old) gentlemen and gentlewomen of birth and quality (as if they were born for no other purpose but to consume their youth, their lives in lascivious dalliances, plays and pastimes, or in pampering, in adorning those idolised living carcases of theirs, which will turn to earth, to dung, to rottenness and worm's-meat ere be long, and to condemn their poor neglected souls) casting by all honest studies, callings, employments, all care of Heaven, of salvation, of their own immortal souls, of that God who made them, that Saviour who redeemed them, that Spirit who should sanctify them, and that Commonweal that fosters them; do, in this idle age of ours, like those Epicures of old most prodigally, most sinfully riot away the very cream and flower of their years, their days in play-houses, in dancing-schools, taverns, ale-houses, dice-houses, tobacco-shops, bowling-allies, and such infamous places, upon those life-devouring, time-exhausting plays and pastimes (that I say not sins beside), as is a shame for pagans, much more for Christians to approve. O that men endued with reason, ennobled with religion; with immortal souls: fit only for the noblest, heavenliest, sublimest and divinest actions, should ever be so desperately besotted as to waste their precious time upon such vain, such childish, base ignoble pleasures, which can no way profit soul or body, Church or State; nor yet advance their temporal, much less their spiritual and eternal good, which they should ever seek.

You therefore, dear Christian brethren, who are, who have been peccant in this kind, for God's sake, for Christ's sake, for the Holy Ghost's sake, for Religion's sake (which now extremely suffers by this your folly), for the Church and Commonweal's sake, for your own soul's sake, which you so much neglect, repent of what is past recalling, and for the future time resolve through God's assistance, never to cast away your time, your money, your estates, your good names, your lives, your salvation, upon these unprofitable spectacles of vanity, lewdness, lasciviousness, or these delights of sin, of which you must necessarily repent and be ashamed, or else be condemned for them at the last; passing all the time of your pilgrimage here in fear, and employing all the remainder of your short inconstant lives, in those honest studies, callings, and pious Christian duties, which have their fruit unto holiness, and the end everlasting life. And because we have now many wanton females of all sorts resorting daily by troups unto our plays, our play-houses, to see and to be seen as they did in Ovid's age; I shall only desire them (if not their parents and Husbands?) to consider: that it hath evermore been the notorious badge of prostituted strumpets and the lewdest harlots, to ramble abroad to plays, to play-houses; whither no honest, chaste, or sober girls or women, but only branded whores and infamous adultresses did usually resort in ancient times: the theatre then being made a common brothel: And that all ages, all places have constantly suspected the chastity, yea branded the honesty of those females who have been so immodest as to resort to theatres, to stage-plays, which either find or make them harlots; inhibiting all married wives and virgins to resort to plays and theatres, as I have here amply proved.

William Prynne

Mr. Thomas Betterton
Totus Mundus Agit Histrionem

4

To the Playhouse

Samuel Pepys (1633–1703), nonpareil of diarists (1660–9) and of playgoers, left in his journal a running commentary on the theatres of the Restoration. This eager, acutely observant, amorous personage, was also a zealous public official; in 1673 he became Secretary to the Admiralty. Another, and very different, diarist, John Evelyn, wrote of him at his death: 'Mr Sam Pepys, a very worthy, industrious, and curious person, none in England exceeding him in knowledge of the navy . . . He was universally belov'd, hospitable, generous, learned in many things, skill'd in music, a very greate cherisher of learned men of whom he had the conversation.'

In these entries he is at, or round, the playhouse. Here, in the order of printing, is a key to the plays and people in our extracts:

Plays

Epicœne; or, The Silent Woman, comedy (1609) by Ben Jonson; *The Lost Lady*, tragi-comedy (1637) by Sir William Berkeley; *All's Lost by Lust*, tragedy (1619) by William Rowley; *Bartholomew Fair*, comedy (1614) by Ben Jonson; *'Tis Pity She's a Whore*, tragedy (1632) by John Ford; *The Wild Gallant*, comedy (1663) by John Dryden; *The Traitor*, tragedy (1631) by James Shirley; *The Custom of the Country*, Jacobean play by John Fletcher and another; *The Humorous Lieutenant*, tragi-comedy (1619) by John Fletcher; *The Duke of Lerma*, comedy (1665) by Sir Robert Howard; *The Man's the Master* (1668) by Sir William Davenant, founded on two plays by Scarron; *Macbeth*, probably Davenant's adaptation; *The Tempest*, adapted by Dryden and Davenant; *Sweet Love; or, The Maiden Queen* (1667) by Dryden; *The Indian Emperor* (1665) by Dryden; *All Mistaken; or, The Mad Couple* (1667) by James Howard.

People

Edward Kynaston (?1640–1706), one of the last male actors of female parts; later a player of majesty and power. Pepys's wife was Elizabeth. 'Tom' was his brother. 'Madame Palmer': Barbara Villiers (1641–1709), daughter of William Villiers, Viscount Grandison; wife of Roger Palmer; became Charles II's mistress and, when her husband was elevated to the Irish peerage (1661), Countess of Castlemaine; made Duchess of Cleveland (1670); had five children by the King. Sir W. Pen[n]: 1621–70; distinguished Admiral, later Commissioner of the Navy, father of the founder of Pennsylvania. Pepys was breaking a domestic vow not to go to the play. 'Knipp': Mrs Mary Knipp (Knepp), popular actress, at her best in light comedy. 'Nelly': Nell (Eleanor) Gwyn. 'Deb': Deborah Willet, Elizabeth Pepys's lady's maid. Nicholas Burt and William Cartwright (d1687), actors. Thomas Betterton (1635–1710): the greatest Restoration actor. Eleanor Gwyn (1650–87) sold oranges in the Theatre Royal, Drury Lane; became an actress and Charles II's mistress; an indifferent player but good in comedy. Her first love was Charles Hart (d1683), actor, said to have been the illegitimate son of William Hart, son of Joan Hart, Shakespeare's sister. In *All Mistaken* Nell and Hart acted Mirida and Philidor who are 'in love with each other but protest against marriage'.

General

January 7, 1660–61. Tom and I and my wife to the Theatre and there saw 'The Silent Woman', the first time that ever I did see it, and it is an excellent play. Among other things here, Kinaston, the boy, had the good turn to appear in three shapes: first as a poor woman in ordinary clothes, to please Morose; then in fine clothes, as a gallant, and in them was clearly the prettiest woman in the whole house, and lastly as a man; and then likewise did appear the handsomest man in the house.

January 19, 1660–61. Myself went to the Theatre, where I saw 'The Lost Lady', which do not please me much. Here I was troubled to be seen by four of our office clerks, which sat in the half-crown box and I in the 1s6d.

January 28, 1660–61. To the Theatre, where I saw again 'The Lost Lady', which do now please me better than before; and here I sitting behind in a dark place, a lady spit backward upon me by a mistake, not seeing me, but after seeing her to be a very pretty lady, I was not troubled by it at all.

March 23, 1660–61. At last into the pitt [at the Red Bull Playhouse] where I think there was not above ten more than myself, and not one hundred in the whole house. And the play, which is called 'All's lost by Lust', poorly done; and with so much disorder, among others, in the musique-room, the boy that was to sing a song, not singing it right, his master fell about his ears and beat him so, that it put the whole house into an uprore.

September 7, 1661. I having appointed the young ladies at the Wardrobe to go with them to the play today . . . my wife and I took them to the Theatre, where we seated ourselves close by the King, and Duke of York, and Madame Palmer, which was great content; and, indeed, I can never enough admire her beauty. And here was 'Bartholomew Fayre', with the puppet-show, acted today, which had not been these forty years, (it being so satyricall against Puritanism, they durst not till now, which is strange they should already dare to do it, and the King to countenance it), but I do never a whit like it the better for the puppets, but rather the worse. Thence home with the ladies, it being by reason of our staying for the King's coming, and the length of the play, near nine o'clock before it was done.

September 9, 1661. Thence to Salisbury Court playhouse, where was acted the first time, 'Tis pity Shee's a Whore', a simple play and ill acted, only it was my fortune to sit by a most pretty and most ingenious lady, which pleased me much.

February 23, 1662–63. We took coach and to Court, and there got good places, and saw 'The Wilde Gallant', performed by the King's house, but it was ill acted, and the play so poor a thing as I never saw in my life almost, and so little answering the name, that from beginning to end, I could not, nor can at this time, tell certainly which was the Wild Gallant. The King did not seem pleased at all, all the whole play, nor any body else, though Mr Clerke whom we met here did commend it to us.

January 13, 1664–5. To the King's house, to a play, 'The Traytor', where, unfortunately, I met with Sir W. Pen, so that I must be forced to confess it to my wife, which troubles me.

January 2, 1666–67. To the King's House, and there saw 'The Custome of the Country', the second time of its being acted, wherein Knipp does the Widow well; but of all the plays that ever I did see, the worst—having neither plot, language, not anything in the earth that is acceptable; only Knipp sings a little song admirably. But fully the worst play that ever I saw or I believe shall see.

January 23, 1666–67. Thence to the King's house, and there saw 'The Humerous Lieutenant'; a silly play, I think; only the Spirit in it that grows very tall, and then sinks again to nothing, having two heads breeding upon one, and then Knipp's singing, did please us. . . . Knipp took us all in, and brought to us Nelly, a most pretty woman, who acted the part of Cœlia today very fine, and did it pretty well; I kissed her, and so did my wife; and a mighty pretty soul she is.

February 20, 1667–68. By one o'clock to the King's house: a new play, 'The Duke of Lerma' of Sir Robert Howard's: where the King and the Court was; and Knepp and Nell spoke the prologue most excellently, especially Knepp, who spoke beyond any creature I ever heard. The play designed to reproach our

King with his mistresses, that I was troubled for it, and expected it should be interrupted; but it ended all well, which salved all. The play a well-writ and good play, only its design I did not like of reproaching the King, but altogether a very good and most serious play.

March 26, 1667–68. To the Duke of York's house, to see the new play, called 'The Man is Master', where the house was, it not being above one o'clock, very full. But my wife and Deb. being there before, . . . they made me room; and there I sat, it costing me 8s upon them in oranges, at 6d a-piece. By and by the King come; and we sat just under him, so that I durst not turn my back all the play. The play is a translation out of French, and the plot Spanish, but not anything extraordinary at all in it, though translated by Sir W. Davenant, and so I found the King and his company did think meanly of it though there was here and there something pretty: but the most of the mirth was sorry poor stuffe, of eating of sack posset and slabbering themselves, and mirth fit for clownes; the prologue but poor, and the epilogue little in it but the extraordinariness of it, being sung by Harris and another in the form of a ballet.

February 22, 1668–9. To White Hall, and there did without trouble get [the ladies] into the playhouse, there in a good place among the Ladies of Honour, and myself also sat in the pit, and there by and by come the King and Queen, and they begin 'Bartholomew Fayre'. But I like no play here so well as at the common playhouse; beside that, my eyes being very ill since last Sunday and this day se'n-night, with the light of the candles, I was in mighty pain to defend myself now from the light of the candles.

Shakespeare

October 11, 1660. To the Cockpit to see 'The Moore of Venice', which was well done. Burt acted the Moor; by the same token, a very pretty lady that sat by me, called out to see Desdemona smothered.

March 1, 1661–2. Thence to the Opera, and there saw 'Romeo and Juliet', the first time it was ever acted [since the Restoration]; but it is a play of itself the worst that ever I heard in my life, and the worst acted that ever I saw these people do, and I am resolved to go no more to see the first time of acting, for they were all of them out more or less.

September 29, 1662. Then to the King's Theatre, where we saw 'Midsummer Night's Dream', which I had never seen before, nor shall ever again, for it is the most insipid ridiculous play that ever I saw in my life. I saw, I confess, some good dancing and some handsome women which was all my pleasure.

January 6, 1662–63. To the Duke's house, and there saw 'Twelfth Night' acted well, though it be but a silly play, and not related at all to the name or day.

January 1, 1663–64. To the Duke's house, the first play I have been at these six months, according to my last vowe, and here saw the so much cried-up play of 'Henry the Eighth'; which, though I went with resolution to like it, is so simple a thing made up of a great many patches that, besides the shows and processions in it, there is nothing in the world good or well done. Thence mightily dissatisfied.

January 7, 1666–7. To the Duke's house, and saw 'Macbeth', which . . . appears a most excellent play in all respects, but especially in divertisement, though it be a deep tragedy; which is a strange perfection in a tragedy, it being most proper here and suitable.

April 19, 1667. So to the playhouse, not much company come, which I impute to the heat of the weather, it being very hot. Here we saw 'Macbeth' which, though I have seen it often, yet it is one of the best plays for a stage, and variety of dancing and musique, that ever I saw. So, being very much pleased, thence home.

November 2, 1667. To the King's playhouse, and there saw 'Henry the Fourth'; and contrary to expectation, was pleased in nothing more than in Cartwright's speaking of Falstaffe's speech about 'What is Honour?' The house full of Parliament-men, it being holyday with them.

November 13, 1667. To the Duke of York's house, and there

saw the Tempest again, which is very pleasant, and full of so good variety that I cannot be more pleased almost in a comedy, only the seamen's part is a little tedious.

August 31, 1668. Saw 'Hamlet', [at the Duke of York's playhouse] which we have not seen this year before, or more; and mightily pleased with it; but, above all, with Betterton, the best part, I believe, that ever man acted.

Nell Gwyn

March 2, 1666–67. To the King's house to see 'The Mayden Queene', a new play of Dryden's . . . and, the truth is, there is a comical part done by Nell, which is Florimell, that I never can hope ever to see the like done again, by man or women. The King and Duke of York were at the play. But so great a performance of a comical part was never, I believe, in the world before as Nell do this, both as a mad girle, then most and best of all when she comes in like a young gallant; and hath the motions and carriage of a spark the most that ever I saw any man have. It makes me, I confess, admire her.

May 1, 1667. Saw pretty Nelly standing at her lodgings' door in Drury-lane, in her smock sleeves and bodice, looking upon one: she seemed a mighty pretty creature.

August 22, 1667. To the King's playhouse, and there saw 'The Indian Emperour'; where I find Nell come again, which I am glad of; but was most infinitely displeased with her being put to act the Emperour's daughter; which is a great and serious part which she do most basely.

October 5, 1667. To the women's shift, where Nell was dressing herself, and was all unready, and is very pretty, prettier than I thought . . . But to see how Nell cursed, for having so few people in the pit, was pretty.

December 28, 1667. Nell and Hart's mad parts ['The Mad Couple'] are most excellently done, but especially her's: which makes it a miracle to me to think how ill she do any serious part, as, the other day, just like a fool or changeling; and, in a mad part, do beyond all imitation almost.

May 7, 1668. Nell, in her boy's clothes, mighty pretty [in the greenroom of the King's theatre]. But Lord! their confidence! and how many men do hover about them as soon as they come off the stage, and how confident they are in their talk.

Samuel Pepys

5

His Father's Spirit

Colley Cibber (1671–1757), a sculptor's son, was dramatist, manager, actor, and eventually an inferior Poet Laureate (1730 until his death), but we think of him first for his shrewdly delightful discursive autobiography (1740), *An Apology for the Life of Mr Colley Cibber, Comedian*, from which our extract is taken. Born two years after Pepys ceased to write, his was another theatre, though some of the famous players noted by Pepys were still acting in Cibber's youth. The veteran Thomas Betterton (1635–1710) was their king, in the direct line of the First Players of the English stage (Burbage, Betterton, Garrick . . .). Though short-necked, pock-marked, and inclined to be plump, he had superb tragic power; Pepys thought his Hamlet 'beyond imagination'. Offstage he was not a particularly pleasant character.

Cibber (who here celebrates a scene from *Hamlet*) was pale and meagre in aspect. He could play fops with uncommon address (Sir Novelty Fashion, Lord Foppington, and so forth), and he had a way with villains (Iago, Richard III). Author of several plays—one of them *Love's Last Shift*—he is remembered for the celebrated adaptation of *Richard III* (1700) which held the stage until well into the nineteenth century and contained the lines, 'Off with his head!—so much for Buckingham!' and 'Conscience avaunt, Richard's himself again!' Pope made him, unkindly, the butt of *The Dunciad*; but Hazlitt would say: 'A gentleman and scholar of the old school; a man of wit and pleasantry in conversation, a diverting mimic, an excellent actor, an admirable dramatic critic, and one of the best comic writers of his age.'

Betterton was an actor, as Shakespeare was an author, both without competitors! form'd for the mutual assistance and illustration of each other's genius . . .

You have seen a Hamlet, perhaps, who on the first appearance of his father's spirit, has thrown himself into all the straining vociferation requisite to express rage and fury, and the house has thunder'd with applause; tho' the misguided actor was all the while (as Shakespeare terms it) tearing a passion into rags.—I am the more bold to offer you this particular instance, because the late Mr Addison, while I sate by him to see this scene acted, made the same observation, asking me with some surprise if I thought Hamlet should be in so violent a passion with the Ghost, which tho' it might have astonish'd, it had not provok'd him? for you may observe that in this beautiful speech, the passion never rises beyond an almost breathless astonishment, or an impatience, limited by filial reverence, to enquire into the suspected wrongs that may have rais'd him from his peaceful tomb! and a desire to know what a spirit so seemingly distrest, might wish or enjoin a sorrowful son to execute towards his future quiet in the grave? This was the light into which Betterton threw this scene; which he open'd with a pause of mute amazement! then rising slowly to a solemn, trembling voice, he made the ghost equally terrible to the spectator as to himself! and in the descriptive part of the natural emotions which the ghastly vision gave him, the boldness of his expostulation was still govern'd by decency, manly, but not braving; his voice never rising into that seeming outrage, or wild defiance of what he naturally rever'd. But alas! to preserve this medium, between mouthing and meaning too little, to keep the attention more pleasingly awake, by a temper'd spirit than by mere vehemence of voice, is of all the master-strokes of an actor the most difficult to reach. In this none yet have equalled Betterton.

Colley Cibber

6

So Fond of Humour

Colley Cibber calls his enchanting actress Mrs Monfort. She was Mrs Susanna Mountford (1667–1703), an actor's daughter who had been in the theatre since childhood. Her first husband, William (1664–92), a player of much elegance, winning in aspect ('tall, well-made, fair,' said Cibber) and in voice ('clear, full, and melodious'), was murdered in the street one December night by a Captain Hill, the unaccepted lover of the actress Mrs Bracegirdle. Hill was said to be jealous of Mountford who played Alexander to Mrs Bracegirdle's Statira in Nathaniel Lee's *The Rival Queens; or, The Death of Alexander the Great*. According to Cibber, Mountford in tragedy 'was the most affecting lover within my memory . . . In comedy he gave the truest life to what we call the *fine* gentleman; his spirit shone the brighter for being polish'd with decency.' He and Susanna Percival were married only six years before his death. Her second husband was the actor John Baptist Verbruggen. In her last years she became deranged. The Revd John Genest (*Some Account of the English Stage*) says that, in a lucid interval, learning that Ophelia was to be played that night, she eluded her attendants, reached the theatre, and pushed on the stage in the Mad Scene before the official actress. There 'she exhibited a representation . . . that astonished the performers as well as the audience. She exhausted her vital powers in this effort, was taken home, and died soon after.'

The ensuing passage is from *An Apology for the Life of Colley Cibber, Comedian*, 1740. *The Rehearsal* was by George Villiers, Duke of Buckingham (1671), and *Marriage A-la-Mode* by John Dryden (1672). Mrs Anne Bracegirdle, actress (*c*1674–1748).

Mrs Monfort, whose second marriage gave her the name of Verbruggen, was mistress of more variety of humour than I ever knew in any one woman actress. This variety, too, was attended with an equal vivacity, which made her excellent in characters extremely different. As she was naturally a pleasant mimick, she had the skill to make that talent useful on the stage, a talent which may be surprising in a conversation, and yet be lost when brought to the theatre, which was the case of Estcourt. But where the elocution is round, distinct, voluble, and various, as Mrs Monfort's was, the mimick, there, is a great assistant to the actor. Nothing, tho' ever so barren, if within the bounds of nature, could be flat in her hands. She gave many heightening touches to characters but coldly written, and often made an actor vain of his work that in itself had but little merit. She was so fond of humour, in what low part soever to be found, that she would make no scruple of defacing her fair form, to come heartily into it; for when she was eminent in several desirable characters of wit and humour in higher life, she would be, in as much fancy, when descending into the antiquated Abigail of Fletcher, as when triumphing in all the airs and vain graces of a fine lady; a merit that few actresses care for. In a play of D'urfey's, now forgotten, call'd *The Western Lass*, which part she acted, she transform'd her whole being, body, shape, voice, language, look, and features, into almost another animal; with a strong Devonshire dialect, a broad laughing voice, a poking head, round shoulders, an unonceiving eye, and the most bediz'ning dowdy dress that ever cover'd the untrain'd limbs of a Joan Trot. To have seen her here, you would have thought it impossible the same creature could ever have been recover'd to what was as easy to her, the gay, the lively, and the desirable. Nor was her humour limited to her sex; for, while her shape permitted, she was a more adroit pretty fellow than is usually seen upon the stage. Her easy air, action, mien, and gesture, quite chang'd from the quoif to the cock'd hat and cavalier in fashion. People were so fond of seeing her a man, that when the part of Bay[e]s in the *Rehearsal*, had for some time lain dormant, she was desired to take it up, which I have seen her act with all the true, coxcombly spirit, and humour that the sufficiency of the character required.

But what found most employment for her whole various excellence at once was the part of Melantha, in *Marriage-Alamode*. Melantha is as finish'd an impertinent as ever flutter'd in a drawing-room, and seems to contain the most complete system of female foppery that could possibly be crowded into the tortured form of a fine lady. Her language, dress, motion, manners, soul, and body are in a continual hurry to be something more than is necessary or commendable. And though I doubt it will be a vain labour, to offer you a just likeness of Mrs Monfort's action, yet the fantastick impression is still so strong in my memory that I cannot help saying something, tho' fantastically, about it. The first ridiculous airs that break from her are upon a gallant, never seen before, who delivers her a letter from her father, recommending him to her good graces as an honourable lover. Here now one would think she might naturally shew a little of the sex's decent reserve, tho' never so slightly cover'd! No, sir; not a tittle of it; modesty is the virtue of a poor soul'd country gentlewoman; she is too much a court lady to be under so vulgar a confusion; she reads the letter, therefore, with a careless, dropping lip and an erected brow, humming it hastily over, as if she were impatient to outgo her father's commands by making a compleat conquest of him at once; and that the letter might not embarrass her attack, crack! she crumbles it at once into her palm, and pours upon him her whole artillery of airs, eyes, and motion; down goes her dainty, diving body to the ground as if she were sinking under the conscious load of her own attractions; then launches into a flood of fine language, and compliment, still playing her chest forward in fifty falls and risings, like a swan upon waving water; and, to complete her impatience, she is so rapidly fond of her own wit that she will not give her lover leave to praise it. Silent assenting bows, and vain endeavours to speak, are all the share of the conversation he is admitted to, which at last he is relieved from by her engagement to half a score visits, which she *swims* from him to make, with a promise to return in a twinkling.

If this sketch has colour enough to give you any near conception of her, I then need only tell you that throughout the whole character, her variety of humour was every way proportionable; as, indeed, in most parts that she thought worth her care, or that had the least matter for her fancy to work upon, I may justly say that no actress, from her own conception, could have heighten'd them with more likely strokes of nature.

Colley Cibber

7

Hearty Wishes

This is the final scene of Nahum Tate's adaptation of *King Lear* (1681), a text—praised by Dr Samuel Johnson—that had a life of more than a century and a half before Macready, in 1838, revived Shakespeare's tragedy with the Fool Tate had dismissed. The alterations are sad stuff; but Tate, like other men, was simply serving the taste of his day. In a dedication to 'my esteem'd friend Thomas Boteler, Esq.', he wrote:

> I found the Whole to answer your Account of it, a Heap of Jewels, unstrung, and unpolish'd; yet so dazzling in their Disorder, that I soon perceiv'd I had seiz'd a Treasure. 'Twas my good Fortune to light on one Expedient to rectifie what was wanting in the Regularity and Probability of the Tale, which was to run through the Whole, as Love betwixt Edgar and Cordelia; that never chang'd Word with each other in the Original. This renders Cordelia's Indifference, and her Father's Passion in the first Scene, probable. It likewise gives Countenance to Edgar's Disguise, making that a generous Design that was before a poor Shift to save his Life.
>
> The Distress of the Story is evidently heightened by it; and it particularly gave Occasion of a new Scene, or Two, of more Success (perhaps) than Merit. This Method necessarily threw me on making the Tale conclude in a success to the innocent destrest Persons: Otherwise I must have incumbered the Stage with dead Bodies, which Conduct makes many Tragedies conclude with unseasonable Jests. Yet was I wrack'd with no small Fears for so bold a Change, 'till I found it well receiv'd by my Audience...

My favourite observation in the mauled tragedy itself is one of Tate's own lines. Lear and Cordelia are spared at the end; Lear hands her to

Edgar with suitable expressions ('Take her Crown'd; Th'imperial Grace fresh blooming on her Brow'); and suddenly there is a resolute voice, 'Old Kent throws in his hearty Wishes too.' We gather that he and Lear propose to retire reflectively to 'some cool Cell' and gently pass their 'short reserves of Time'.

Thomas Betterton was the original Lear. If he could have looked into the future, he might have been happy about Samuel Johnson's commendation of Tate's text: 'A play in which the wicked prosper, and the virtuous miscarry, may doubtless be good because it is a just representation of the common events of human life; but since all reasonable beings naturally love justice. I cannot easily be persuaded that the observation of justice makes a play worse; or, that if other excellencies are equal, the audience will not always rise better pleased from the final triumph of persecuted virtue. In the present case the public has decided. Cordelia, from the time of Tate, has always retired with victory and felicity. And, if my sensations could add anything to the general suffrage, I might relate, I was many years ago so shocked by Cordelia's death that I know not whether I ever endured to read again the last scenes of the play till I undertook to revise them as editor.'

Tate (1652–1715) was Poet Laureate from 1692–1715; he died a pauper. Though he wrote various plays, his best memorial maybe is the hymn, 'While shepherds watched their flocks by night'.

Re-enter Edgar with Gloster

Albany Look, Sir, where pious Edgar comes,
Leading his Eye-less Father. O my Liege!
His wond'rous Story will deserve your Leisure;
What he has done and suffer'd for your Sake,
What for the fair Cordelia's.

Gloster Where's my Liege? Conduct me to his Knees, to hail
His second Birth of Empire; my dear Edgar
Has, with himself, reveal'd the King's blest
Restauration.

Lear My poor dark Gloster.

Gloster O let me kiss that once more sceptred Hand!

Lear Hold, thou mistak'st the Majesty, kneel here;
Cordelia has our Pow'r, Cordelia's Queen.

Gloster My pious son, more dear than my lost Eyes.

Lear I wrong'd him too, but here's the fair Amends.

Edgar Your Leave, my Liege, for an unwelcome Message.
Edmund (but that's a Trifle) is expir'd;
What more will touch you, your imperious Daughters,
Goneril and haughty Regan, both are dead,
Each by the other poison'd at a Banquet;
This, Dying, they confest.

Cordelia O fatal Period of ill-govern'd Life!

Lear Ingratefull as they were, my Heart feels yet
A Pang of Nature for their wretched Fall;—
But, Edgar, I defer thy Joys too long:
Thou serv'dst distrest Cordelia; take her Crown'd;
Th'imperial Grace fresh blooming on her Brow;
Nay, Gloster, thou hast here a Father's Right,
Thy helping Hand t'heap Blessings on their Heads.

Kent Old Kent throws in his hearty Wishes too.

Edgar The Gods and you too largely Recompence
What I have done; the Gift strikes Merit dumb.

Cordelia Nor do I blush to own my Self o'er-paid
For all my Suff'rings past.

Gloster Now, gentle Gods, give Gloster his Discharge.

Lear No, Gloster, though hast Business yet for Life;

Thou, Kent, and I, retir'd to some cool Cell
Will gently pass our short Reserves of Time
In calm Reflections on our Fortunes past,
Cheer'd with Relation of the prosperous Reign
Of this celestial Pair; thus our Remains
Shall in an even Course of Thoughts be past,
Enjoy the present Hour, nor fear the last.

Edgar Our drooping Country now erects her Head,
Peace spreads her balmy Wings, and Plenty blooms.
Divine Cordelia, all the Gods can witness
How much thy Love to Empire I prefer!
Thy bright Example shall convince the World
(Whatever Storms of Fortune are decreed)
That Truth and Vertue shall at last succeed.

(*Exeunt Omnes.*)

Nahum Tate

8

Handkerchief

Macaulay took the desperate classicist, Thomas Rymer (1641–1713), author and archaeologist, graduate of Cambridge, barrister of Gray's Inn, to have been 'the worst critic that ever lived'. Rymer's opinion of *Othello* we quote now from *A Short View of Tragedy* (1693). His own 'heroick tragedy', *Edgar, or The English Monarch* (1678) was unactable.

What ever rubs or difficulties may stick on the Bark, the Moral, sure, of this Fable is very instructive.

1. First. This may be a caution to all Maidens of Quality how, without their Parents consent, they run away with Blackamoors.

Secondly, this may be a warning to all good Wives, that they look well to their Linnen.

Thirdly, this may be a lesson to Husbands, that before their Jealousie be Tragical, the proofs may be Mathematical . . .

In the *Neighing* of an horse, or in the *growling* of a Mastiff, there is a meaning, there is as lively expression, and, may I say, more humanity, than many times in the Tragical flights of *Shakespear* . . .

So much ado, so much stress, so much passion and repetition about an Handkerchief! Why was not this called the *Tragedy of the Handkerchief*? Had it been *Desdemona*'s Garter, the Sagacious Moor might have smelt a Rat; but the Handkerchief is so remote a trifle, no Booby, on this side *Mauritania*, cou'd make any consequence from it . . .

What can remain with the Audience to carry home with them from this sort of Poetry, for their use and edification? how can it work, unless (instead of settling the mind, and purging our passions) to delude our senses, disorder our thoughts, addle our brain, pervert our affections, hair our imaginations, corrupt our appetite, and fill our head with vanity, confusion, *Tintamarre*, and Jingle-jangle beyond what all the Parish Clerks of *London*, with their *old Testament* farces, and interludes, in Richard the seconds time cou'd ever pretend to? Our only hopes, for the good of their Souls, can be, that these people go to the Playhouse, as they do to Church, to sit still, look on one another, make no reflection, nor mind the Play, more than they would a Sermon.

There is in this Play, some burlesk, some humour, and ramble of Comical Wit, some shew, and some *Mimickry* to divert the spectators; but the tragical part is, plainly, none other, than a Bloody Farce, without salt or savour.

Thomas Rymer

9

Playgoing with Partridge

Henry Fielding (1707–54) published his most famous novel, *The History of Tom Jones, a Foundling*, in 1749. Mr Partridge, who attends the performance of *Hamlet*, is a Somerset village schoolmaster, barber, and clerk, 'one of the best-natured fellows in the world', but neither the most learned nor the most modest. In London with Tom Jones, he goes to the play; the Hamlet is David Garrick.

In the first row then of the first gallery did Mr Jones, Mrs Miller, her youngest daughter, and Partridge, take their places. Partridge immediately declared it was the finest place he had ever been in. When the first music was played, he said, 'It was a wonder how so many fiddlers could play at one time, without putting one another out.' While the fellow was lighting the upper candles, he cried out to Mrs Miller, 'Look, look, madam, the very picture of the man in the end of the common-prayer book before the gunpowder-treason service.' Nor could he help observing, with a sigh, when all the candles were lighted, 'That here were candles enough burnt in one night to keep an honest poor family for a whole twelvemonth.'

As soon as the play, which was *Hamlet, Prince of Denmark*, began, Partridge was all attention, nor did he break silence until the entrance of the ghost; upon which he asked Jones, 'What man that was in the strange dress; something,' said he, 'like what I have seen in the picture. Sure it is not armour, is it?' Jones answered, 'That is the ghost.' To which Partridge replied with a smile, 'Persuade me to that, sir, if you can. Though I can't say I ever actually saw a ghost in my life, yet I am certain I should know one, if I saw him, better than that comes to. No, no, sir, ghosts don't appear in such dresses as that, neither.' In this mistake, which caused much laughter in the neighbourhood of Partridge, he was suffered to continue, till the scene between the ghost and Hamlet, when Partridge gave that credit to Mr Garrick, which he had denied to Jones, and fell into so violent a trembling that his knees knocked against each other. Jones asked him what was the matter, and whether he was afraid of the warrior upon the stage. 'O la! sir,' said he, 'I perceive now it is what you told me. I am not afraid of anything; for I know it is but a play. And if it was really a ghost, it could do no one harm at such a distance, and in so much company; and yet if I was frightened, I am not the only person.' 'Why, who,' cries Jones, 'dost thou take to be such a coward here besides thyself?' 'Nay, you may call me coward if you will; but if that little man there upon the stage is not frightened, I never saw any man frightened in my life. Ay, ay: go along with you! Ay, to be sure!

Who's fool then? Will you? Lud have mercy upon such foolhardiness? Whatever happens, it is good enough for you. Follow you? I'll follow the devil as soon. Nay, perhaps it is the devil—for they say, he can put on what likeness he pleases. Oh! here he is again. No farther! No, you have gone far enough already; farther than I'd have gone for all the king's dominions.' Jones offered to speak, but Partridge cried, 'Hush! Hush! dear sir, don't you hear him?' And during the whole speech of the ghost, he sat with his eyes fixed partly on the ghost and partly on Hamlet, and with his mouth open; the same passions which succeeded each other in Hamlet, succeeding likewise in him.

When the scene was over Jones said, 'Why, Partridge, you exceed my expectations. You enjoy the play more than I conceived possible.' 'Nay, sir,' answered Partridge, 'if you are not afraid of the devil, I can't help it; but to be sure, it is natural to be surprised at such things, though I know there is nothing in them: not that it was the ghost that surprised me, neither; for I should have known that to be only a man in a strange dress; but when I saw the little man so frightened himself, it was that which took hold of me.' 'And dost thou imagine, then, Partridge,' cries Jones, 'that he was really frightened?' 'Nay, sir,' said Partridge, 'did not you yourself observe afterwards, when he found it was his own father's spirit, and how he was murdered in the garden, how his fear forsook him by degrees, and he was struck dumb with sorrow, as it were, just as I should have been, had it been my own case. But hush! O la! what noise is that? There he is again. Well, to be certain, though I know there is nothing at all in it, I am glad I am not down yonder, where those men are.' Then turning his eyes again upon Hamlet, 'Ay, you may draw your sword; what signifies a sword against the power of the devil?'

During the second act Partridge made very few remarks. He greatly admired the fineness of the dresses; nor could he help observing upon the king's countenance. 'Well,' said he, 'how people may be deceived by faces! *Nulla fides fronti* is, I find, a true saying. Who would think, by looking in the king's face, that he had ever committed a murder?' He then inquired after the ghost; but Jones, who intended he should be surprised, gave him no other satisfaction than, 'that he might possibly see him again soon, and in a flash of fire'.

Partridge sat in fearful expectation of this; and now, when the ghost made his next appearance, Partridge cried out, 'There, sir, now; what say you now? is he frightened now or no? As much frightened as you think me, and, to be sure, nobody can help some fears. I would not be in so bad a condition as what's his name, squire Hamlet, is there, for all the world. Bless me! what's become of the spirit? As I am a living soul, I thought I saw him sink into the earth.' 'Indeed, you saw right,' answered Jones. 'Well, well,' cries Partridge, 'I know it is only a play; and besides, if there was anything in all this, Madam Miller would not laugh so; for as to you, sir, you would not be afraid, I believe, if the devil was here in person. There, there—Ay, no wonder you are in such a passion, shake the vile wicked wretch to pieces. If she was my own mother, I would serve her so. To be sure all duty to a mother is forfeited by such wicked doings—Ay, go about your business, I hate the sight of you.'

Our critic was now pretty silent till the play which Hamlet introduces before the king. This he did not at first understand, till Jones explained it to him; but he no sooner entered into the spirit of it, than he began to bless himself that he had never committed murder. Then turning to Mrs Miller, he asked her, 'if she did not imagine the king looked as if he was touched; though he is,' said he, 'a good actor, and doth all he can to hide it. Well, I would not have so much to answer for, as that wicked man there hath, to sit upon a much higher chair than he sits upon. No wonder he run away; for your sake I'll never trust an innocent face again.'

The grave-digging scene next engaged the attention of Partridge, who expressed much surprise at the number of skulls thrown upon the stage. To which Jones answered, 'That it was one of the most famous burial-places about town.' 'No wonder then,' cries Partridge, 'that the place is haunted. But I never saw in my life a worse gravedigger. I had a sexton, when I was clerk, that should have dug three graves while he is digging one. The fellow handles a spade as if it was the first time he had ever had one in his hand. Ay, ay, you may sing. You had rather sing than work, I believe.' Upon Hamlet's taking up the skull, he cried out, 'Well! it is strange to see how fearless some men are: I never could bring myself to touch anything belonging to a dead man, on any account. He seemed frightened enough too at the ghost, I thought. *Nemo omnibus horis sapit*.'

Little more worth remembering occurred during the play, at the end of which Jones asked him, 'Which of the players he had liked best?' To this he answered, with some appearance of indignation at the question, 'The king, without doubt.' 'Indeed, Mr Partridge,' says Mrs Miller, 'you are not of the same opinion with the town; for they are all agreed that Hamlet is acted by the best player who ever was on the stage.' 'He the best player!' cries Partridge, with a contemptuous sneer, 'why, I could act as well as he myself. I am sure, if I had seen a ghost, I should have looked in the very same manner, and done just as he did. And then, to be sure, in that scene, as you called it, between him and his mother, where you told me he acted so fine, why, Lord help me, any man, that is, any good man, that had such a mother, would have done exactly the same. I know you are only joking with me; but indeed, madam, though I was never to a play in London, yet I have seen acting before in the country; and the king for my money; he speaks all his words distinctly, half as loud again as the other. Anybody may see he is an actor.'

Henry Fielding

David Garrick

10

Sick of Fiction

Horace (Horatio) Walpole (1717–97), Sir Robert Walpole's son, himself an MP for nearly sixteen years, and ultimately fourth Earl of Orford, is known to us principally for his voluminous gossiping letters (about 4,000 of them), for the romantic novel of *The Castle of Otranto*, and for his 'Gothick' house, Strawberry Hill, Twickenham. He wrote this article in 1753, his earliest days as a writer, for Edward Moore's periodical, *The World*: Moore used the name 'Adam Fitz-Adam'. Some of the people mentioned are John Rich, pantomimist and theatre manager, who produced Gay's *The Beggar's Opera*; and Francesco Bernardi Senesino (*c*1680–*c*1750), who was an Italian opera singer, a male soprano, in London. There are various references to early pantomimes; *Caesar in Egypt* was Colley Cibber's derivative tragedy (1724); Armida is in Handel's opera, *Rinaldo*, and Alexander in Handel's *Alessandro*.

Sir—As you have chosen the whole world for your province, one may reasonably suppose, that you will not neglect that epitome of it, the theatre. Most of your predecessors have bestowed their favourite pains upon it; the learned and the critics (generally two very distinct denominations of men) have employed many hours and much paper in comparing the ancient and modern stage. I shall not undertake to decide a question which seems to me so impossible to be determined, as which have most merit, plays written in a dead language, and which we can only read; or such as we every day see acted inimitably, in a tongue familiar to us and adapted to our common ideas and customs. The only preference that I shall pretend to give to the modern stage over Greece and Rome relates to the subject of the present letter; I mean the daily progress we make towards nature. This will startle any bigot to Euripides, who perhaps will immediately demand, whether Juliet's nurse be a more natural gossip than Electra's or Medea's. But I did not hint at the representation of either persons or characters. The improvement of nature, which I had in view, alluded to those excellent exhibitions of the animal and inanimate parts of the creation; which are furnished by the worthy philosophers, Rich and Garrick; the latter of whom has refined on his competitor; and having perceived that art has become so perfect that it was necessary to mimick it by nature, he has happily introduced a cascade of real water.

I know there are persons of a systematic turn, who affirm that the audience are not delighted with this beautiful waterfall, from the reality of the element, but merely because they are pleased with the novelty of any thing that is out of its proper place. Thus they tell you, that the town is charmed with a genuine cascade upon the stage, and were in raptures last year with one of Tin at Vauxhall. But this is certainly prejudice; the World, Mr Fitz-Adam, though never sated with show, is sick of fiction. I foresee the time approaching, when delusion will not be suffered in any part of the drama; the inimitable Serpent in Orpheus and Eurydice, and the amorous Ostrich in the Sorcerer, shall be replaced by real monsters from Africa. It is well known that the pantomime of the Genii narrowly escaped being damned on my lady Maxim's observing very judiciously, *that the brick-kiln was horridly executed, and did not smell at all like one.*

When this entire castigation of improprieties is brought about, the age will do justice to one of the first reformers of the stage, Mr Cibber, who essayed to introduce a taste for real nature in his Caesar in Egypt, and treated the audience with real—not swans indeed, for that would have been too bold an attempt in the dawn of truth, but very personable geese. The inventor, like other original genius's, was treated ill by a barbarous age; yet I can venture to affirm, that a stricter adherence to reality would have saved even those times from being shocked by absurdities, always incidental to fiction. I myself remember, how, much about that aera, the great Senesino, representing Alexander at the siege of Oxydracae, so far forgot himself in the heat of conquest, as to stick his sword into one of the pasteboard stones of the wall of the town, and bore it in triumph before him as he entered the breach; a puerility so renowned a general could never have committed, if the ramparts had been built, as in this enlightened age they would be, of actual brick and stone. Will you forgive an elderly man, Mr Fitz-Adam, if he cannot help recollecting another passage that happened in his youth, and to the same excellent performer? He was stepping into Armida's enchanted bark; but treading short, as he was more attentive to the accompanyment of the orchestra than to the breadth of the shore, he fell prostrate, and lay for some time in great pain, with the edge of a wave running into his side. In the present state of things, the worst that could have happened to him, would have been drowning; a fate far more becoming Rinaldo, especially in the sight of a British audience! . . .

Horace Walpole

Philip Kemble

11

Dirty Faces & The Same Thing

'The eminent Lewis Riccoboni', who wrote in the mid-eighteenth century, *A General History of the Stage, from its Origin*—the title continues for another seventy words—was Luigi Riccoboni (*c*1675–1753), known as Lelio, himself an actor and son of another celebrated player of the *commedia dell'arte*. Luigi had directed the Italian company in Paris; under him it first played in French. He wrote some valuable books. To the second English edition (1754) of the *General History* its anonymous translator prefixed 'An Introductory Discourse concerning the Present State of the English Stage and Players', from which the ensuing extracts are taken. David Garrick was then in his prime as leader of the theatre, and the translator dedicated the second edition to him.

There are references to:

David Garrick (1717–79), actor, manager, dramatist; as an actor (opposed to the old declamatory school) magnificent in both tragedy and comedy; a small, lithe man with extremely expressive eyes. He was buried in Westminster Abbey;

Thomas Otway's tragedy, *Venice Preserv'd* (1682) and its character, Pierre; the actor Spranger Barry (1719–77) as Essex in Henry Jones's tragedy, *The Earl of Essex* (1753); Richard Glover's *Boadicea* (1753) in which Mrs Pritchard was the heroine, Garrick was Dumnorix, 'chief of the Trinobantians', and Mrs Cibber his wife Venutia; Susannah Cibber (1714–66), Colley's daughter-in-law and sister of Dr Thomas Arne, the composer, a favourite leading actress at both Drury Lane and Covent Garden; Indiana, a character in Richard Steele's *The Conscious Lovers* (1722); Constance, in Shakespeare's

King John; Mrs Hannah Pritchard (1711–65), for long Garrick's leading lady and a fine Lady Macbeth; Aaron Hill's *Mérope* (1749), from Voltaire; Hermione, a character in Ambrose Philips's tragedy, *The Distrest Mother* (1712).

Dirty faces

. . . It were foolish to join the Mob in hollowing at the thin Seats in a *Venetian* Senate; for that is right: a Council of Six determines all Things of Importance there; but then the Six might look like Counsellors. One is offended at the dirty Faces and the dirty Shoes of these *most potent Grave and Reverends*; and in the same Manner one cannot help being disgusted with the Conspirators who join with *Pierre*. We conceive of them as great Men engaged in a great Enterprize; the principal Persons in one of the most powerful States in the World, joined to its Destruction: How is this idea satisfied, when we see the Band of Big-coated Candle-Snuffers? Embroidery and Dirt; unfit Embroidery, and Dirt that sits too naturally, striving at an impossible Union: and we hear the better Sort of them speak, those who are judged fit to be intrusted with a Line and half, how are we disgusted! These, Men to form Conspiracies, to overturn States, and set the World in Uproar! Sense and Reason contradict it! The Force of the Scene is wholly destroy'd by the unnatural Aspect. We cannot expect Pierre shall be successful; we see these People must betray him. When he is in the midst of them he seems a Hero encircled by a Race of Pickpockets; and we blush to see him embrace Men who are fitter to wipe his Shoes.

There are many Instances of the like Kind in other Tragedies; and they are the great Disgrace of the present Theatre. The Manager will say 'tis difficult for him to remove them; for Men who have a Mien and Aspect have generally Parts joined with it, and will not be placed as Cyphers: and those who are able to perform a Character of Consequence will not accept these Parts of a Line or two. It may be difficult to get the better of this; but it cannot be impossible. It will offend these Gentlemen of better Figure and higher Rank, to be used occasionally in low and trifling Characters; but they should remember it is only occasionally: and he should remember that they are his Servants. The Army submits in some degree to these Regulations; and the best Players, probably, would not be for demanding a Rank above the superior Officers: if so, the Secondaries cannot be placed higher than Subalterns. The Remedy will follow. The Superior among the Forces has Power to make them serve in any Capacity. The Sergeant raised from a private Man must descend into a private Man again, if the Necessity of the Service require it; and why should not the same be practised in these Forces of the Stage? This is wanting: This is the great, nay one might almost say, it is the only Thing wanting to raise the present theatre to the highest Pitch of Excellence: And why should it not be done? The Publick give sufficient encouragement; the Manager has Abilities and Spirit; and if this be the only Reform necessary, why should he delay to make it?

The same thing

The other Thing it would be well that our Actors would imitate from the Italians, is their Variety. This would do them much more Honour than their constant Sameness, and certainly would give their Audiences greatly more Pleasure. With us the same Scene is always play'd in the same Manner, not only by the same Actor, but by every Actor who performs it: We know, therefore, before it comes, all that we are to admire. Perhaps there never was a greater or a juster Piece of Action upon the Theatre of any Country, than that consummate Player Mr *Barry* threw into his character of the Earl of *Essex*, when his Wife fell into a Swoon, and he was going to Execution; but 'twas every Night the same. In this Manner also that beautiful, though perhaps not proper, Attitude of *Romeo* at the Tomb, is always the same, not only in Mr *Barry* and in Mr *Garrick*, every Time each plays, but 'tis the same in Both: On the contrary, let an Italian pleade ever so greatly once in his Scene, he never courts a second Applause by the same Attitude. It seems that those of our Performers are practised at the Glass, those of the *Italians* rise from Nature: these People having that true Enthusiasm to conceive themselves really the Persons they represent. In Comedy this fault is more frequent and more conspicuous in our People than in *Tragedy*; with the *Italians* it is more avoided . . .

We are weary of seeing the same Thing in the same Manner, though we could very well receive it with the advantage of but a little Variety. If we are content to recollect the Sentiments, and from our imperfect Remembrance of the Words in which they are cloathed acknowledge a sort of Novelty, that greatest of all Charms, in the Repetition of them; we are disgusted at having the same Gestures, Looks, and Attitudes repeated to us nine Times over. To remember these, and expect them over and over again, is insupportable; and it argues a strange Dearth of Invention in those who practise them; at least it would argue this, if Custom did not too much authorise it: and it will when that Custom shall be condemned by all Persons as unnatural and vicious.

In the Tragedy of *Boadicea*, which but for this cloying Repetition would certainly have pleased more than nine Nights, we had an instance of the Fault in the greatest Player in the World: It is no particular Censure to charge him with it, because 'tis customary; and nothing else was expected from him; but he will own the Impropriety when he submits the Question not to Custom, but to his own discerning and impartial Reason.

Mr *Garrick*, in the Character of *Dumnorix*, in this Play, drew his Sword on the first Night in the midst of a Prayer; and full of the Uprightness of his Cause, brandished it in the Face of Heaven. It was disputed whether this were proper; but there could be no Dispute whether a Repetition of it could be proper: that was impossible. The Suddenness of a virtuous Emotion might excuse him once in doing it; but nothing could justify the cold Repetition; nor could anything be more unpleasing to an Audience than to know beforehand what was to happen at the Start of a Passion, and to be able to say at what Word the Hero was to draw forth his Weapon. This, taking away the Appearance of Nature and Reality, debases in the greatest Degree a Player who is full of her true Feelings, and places Mr Garrick upon almost a Level with the Automatons who attend upon him in that Scene, to whom he is to give a Look at their Cue for drawing their Swords, as the Word in the Prayer is his . . .

The Women of the present Stage are much less liable to this

Censure than the Men; they may therefore with Justice, and greatly to their Honour, claim a Reserve for themselves in the Sentence: Not that they are wholly free from the Fault, but that they are not so guilty of it; and this is the more to their Honour, because if they had fallen into it, and pleaded the Example of the Men, it would have been an Authority. Whoever observes Mrs *Cibber*, in her repeated playing of *Indiana*, will find continually something new in her Manner, her Gesture, and Deportment. All her Attitudes in her Distress speak the same Emotions of Despair; but the whole Frame is as capable of Variety in Expression, as the Voice. This is not the only Proof we have of that Actress's really possessing that Enthusiasm of the Theatre; on which all great Acting depends, and of her perfectly losing herself in the Character: of her being not Mrs *Cibber*, but very *Indiana*; very *Lady Macbeth*; and very very *Constance*.

Her Variety is nowhere seen so much as in this last named Character: It has been indeed so great, that many have questioned whether she now play'd it so well as some Years since; but they answer themselves by the very Conduct of the Question. While one insists she is not equal to her former self, and another that she is greater than ever: Enquire more strictly, and you will find they saw her on different Nights: The Question is not, whether Mrs *Cibber* acted *Constance* better some Years ago or now, but whether she acted it better on *Tuesday* or on *Thursday*, and the whole Result is, that Mrs *Cibber* has great Variety. The Spirit and Gesture of one Night please some; those of another Night others; according to their different Judgments. Mrs *Cibber* is equal and alike worthy their Applause in all.

It were Injustice to pass by Mrs *Pritchard*, without her Share of this Praise; and those must have seen *Merope* but once, who want a lively Instance of it. But this Variety is more surprising in that new Actress named before, who, tho' always the same haughty, jealous, fond *Hermione*, never was twice indebted to the same set of Attitudes and Gestures to express that Excellence.

Anon

12

David Garrick

After a 'Club' dinner in the spring of 1774 at the St James's Coffee-House, the members joined in a contest of epitaphs. Garrick began it with the couplet:

> Here lies Nolly Goldsmith, for shortness called Noll,
> He wrote like an angel, but talked like poor Poll.

There were others. Oliver Goldsmith (1728–74), endearing Irish-bred dramatist, novelist, essayist, and poet, promised his reply later; but when he died in 1774, at the age of 46, he had not completed his *Retaliation*; it broke off in the middle of his epitaph on Sir Joshua Reynolds. The best of those he did—others were on Dean Barnard, three Burkes (Edmund, William, Richard), the dramatist Richard Cumberland, Dr Douglas, the lawyer Joseph Hickey—was a full-length of the actor David Garrick. William Kenrick (*c*1725–79) was a waspishly attacking miscellaneous writer who 'libelled almost every successful actor and author'. Hugh Kelly (1739–77) was a dramatist, and William Woodfall, the critic and Parliamentary journalist (*Morning Chronicle*). Beaumont and Ben are the dramatists, Sir Francis Beaumont (1584–1616) and Ben Jonson (1572–1637).

Here lies David Garrick, describe me, who can,
An abridgment of all that was pleasant in man;
As an actor, confessed without rival to shine:
As a wit, if not first, in the very first line:
Yet, with talents like these, and an excellent heart,
The man had his failings, a dupe to his art.
Like an ill-judging beauty, his colours he spread,
And beplaster'd with rouge his own natural red.
On the stage he was natural, simple, affecting;
'Twas only that when he was off he was acting.
With no reason on earth to go out of his way,
He turn'd and he varied full ten times a day.
Though secure of our hearts, yet confoundedly sick
If they were not his own by finessing and trick;
He cast off his friends, as a huntsman his pack,
For he knew when he pleas'd he could whistle them back.
Of praise a mere glutton, he swallow'd what came,
And the puff of a dunce he mistook it for fame;
Till his relish grown callous, almost to disease,
Who pepper'd the highest was surest to please.
But let us be candid, and speak out our mind,
If dunces applauded, he paid them in kind.
Ye Kenricks, ye Kellys, and Woodfalls so grave,
What a commerce was yours, while you got and you gave!
How did Grub-street re-echo the shouts that you rais'd,
While he was be-Roscius'd, and you were be-prais'd!
But peace to his spirit, wherever it flies,
To act as an angel, and mix with the skies:
Those poets, who owe their best fame to his skill,
Shall still be his flatterers, go where he will.
Old Shakespeare, receive him, with praise and with love,
And Beaumonts and Bens be his Kellys above.

Oliver Goldsmith

13

Rival Queens

Tate Wilkinson (1739–1803), who called himself 'the wandering patentee' in the reminiscences published at York in 1795—there had been an earlier book, the *Memoirs of His Own Life*—was as garrulous, as eccentric, and as likeable as the seventeenth-century gossip, John Aubrey. Originally a moderate London actor and an excellent mimic, he belongs theatrically to the provinces, and especially to his York circuit which he managed for some thirty years. York and Hull (for which in time he obtained Royal patents) and Leeds were his principal theatres; but presently he took in Doncaster and Wakefield and, ultimately, Pontefract. He would be in Hull from October to January, and in York during February to May (also in the August race week). At this time Wilkinson's circuit knew the leaders of the English stage, coming or arrived: for example, John Philip Kemble ('great propriety and startling merit'); George Frederick Cooke ('where his character suits, his merit would be undoubted on any stage, however critical'), Mrs Jordan (during 1782–5 'her plaintive tragedy . . . had great merit'), and, especially, Sarah Siddons ('Were a wild Indian to ask me, What was like a queen? I would have bade him look at Mrs Siddons in . . . *Henry VIII*').

These are some of the plays and personages mentioned in the following extracts:

Plays

Percy (1777), tragedy by Hannah More; *Isabella; or, The Fatal Marriage* (1757), altered from Thomas Southerne by David Garrick;

The Irish Widow (1772), two-act comedy by David Garrick (stage direction in last scene: 'Enter Widow Brady, as Lieutenant O'Neale, seemingly fluttered, and putting up her sword'); *The Roman Father* (1750), a tragedy by William Whitehead ('Enter Horatia, wounded . . . dies'); *Lethe; or, Aesop in the Shade* (1740), brief Garrick farce, written eighteen months before his first stage triumph as an actor; *The Grecian Daughter* (1772), by Arthur Murphy, with its famous title-part of Euphrasia ('No, tyrant, hold!'); *Mary Queen of Scots* (1789) by the Hon John St John; and *The Battle of Hexham; or, Days of Old* (1789), in three acts, by George Colman the younger.

Personages

Mrs (Williams Perkins) Taylor had been Mrs Hannah Henrietta Robinson, wife of an actor who died in 1786 from 'a rapid decay which baffled all art'. Mrs Dorothy (Dorothea) Jordan, 1761–1816, the hoyden of her theatre. She was the illegitimate daughter of Frances Bland. Tate Wilkinson suggested her stage name—'a good name it has proved for her credit'. Immensely successful in London, from 1791 to 1811 she was the mistress of the Duke of Clarence (afterwards William IV) by whom she had several children. Her last years were unhappy, and she died in Paris. Leigh Hunt said of her: 'She was nature herself in one of her most genial forms . . . She was inimitable in exemplifying the consequence of too much restraint in ill-educated Country Girls, in Romps, in Hoydens, and in Wards on whom the mercenary have designs.' Mrs (Susan) Fawcett was the first wife—she had been Mrs John Mills—of John Fawcett, the comedian (1768–1837); he joined the York circuit in 1787 and made such a success that, four years later, he reached London at Covent Garden. Wilkinson admired Mrs Fawcett very much: 'She really was ready for everything; her study was rapid; her will was great; in short, for the laws of wit and humour, she was my only woman.'

Leeds, May 1785

Mrs Robinson was to act four nights at Leeds, and on the Wednesday I arrived from Manchester, she made her first appearance in that heavy plaintive part of Elwina in *Percy*, which she played with credit, but not equal to her forms of fancy. After the play she acted the Irish Widow, which not only in my judgment but everybody's, was much superior to her tragedy.

Her figure in the small clothes was neat to a degree of perfection, and her deportment, spirit, and conception of the part was, I think, the best I had then or have since seen. Her second night was Isabella in *The Fatal Marriage*. Mrs Jordan's mother, Mrs Bland, who was sitting at the stage door while Mrs Robinson was acting, frequently took hold of me by the hand or coat, clapping her apron before her eyes, and begging, as an act of kindness, I would inform her when that fright had done acting and speaking; for it was so horrid she could not look at her.

On the other hand, one evening when I was chatting with Mrs Robinson, she wondered I could allow the merit I did to that Mrs Jordan; for her own part, she could not discover any, or, if any, it was not beyond a small share of mediocrity. She thought she possessed some judgment, and would venture to pronounce when I lost *my great treasure* (as I termed Mrs Jordan) in the autumn, and *it* went to London *it* would soon be turned back again upon my hands, and *it* would be glad to come if I would accept *it*. But that prophecy was not verified, of which I wish Mrs Jordan joy, though my compliments may not be worth her acceptance in her present station.

Leeds, June 1786

Mrs Robinson had only a few nights to play before she finished her engagement that season, 1786. Her last night was for her own benefit on Friday, June 16. She acted Horatia in *The Roman Father*; and in the farce, *The Irish Widow*. The house, I am sorry to remark, was very inferior to that when she appeared in 1785, and to make the circumstance still more mortifying, who should suddenly appear to make it additionally provoking but Mrs Jordan, attended by mamma and sister, on a tour to Edinburgh and Glasgow Theatres, as her trumpet had sounded to the North Pole and excited offers of bewitching golden fire.

I have remarked that no violent love or cordiality had subsisted between these two ladies. Mrs Jordan, of course, after displaying herself in the upper-box, and making the gazers look at Mrs Somebody, who but twelve months before was only held as Mrs Nobody. That gratification being by her accomplished,—in the farce she kindly descended to come behind the scenes and ask the manager and her old friends and acquaintance in that part of the theatre, how they all did, and not without the additional grace of an alluring nod and smile, which had been purchased at the London market of fashion during a whole winter's residence of good luck, fortune, and everything that was enviable. So after the noble greeting and salutation to us all, the Jordan, after having been recognised by her old Leeds audience in profile, from the front row of the balcony, determined on being viewed at full-length; which (as the Fine Gentleman in *Lethe* observes) makes the gods look angry. But how could they be angry with their dearly beloved Jordan? In short, by slow degrees, she advanced so far on the stage that, at the first-hold of her sister's arm, she was at the very edge of the wing on the stage part. This was during the *small clothes* scene in *The Irish Widow*, in the last act of that farce.

This enraged the widow Robinson to a degree, and it added to her anger of a bad benefit, when from the sample of the year before, she expected it to rise, not to fall off, which would naturally irritate any lady. But this said benefit, be it known to all men, was on a Friday, though not a *good* Friday. She, however, kept up her spirits to let the Jordan see how well she could act, and with a sneer, not the gentlest, darted a glance at the Jordan, insinuating,—'Can you act like this?' The other, with all the nonchalance of fashion, said a great deal without ever speaking a word,—for her gestures and pantomime action were inimitable; and as she leaned on her sister, she pointed at Widow Brady's buckles, then at her figure, next with a significant shrug that the whole was intolerable, and at last, after giving the torture in an elegant and truly significant manner, she gave her a last look and turned away with the grandest contempt and hauteur.

Now, it may be asked, why did not I prevail on Mrs Jordan to quit so improper a situation for herself, and cruel to a degree, as Mrs Jordan's marks of disapprobation were of great consequence in the minds of men that year, though the effect might have been widely different the year before. But in answer, it is probable my request would not have been complied with; for the manager she had looked up to was no longer the man of terror or command, but *then* looked down upon, if he dared to assume authority. And another hidden reason might be the cause, had my desire of her quitting so very conspicuous a situation been complied with, it might not have given me the ill-natured satisfaction I enjoyed; for Mrs Robinson had quarrelled with me violently the day before, and I love a little mischief,—'tis in my nature; and oh Nature! Nature! who can stop thy course? I felt for Mrs Robinson, yet at the same time I immoderately chuckled at the mischief I witnessed going forward; and had I ventured to be the mediator, like Milton's Chaos I should 'as umpire sat, And by decision more embroil'd the fray'.

'So, if that be a truth, why, Mr Wilkinson, who do not like being vexed, do you not grow more pliant, from your own feelings?' Why it is a fair question, but it is a picture of life in general more than the reader will suppose, for all are made more or less of the same whimsical disposition, and I will take the hint as well as I can, and mend with all convenient speed; but it was in fact only retaliation. For Mrs Robinson had foretold that Mrs Jordan would be back with me before twelve months were gone and over; and so far her gift of double-sight was verified (so were the Witches' prophecies to Macbeth); but not as either Mrs Robinson or Mr Wilkinson in so high a degree expected, for instead of the *suppliant*, she came splish, splash, dish, dash, to the Leeds play-house, and tassels dangling, and etc.—Oh! it's a charming thing to be a woman of quality,—and in lieu of her asking me for an engagement, the case was greatly altered. I was obliged to solicit the lady who formerly solicited me, and it was no more than a comic adventure between us three, like a party of pleasure at quadrille, where all should play and pay alike. Ay, but sayd Mrs Robinson, you have made me at this game pay more than my share. Well, Mrs Robinson, never mind it, I will pay two-thirds at our next meeting to clear the debt; I am a rich man in that respect and will treat most cheerfully and liberally. And I hope this nonsense will be read by the two ladies as I mean it whimsically, and for us all three to laugh at . . . A wiser head than mine, and a particular good friend at Hull, many years ago, dubb'd Wilkinson 'One of God Almighty's Unaccountables.'

Hull, 1789

Mrs Taylor (late Mrs Robinson) was that year engaged once more. We met so lovingly, and with such apparent friendship, that a bystander would have thought it difficult to have sown the seeds of discord between such sincere friends: and I do aver, *on the probity of a manager*, mine was sincere, depend upon it; but in three days after our meeting, I neglected to *bottom her* (as is the phrase) for the Irish Widow, or the Grecian Daughter, I forget which, but do not forget that she refused to play, and broke out most violently, and run over her catalogue of wrongs, such as 'indignity—lowering of consequence—mean under-mining arts—would have a redress of grievances', and a hundred exclamations, lamentations, provocations, revenge, contempt, etc. This being accompanied with several notes from the enraged lady, brought on a rupture no doctor could cure, and we, who were never to have parted, dissolved all engagement in a few days. She unfortunately depended upon that fatal word, *consequence*, thinking from the high estimation with which she was received at Hull in the year 1785, that her fame was increased, not diminished. But she was wrong, for the furor had ceased; and she should have known that audiences are as changeable as actors and actresses, and that when she left Hull a few seasons before, she claimed pity as well as admiration, being a lovely widow overwhelmed with grief most poignant. But in the year 1789 she was not the matron Robinson but the blooming bride Taylor, with a clever, sensible young gentleman of abilities, to love and to cherish her.

We parted in a rage; not with such civility as we met—I mean the lady;—for I flew to my philosophy to sustain the shock. We have been since nearly coming together once more, but an unlucky word or phrase in one of my none-such epistles, set us again at variance, and peace has never yet been perfectly established . . .

Great indecorum

When Mrs Siddons appointed the new play of Queen Mary for her benefit at York in May 1789, I sent Queen Elizabeth to Mrs Fawcett, which she accepted conditionally, that she would willingly submit to a forfeiture without murmur, than play a character that she judged so ill-drawn; but she at the same time cheerfully accepted the part to act under Mrs Siddons, but did not choose to be compelled to act it under any inferior actress. I to that proviso agreed; assured her she should not perform the part if the play was again wanted. Mrs Fawcett in consequence acted the part, and I thought the matter would there have rested; but Hull winter season will prove it otherwise.

A Mrs Rivers was engaged that season. She was a handsome figure; a fine face; fine eyes; and a set of teeth to be admired and wished for: very tall, and what was more, there was enough for any man. I engaged her as a useful actress, which she could have made herself, as she had no objection to the small-clothes parts. Mrs Taylor, unfortunately, for her benefit and her last night of performing, fixed on Mary Queen of Scots. From the idea the reader will form from what I have just said relative to Mrs Rivers, it will be readily admitted that her figure was highly proper for Queen Elizabeth. I sent her the part which that lady, in a very vehement manner, sent back, wondering how I dared insult her with such an intentional affront. I persisted on her performance, or forfeiting her salary; and as she would not receive the part or attend rehearsal, I sent Mrs Fawcett an account of the dilemma I was in, and desired her assistance. She said that it was true she had requested not to do the part after Mrs Siddons's departure, but did not mean that any disappointment should happen to the audience or me, if at any time in her power to obviate; and was happy that she was ready in the character, and would play it on Tuesday, December 29, with the greatest pleasure. Mrs Fawcett's name, therefore, was inserted for Queen Elizabeth in the distribution of the day, but Mrs Rivers's name being in the bills all the preceding week, a certain part of the audience either did not or would not understand the reason, or were very likely instigated by the charms of Rivers.

However, be it as it may, when Mrs Fawcett made her appearance (though an established favourite as an actress) she was severely hissed. This certainly was extremely hard, ungenerous, and unthinking to a lady who came forward in the time of distress to promote the entertainment of the public, and to act, not read, the character. She explained the matter, but they would not be convinced; they entertained secret thoughts that the poor devil of a manager meant some imposition—(for in town or village that is ever a ready suggestion)—and thus the play was got through, but not without murmurs, for which I was truly sorry for Mrs Fawcett, as such treatment was a bar to her stepping forward, or any other person, on a similar occasion; and so long after as December the 29th to January 13th was Mrs Rivers's next appearance, which was the Queen in *The Battle of Hexham*. It was accident my being at the theatre so early as the beginning of the play, nor could I have the slightest surmise that Queen Elizabeth could be a matter of discord between the public and myself, or have any repeating of grievances, never having heard it mentioned; but on Mrs Rivers's entrance they called to her for an apology for not acting the Queen on Mrs Taylor's benefit. The lady, without any perturbation of spirit, with infinite dignity and one half stride, stalked over my little stage; she enumerated her wrongs most pathetically; that she was a defenceless woman, used with a rod of iron by that barbarous of most barbarous men, the manager; and went through her exercise so well that she received repeated bursts of applause. I felt rather angry that she should have all the triumph, therefore was determined to partake the gale, which was rather awkward, as I had not been on that stage from January 1788 to that time, was in déshabille, and not in training to make my lame bow.

However, with my short stick I hobbled on, and as she was raging with her wrongs (and never acted half so well in her life—that I had seen) with arm uplifted like the Grecian Daughter in the last act, and not perceiving me who was at her elbow till she turned. My being there so very unexpectedly made her stop in an attitude of surprise which to the spectators must have been truly whimsical, and looked as much as to say, 'Who sent for you? All was going on right until you came.' I endeavoured to explain how the lady had insolently returned the part; that I continued her name in the bills till the day, in hopes her good sense would convince her how wrong she was to quarrel with me, or give the least offence to the public; and she herself must be convinced, as well as those who then saw her, that her figure was highly proper for Queen Elizabeth, and that what she had urged, that she was engaged to act the principal characters only in any play, I could evidently prove to the contrary by the call of parts under her own hand, which were chiefly *second*, and many of them even *third*, characters.

I did not obtain victory against the female until a *gentleman*, to whom I begged leave to deliver her *own* written cast, instead of receiving the said paper like a gentleman, a critic, or a wise man, threw it at me in a most indignant manner: this flagrant instance of pride (and as flagrantly ill-bred) made the pit and galleries unanimous in my favour. For the audience, perceiving intentional insult on that occasion, revolted and flew to the weaker side; and I retired with applause, and indeed a complete victory, if I might judge from the great superiority of plaudits; though a few minutes before, the conflict was strong, and like other battles remained doubtful: but what is at times rebellion, when attended with brilliant success and good fortune, changes to the word *revolution.* The lady went through the part with applause, and also marks of disapprobation, for the people were then convinced that she had assumed more consequence than became her; and her acting also proved, to full conviction, that the first characters were disposed of in abler hands.

The next day everybody agreed that Mr Wilkinson was treated

with great indecorum, and that he, as manager, should be supported in his disputes with the actors: for if the audience were to interfere with the never-endless quarrels between the performers and the director, a theatre would be a perpetual scene of discord, and his life would be degraded and insupportable. Of this I am certain, that on Mr Paine's levelling scheme, no theatre could be conducted without a government; they might indeed elect a manager, but that manager would be proclaimed not duly elected, and on the first supposed offence would be tumbled from his chair and guillotined, unpitied.

From these reflections Mrs Rivers was received with much severity when she next made her appearance; but some bucks supported her;—she made an apology. She was a woman and a handsome woman, and all terminated happily as it should be; and again it was as it should be, for the little affray brought money, and that was a good poultice for my aching bones.

On Tuesday, January 19th, I made my appearance in Shylock, after two years' confinement; had a wonderful reception and a brilliant and crowded audience . . .

Tate Wilkinson

14

Hannah Brand

Now, in his kindly way, Tate Wilkinson flashes up for us the eccentric actress, Hannah Brand, originally a governess. She arrived in his York company during the spring of 1794, appearing first as Lady Townly in Cibber's comedy, *The Provok'd Husband; or, A Journey to London* ('You would really have a woman of my rank and spirit stay at home to comfort her husband! Lord, what notions of life some men have!') According to a historian (Genest), Hannah Brand was 'much too formal'.

She had acted two years earlier, with John Philip Kemble, in a play of her own, *Huniades*, for the Drury Lane company; this was established temporarily at the new King's Theatre in Haymarket. Hannah's tragedy was about the Turkish siege of Belgrade in 1456; the gallant Huniades (Kemble) led the defenders. James Boaden says of the production in *Memoirs of the Life of John Philip Kemble, Esq.* (1825): 'The authoress herself acted the heroine Agmunda. How it was effected I now forget, but she absolutely withdrew the play for the purpose of cutting out the hero, and the tragedy was evidently not the worse for his departure; for the audience were not a jot more indifferent to the new title of *Agmunda* than they had been to the more barbarous name of *Huniades*. If my memory does not deceive me, the costume in the play was somewhat unusual, and provoked a laugh—I think, black with gold ornaments.'

Hannah Brand's *Plays and Poems* (Norwich, 1798) contained *Huniades; or, The Siege of Belgrade* and two adaptations from the French. She became the mistress of 'a respectable seminary for French education' at Norwich and died in 1821.

The extract is from Wilkinson's *The Wandering Patentee* (1795). Calista is the heroine of Nicholas Rowe's *The Fair Penitent* (1703), based on *The Fatal Dowry* of Massinger and Field; a character in this is the luckless 'haughty, gallant, gay Lothario'. The journalist William Woodfall (he first called Wilkinson 'the wandering patentee') wrote for the London *Morning Chronicle*.

On Tuesday, March 20 [1794; at York] came forth Miss Hannah Brand, with credentials in her hand, from Mr Woodfall. Perhaps there is not any character, as a romantic stage-struck princess, possesses a more extraordinary set of contradictory passions than the said lady, Miss Hannah Brand. She is very sensible, but too learned. She knows herself to be an actress of such sterling worth, that every bar to her success is created from the envy, fear, of Mrs Siddons, and that of all the Kembles; and from their interests, every manager in the kingdom of Great Britain is a determined enemy. She values herself at not holding up her train as her constant use of large drawing-rooms, and a frequent habit of brilliant assemblies, prevents such trifles ever to occur as necessary. A tolerable room looks very insignificant, from the always living in those of expanse, as to width, length, and heighth. Fielding's works are not deserving the perusal; they cannot be termed poetry, but if they are, it can only be admitted as of the lowest kind, and as the very dregs of verse. No! when she has a mind to be entertained with works of humour, she has recourse to certain entertainment in the Latin authors, in their original purity of language; it is there only, that she finds ample field for comic entertainment. No sensible person surely ever sat to see a farce; it was not only a loss of time, but degrading to taste; she never murdered time in that manner but once, and that was to see *My Grandmother* at York, to gratify her curiosity as a compliment to Mrs John Wilkinson.

My son, casually asking her what farce she would approve for her benefit, after a solemn grand pause, she said—'Why, Sir, should I strike the anvil of my brain, when there is nothing to hammer out?' She sent me a note one morning that contained rather, I thought, an absurd expression as to correctness, which I mentioned to her, when she erected her chest with infinite majesty, and said: 'Mr Wil-kin-son, had I wrote that note to Mrs Wil-kin-son, I had not been so precisely exact as to grammatical points, but when I considered that I was addressing a classical gentleman, I judged it obviously unnecessary to be careful of any unguarded slip; for if you would attentively re-peruse the note, you will quickly perceive that the line alluded to was appertaining to the *plural* not the *singular* number.' I could not refrain a burst of immoderate laughter; but as soon as my breath recovered, and gave me leave, with resumed gravity, I assured her, the gods had neither made me poetical or learnedly classical . . .

'Well,' says Mrs Hannah, 'it is wonderful not to converse with the ancients, the Italians, French, Latin and the Greek authors, all which I can read, perfectly understand, and speak fluently.' When immediately she could not instantly recollect whether a word she had just then pronounced was from any expression of the Greeks or the Romans; and quoted a line of each to ascertain which it belonged to . . .

A lady of rank assured me that she sat in a box where Mrs Hannah was in the row behind, at the Opera House or the Play House, I do not recollect which, where she was accoutred in an old-fashioned jacket, with deep flaps (as all York can remember and testify the said remarkable habit) with a tremendous long bosom-frill, over which the right hand was plunged, and in a fixed attitude she continued pensively superior from the beginning of the evening's entertainment to the finale. She seldom went or came from the theatre at York but in a chair, so dreadfully fearful was she in that quiet city of the insulter, man. At the time she was at York were the Lent Assizes, and in the last season, March, 1794, there were more carriages than I have remembered for some years; so many that at noon it really bore a little resemblance of the streets near Grosvenor Square, but as a proof of home partiality (Hannah being of Norfolk breed), I asked her if she did not like the flitting of the various carriages in York at that particular time? She said, 'Yes; she certainly thought there was an appearance of much and elegant company, but when she allowed that circumstance, begged leave to lament her not being at Norwich; and implored leave to observe that, being accustomed to Norfolk, where she received the daily pleasure of viewing horses of the highest breed, health, and condition, it was deplorable at York not to see any one carriage with decent cattle.' 'Why, surely, Miss Brand, you are not serious?' 'Indeed, Mr Wil-kin-son, I am.' 'Why, Madam, you certainly cannot be ignorant that in the breed of horses and grooms, Yorkshire is universally known and allowed to be the foremost county in the kingdom.' She said she would not contradict me, but it was the first time she ever heard it averred that Yorkshire was remarkable for races, grooms, or horses! A certain instance that her knowledge, not only in that point, but many others, was more in the vortex of her brain than in the real experience. Her dresses were more than good, and her linen fine, they would not have disgraced a drawing-room on the royal birth-day, but they were all romantic; and either in the street or the room, she wanted only a spear and shield, to have awed the wondering beholders with her grand and majestic portly bearing.

It is no more extraordinary than true, that Miss Brand'*s* dialect was as provincial as if her education had been utterly neglected: For instance (one as good as a hundred) I might receive your whole *ustate* instead of *estate*, &c. *arkangel,—archangel*, as the *arch* of a bridge. Her dresses on the stage I have mentioned as elegant, but all the effect was lost owing to her wearing stays not of the *new* but the *old* fashion, which barriers defended her charms from all unhallowed eyes: For at present all beholders need not want a peep but look full and be perfectly satisfied whether the view will cause many bidders. But Hannah Brand would not unveil her beauties even to the chaste Diana; therefore she, with well-bound bone, forbid all access . . . Troy was not more impregnable within her walls, her bulwarks, and her gates of brass than was the fearless Hannah, unless indeed that fair heroine was assailed with lavish praises on her play or her acting, and then the gods (to whom she would appeal) have mercy on her, for on that theme she would be as vulnerable as the invulnerable Prince Achilles was in his heel. It was no more than strictly true that her generosity was boundless, as she would (like Sheva the Jew) stint her appetite to pamper her affections, and live on a crust to gratify others, to whom she thought herself in the least obliged.

Her first appearance in Lady Townly, so far from being well received, met with rude remarks of disgustful behaviour, and that from ladies who did not add by such demeanour to their politeness or good understanding; but I must grant that Hannah's Lady Townly was too formal for the school of gaiety in 1794. Her play of *Agmunda* was acted the last night in the season, May 21, 1794. So tenacious was she of such her invaluable treasure being purloined, that she would not suffer the original Drury Lane manuscript to be in the dangerous prompter's hands, but wrote out an entire copy herself, actually without one line of her own part being inserted, as a certain safeguard to her property, for on that she constantly placed a steady hand. At the end of an act she found the altar-table too high, and exclaimed, 'If the theatre were to fall in one momentous crush, she would not begin unless it was more advanced'; and with great composure at the end of the fourth act, assured Mr Earby (the prompter) 'That she would not proceed in her business unless he first assured her she might depend upon *two flourishes* previous to her entrance.' The play ended as a comic, not as the tale of woe; and certainly as a tragedy neither was, is, or ever will be able to retain a place on the boards. I cannot omit noticing that, at the rehearsal, after a pause of considerable length, when all were in amazement lost, she turned profoundly round, and in blank-verse tone said, 'Observe, Mr Warren, I have stopped thus long that you may remember at night, all this length of time *I shall be weeping*.'

She engaged after that exploit the last summer at Liverpool, where she treated the audience with Calista, with much the same success, I believe, as her tragedy met with at York, for which I am told she ushered a complaining publication to the inhabitants of Liverpool . . . Her performance at York by no means merited the sarcastic manner in which she was treated; the which, though certainly as unkind as ungenerous, could only be palliated by the uncommon stiffness of deportment that the Lady Townly by custom had habituated herself to. Indeed the *School* formality she possesses, I may almost say from instinct.

One day, rapping at my room door, 'Who's there?' says I, to which she replied as awfully as the Ghost in *Hamlet*, 'It is Hannah Brand.' Now take this lady from her tragedy and her acting, and she possesses many good, ay shining qualities; that is, she would rather give than take, and does not know sufficiently how to content her mind, without making more than ample restitution for any received civilities. To that generosity of temper she unites a good understanding, and is certainly worthy of much esteem as to her private character; and I sincerely hope that the experience she has had, will make her enjoy both health and comfort, far, ay very far, preferable to the buffets of the stage, unless where great profits may come home.

Tate Wilkinson

Theatre-Royal, Newcastle.

FOR THREE NIGHTS ONLY.

Miss Clara Fisher's
SECOND NIGHT.

On TUESDAY, May the 18th, 1819,
Will be presented Shakespeare's Comedy of

THE MERCHANT OF VENICE.

Shylock, MISS CLARA FISHER

The Duke of Venice,	MR AMHERST	Salanio,	MR HILL
Anthonio, (the Merchant)	MR GRANT	Launcelot,	MR DANBY
Bassanio	MR YOUNG	Gobbo,	MR HODGSON
Gratiano,	MR DE CAMP	Balthazer,	MR MOORE
Lorenzo,	MR KING	Tubal,	MR FORRESTER
Salarino,	MR UDALE		

Nerissa, MISS AMELIA FISHER
Portia - MISS CAROLINE FISHER
Jessica, MISS HILL

AFTER THE PLAY,

A COMIC SONG,
(IN CHARACTER)
BY MISS CLARA FISHER.

To conclude with the interesting Melo-Drame of

The Dog of Montargis;
Or, The Forest of Bondy.

Florian, (the Dumb Orphan) MISS POVEY

Colonel Gontram,	MR FORRESTER	Lieutenant Macaire,	MR YOUNG
Seneschal,	MR HODGSON	Landre,	MR KING
Captain Aubri,	MR DE CAMP	Blaize,	MR DANBY
Dame Gertrude,	MISS WALDRON	Lucille,	MISS HILL

In Consequence of the almost immediate Departure of the **MILITARY BAND** of the Royal 18th Hussars, **COLONEL GRANT** has obligingly permitted their Attendance at the Theatre for this Evening, when they will play several **POPULAR** and **FASHIONABLE AIRS.**

Tickets and Places to be had of Mr Tadman, at the Saloon, every Day from 12 till 3.

Printed by E. Humble, at the Shakespeare Press.

15

'Unpolished Gem'

This article appeared (July 1874) in *All the Year Round*, the weekly miscellany founded by Charles Dickens. The anonymous writer celebrated a remarkable business woman, Mrs Sarah Baker (*c*1736–1816), daughter of an acrobatic dancer who became a touring manager. In time, Sarah went on to own theatres in several places in Kent, notably Canterbury and Rochester. Her daughter Sally (1768–1817) married the actor William Dowton (1764–1851)—'a genuine and excellent comedian', said Hazlitt—before he made his London successes. Edmund Kean, as a young man, acted with Sarah Baker during 1806–7.

Mrs Jarley was the proprietor of Jarley's Wax-work; Nell travelled with her in Dickens's *The Old Curiosity Shop*. *Who's the Dupe?* (1779) was a farce by Mrs Hannah Cowley.

A famous provincial manager, or manageress, was one Mrs Baker, who owned theatres at Canterbury, Rochester, Maidstone, Tunbridge Wells, Faversham, and other places, but was understood to have commenced her professional career with a puppet-show, or even the homely entertainment of Punch and Judy. But her energy, enterprise, and industry were of an indomitable kind. She generally lived in her theatres, and rising early to accomplish her marketing and other household duties, she proceeded to take up her position in the box-office, with the box-book open before her, and resting upon it 'a massy silver inkstand, which, with a superb pair of silver trumpets, several cups, tankards, and candlesticks of the same pure metal, it was her honest pride to say she had paid for with her own hard earnings'. While awaiting the visits of those desirous to book their places for the evening, she arranged her programme of the entertainments. Her education was far from complete, however, for although she could read, she was but an indifferent scribe. By the help of scissors, needle, thread, and a bundle of old playbills, she achieved her purpose. She cut a play from one bill, an interlude from another, a farce from another, and sewing the slips neatly together avoided the use of pen and ink. When the name of a new performer had to be introduced, she left a blank to be filled up by the first of her actors she happened to encounter, presuming him to be equal to the use of a pen.

She sometimes beat the drum, or tolled the bell behind the scenes, when the representation needed such embellishments, and occasionally fulfilled the duties of prompter. In this respect it was unavoidable that she should now and then be rather over-tasked. On one special evening she held the book during the performance of the old farce of *Who's the Dupe?* The part of Gradus was undertaken by her leading actor, one Gardner, and in the scene of Gradus's attempt to impose upon the gentleman of the story by affecting to speak Greek, the performer's memory unfortunately failed him. He glanced appealingly towards the prompt-side of the stage. Mrs Baker was mute, examining the play-book with a puzzled air. 'Give me the word, madam,' whispered the actor. 'It's a hard word, Jem,' the lady replied. 'Then give me the next.' 'That's harder.' The performance was at a standstill. 'The next,' cried Gardner, furiously. 'Harder still!' answered the prompter, and then, perplexed beyond bearing, she flung the book on the stage, and exclaimed aloud: 'There, now, you have them all; take your choice.'

But the lady's usual station was in front of the house. She was her own money-taker, and to this fact has been ascribed the great good fortune she enjoyed as a manager. 'Now then, pit or box, pit or gallery, box or pit?' she cried incessantly. 'Pit! Pit!' half-a-dozen voices might cry. 'Then pay two shillings. Pass on, Tom Fool!' for so, on busy nights, she invariably addressed her patrons of all classes. To a woman who had to quit the theatre, owing to the cries of the child she bore in her arms disturbing the audience, Mrs Baker observed, as she returned the entrance money, 'Foolish woman! Foolish woman! Don't come another night until half-price, and then give your baby some Dalby's Carminative.' 'I remember,' writes Dibdin, 'one very crowded night, patronised by a royal duke at Tunbridge Wells, when Mrs Baker was taking money for three doors at once, her anxiety and very proper tact led her, while receiving cash from one customer, to keep an eye in perspective on the next, to save time, as thus: "Little girl! get your money ready, while this gentleman pays. My Lord! I'm sure your lordship has silver. Let that little boy go in while I give his lordship change. Shan't count after your ladyship. Here comes the duke! Make haste! His royal highness will please to get his ticket ready while my lady—now sir! Now your royal highness!" "Oh dear, Mrs Baker! I've left my ticket in another coat pocket!" "To be sure you have! Take your royal highness's word! Let his royal highness pass! His royal highness has left his ticket in his *other* coat-pocket." Great laughter followed, and I believe the rank and fashion of the evening found more entertainment in the lobby than on the stage.'

On the occasion of Grimaldi's engagement 'for one night only', it was found necessary to open the doors of the Maidstone Theatre at a very early hour, to relieve the thoroughfare of the dense crowd which had assembled. The house being quite full,

Mrs Baker locked up the box in which the receipts of the evening had been deposited, and going round to the stage, directed the performance to begin forthwith, remarking, reasonably enough, 'that the house could but be full, and being full to the ceiling now, they might just as well begin at once, and have business over so much the sooner'. Greatly to the satisfaction of the audience, the representation accordingly began without delay, and ended shortly after nine o'clock.

It should be added that Mrs Baker had been a dancer in early life, and was long famed for the grace of her carriage and the elegance of her curtsey. Occasionally she ventured upon the stage dressed in the bonnet and shawl she had worn while receiving money and issuing checks at the door, and in audible tones announced the performances arranged for future evenings, the audience enthusiastically welcoming her. A measure of her manifold talents was shared by other members of her family. Her sister, Miss Wakelin, was principal comic dancer to the theatre, occasional actress, wardrobe-keeper, and professed cook, being rewarded for her various services by board and lodging, a salary of a guinea and a half per week, and a benefit in every town Mrs Baker visited, with other emoluments by way of perquisites. Two of Mrs Baker's daughters were also members of her company and divided between them the heroines of tragedy and comedy. One Miss Baker subsequently became the wife of Mr Dowton, the actor.

A settled distrust of the Bank of England was one of Mrs Baker's most marked peculiarities. At the close of the performance she resigned the position she had occupied for some five hours as money-taker for pit, boxes, and gallery, and retired to her chamber, carrying the receipts of the evening in a large front pocket. This money she added to a store contained in half-a-dozen large china punch-bowls, ranged upon the top shelf of an old bureau. For many years she carried her savings about with her from town to town, sometimes retaining upon her person gold in rouleaux to a large amount. She is even said to have kept in her pocket for seven years a note for two hundred pounds. At length her wealth became a positive embarrassment to her. She invested sums in county banks and in the hands of respectable tradesmen, at three per cent, sometimes without receiving any interest whatever, but merely with a view to the safer custody of her resources. It was with exceeding difficulty that she was eventually persuaded to become a fund-holder. She handed over her store of gold to her stockbroker with extraordinary trepidation. It is satisfactory to be assured that at last she accorded perfect confidence to the Bank, increased her investments from time to time, and learned to find pleasure in visiting London half-yearly to receive her dividends. Altogether, Mrs Baker appears to have been a thoroughly estimable woman, cordially regarded by the considerate members of the theatrical profession with whom she had dealings. While recording her eccentricities and conceding that occasionally her language was more forcible and idiomatic than tasteful or refined, Dibdin hastens to add that 'she owned an excellent heart, with much of the appearance and manners of a gentlewoman'. Grimaldi was not less prompt in expressing his complete satisfaction with 'the manageress'. Dibdin wrote the epitaph inscribed above her grave in the cathedral yard of Rochester. A few lines may be extracted, but it must be said that the composition is of inferior quality:

Alone, untaught,
And self-assisted (save by Heaven), she taught
To render each his own, and fairly save
What might help others when she found a grave,
By prudence taught life's troubled waves to stem,
In death her memory shines, a rich, unpolished gem.

It is conceivable—so much may perhaps be added—that Mrs Baker unconsciously posed as a model, and lent a feature or two, when the portrait came to be painted of an even more distinguished manageress, whose theatre, however, was a caravan, whose company consisted of waxen effigies, and who bore the name of Jarley.

All the Year Round

Theatre-Royal, Newcastle.

Unition of superior Talent!!!

Miss O'NEILL and Mr W. M'CREADY,

And probably the *only Opportunity* that ever may occur of those Performers *appearing at the same Time* on the Newcastle Stage.

LAST NIGHT OF

Miss O'NEILL

AND

Mr W. M'Cready's

ENGAGEMENT.

***On SATURDAY Evening, August 22nd,* 1818,**

Will be presented, the new TRAGEDY, called

BELLAMIRA

Or, THE FALL OF TUNIS.

Written by Richard Sheil, Esq. Author of *The Apostate.*

The Part of Bellamira, by Miss O'NEILL

And the Part of Amurath, by Mr WILLIAM M'CREADY,

As originally performed by them at the Theatre-Royal, Covent-Garden.

Manfredi, - Mr ARMSTRONG

Montalto, Mr HILLINGTON

Salerno, Mr MONK   Kaled, Mr BENNETT

Anselmo, Mr BODDIE - Gonzaga, Mr LEWIS

Sadi, Mr DARLEY   Ganem, Mr FRAZER

END OF THE PLAY,

Comic Song—" *The Cosmetic Doctor,*" by Mr Baker

Comic Song—" *Feyther and I,*" by Mr Newton.

DANCING, by Miss Parr and the Junior Miss Worgman.

To which will be added, the FARCE of

Raising the Wind.

Jeremy Didler, Mr STANLEY

Plainway, Mr BODDIE - Sam, Mr NEWTON

Fainwou'd, Mr BAKER   Richard, Mr MONK

Miss Durable, Mrs MARA

And Peggy Plainway, Miss PATTERSON

MISS O'NEILL's BENEFIT,

And the last Night of her and Mr William M'Cready's performing here.

On MONDAY Evening, August 24, will be presented a Play, called

THE POINT OF HONOUR.

The Part of Birtha, by Miss O'NEILL; and the Part of Durimel, by Mr WILLIAM M'CREADY.

After which, the Farce of THE CITIZEN. The Part of Maria, by Miss O'NEILL.

The Ladies and Gentlemen are most respectfully informed that MISS BOOTH, from the Theatre-Royal, Covent-Garden, is engaged to perform here a FEW NIGHTS, the first of which will be on Tuesday, the 25th August, when will be presented Sheridan's admired Comedy, called THE SCHOOL FOR SCANDAL. The Part of Lady Teazle, by Miss BOOTH; Charles Surface, Mr STANLEY. To which will be added, the musical Farce of THE ROMP; or, *A Cure for the Spleen.* Miss Priscilla Tomboy, (the Romp) Miss BOOTH.

Second Night of Miss Booth's Engagement will be on Wednesday, 26th August.

Printed by E. Humble, at the Shakespeare Press.

16

A Word from Rolla

Pizarro, a melodrama about the Spanish conquistadores in Peru, was produced at Drury Lane on 24 May 1799. Leigh Hunt, in later years, said that 'in its highest flights, it is downright booth at a fair—a tall, spouting gentleman in tinsel'. In the circumstances, it is odd that it should have been adapted from the German dramatist, Kotzebue, by Richard Brinsley Sheridan (1751–1816), who, in *The Critic* twenty years earlier, had laughed so much nonsense off the stage. But the sentimental theatrics of the immensely prolific Kotzebue had become a transient cult. Sheridan, manager of the Lane, had had a lot to do in the previous year with *The Stranger*—this is the piece in which, in Thackeray's *Pendennis*, 'the Fotheringay' acts at a country theatre—and now *Pizarro*, in spite of its naivete, was a tremendous financial success. John Philip Kemble as the Peruvian general, Rolla; Sarah Siddons, as Pizarro's mistress with a long train of crimson velvet; and Mrs Jordan as the distracted Cora, were all in the cast—Sheridan disliked Mrs Jordan's performance exceedingly—and most of the dialogue was stupefying bombast. Pizarro (he was acted by Barrymore) orders Elvira to retire. Whereupon she observes: 'O man, man! ungrateful and perverse! O woman! still affectionate though wronged! The beings to whose eyes you turn for animation, hope, and rapture, through the days of mirth and revelry; and on whose bosoms in the hour of sore calamity you seek for rest and consolation; *them*, when the pompous follies of your mean ambition are the question, you treat as playthings or as slaves!—I shall not retire.'

Sheridan's most effective passages were extracted from his own public eloquence: Rolla might well have been referring to the war with France. Lazily, the dramatist did not trouble to write a new prologue; instead he used one, entirely inappropriate, that had preceded Lady Craven's *Miniature Picture* in 1780. The principals, fortunately quick studies, did not receive the text of the last act until the night of the first performance. *Pizarro* then ran on until nearly midnight, and when the after-piece, the farce of *My Grandmother*, began, only twenty-two people remained in the pit and seventeen in the whole of the dress circle.

Pizarro, for many years, was a familiar hack piece in the country; and Edward Stirling, as a strolling player in Kent in the early 1830s, saw his manager improvise what a direction calls 'The Temple of the Sun; it represents the magnificence of Peruvian idolatry'. The Temple was resplendent with gold and silver foil; the 'altar sacred to the god of Peru', a tea-chest, covered with calico. For moonlight a country boy, perched on a ladder, held two large candles behind a hole cut in the temple and covered with gauze. There were also more opulent revivals. As late as September 1856, Charles Kean staged *Pizarro* at the Princess's 'for the purpose of exemplifying the customs, ceremonies, and religion of Peru at the time of the Spanish invasion'. Thus he introduced at the close of the third act 'the principal square of the country during the grand festival of Raymi, the most magnificent and imposing of all the Peruvian religious ceremonies'. Moreover, according to his hardly objective biographer, John William Cole, 'the glowing luxuriance and warmth of South American vegetation were transferred to the canvas with the delicate finish of the richest cabinet painting'.

That is a long way from the solemnities of Drury Lane in 1799. Our extract is from James Boaden's *Memoirs of the Life of John Philip Kemble, Esq.* (1825). Boaden (1762–1839) was a conscientious biographer, a Shakespearian, a miscellaneous writer, and a dramatist. Naomi Royde-Smith said of him, charmingly, that as a biographer he 'combined the industry of the bee with the inconsequence of the butterfly'.

Mr Kemble had only one novelty of much consequence during the remainder of the season . . . the celebrated part of Rolla in Sheridan's alteration of Kotzebue's *Pizarro*, a play of which the performance is never likely to cease, and of which the heroic character of Rolla is the soul. It had been many months under the correction of Sheridan, who not only gave that sustained character to the dialogue which a German sometimes invades by trivial or familiar language, but he added some very glowing thoughts occasionally, and a passage of infinite value in the address of Rolla to the Peruvian soldiers. As I do not remember that any critic has pointed out these original effusions of the mind of Sheridan; as they are, moreover, the only specimens of tragic composition from his pen; and as [they] were subsequently noticed by Mr Pitt, I shall here insert the most prominent to which Kotzebue never supplies more than a fit place to receive them. Perhaps the trial of Warren Hastings led [Sheridan] to fill his mind generally with images of the higher emotions, expressed in the richest terms, though not in the metre of poetry:

The Address of Rolla to his Soldiers, II. 2.

My brave associates—partners of my toil, my feelings and my fame! Can Rolla's words add vigour to the virtuous energies which inspire your hearts?—No—*you* have judged, as I have, the foulness of the crafty plea by which these bold invaders would delude you.—Your generous spirit has compared as mine has, the motives which, in a war like this, can animate *their* minds, and *ours*. *They*, by a strange frenzy driven, fight for power, for plunder, and extended rule—*We* for our country, our altars, and our homes.—*They* follow an adventurer whom they fear, and obey a power which they hate. *We* serve a Monarch whom we love—a God whom we adore. Where'er they move in anger, desolation tracks their progress!—Where'er they pause in amity, affliction mourns their friendship. They boast, they come but to improve our state, enlarge our thoughts, and free us from the yoke of error!—Yes—*they* will give enlightened freedom to *our* minds, who are themselves the slaves of passion, avarice, and pride. They offer us their protection—Yes, such protection as vultures give to lambs—covering and devouring them!—They call on us to

> barter all of good we have inherited and proved, for the desperate chance of something better which they promise. Be our plain answer this: The throne *we* honour is the *people's choice*—the laws we reverence are our brave fathers' legacy—the faith we follow teaches us to live in bonds of charity with all mankind, and die with hope of bliss beyond the grave. Tell your invaders this, and tell them too, we seek no change: and least of all, such change as *they* would bring us.

. . . Again, in that splendid soliloquy of Elvira's, at the end of the third act:

> 'Tis well! 'tis just I should be humbled.—I had forgot myself, and in the cause of innocence assumed the tone of virtue; 'twas fit I should be rebuked, and by Pizarro. Fall, fall, ye few reluctant drops of weakness—the last these eyes shall ever shed. How a woman can love, Pizarro, thou hast known too well—how she can hate, thou hast yet to learn. Yes, thou undaunted! Thou whom yet no mortal hazard has appalled! Thou on Panama's brow didst make alliance with the raving elements, that tore the silence of that horrid night; when thou didst follow, as thy pioneer, the crashing thunder's drift, and stalking o'er the trembling earth, didst plant thy banner by the red volcano's mouth. Thou, who, when battling on the sea, and thy brave ship was blown to splinters, wast seen—as thou did'st bestride a fragment of the smoaking wreck—to wave thy glittering sword above thy head—as thou woul'st defy the world in that extremity!—Come, fearless man—now meet the last and fellest peril of thy life—meet! and survive—an injured woman's fury, if thou canst.

. . . There are several other additions, but these are the most striking, and, from the first part of the second scene in the fifth act, the translation ceases, new incidents are introduced, and, excepting the death of Rolla, the conclusion is totally different, particularly in the reappearance of Elvira and the fall of Pizarro through her intervention. I am not quite sure, but I think he used a translation made for him by Mr Geisweiler, a German possessing both languages, and who afterwards rendered Sheridan's alteration back into German, confronted page for page by the

English. Every care was taken in the getting up of this splendid drama—scenery and dresses of the most striking beauty were invented, and Kelly, who prepared the music, introduced some very eloquent strains . . .

How unwillingly Sheridan always worked may be judged by the following fact. Instead of preparing a prologue that should bear some remote reference to the interest of his play, he sent King on to speak one, written by himself, to be sure, but which had preceded Lady Craven's *Miniature Picture* in 1780. It breathed of neither heroism nor love—but takes the dust in Rotten Row in the person of a cit on his hack Bucephalus; and, sauntering with white-rob'd Misses in Kensington Gardens, listens to the small questions of the promenade, so vastly usual, that they require no answer . . .

Pizarro was acted thirty-one nights in succession, in the serious drama up to that time, unprecedented . . . There was a political point of no mean importance, obvious in this play; we had Mr Sheridan (formerly furious in the cause of France, invoking destruction upon the heads of the British Cabinet, and coveting for himself the 'blow of vengeance'), now speaking with the heart and voice of his country, his perfect abhorrence of the conduct and the principles of revolution; and urging by every oratorical charm his countrymen to resist and disdain the arms and arts of France. If any very furious Whig, anxious for the political wisdom or the consistency of Sheridan, should remind me that this intruded harangue is in the character of a Peruvian, and its invective pointed at a Spanish invader; I think myself able to prove that they were inserted because they applied to the condition of the country. If he were to add that even this concluded nothing as to the *real* sentiments of Mr Sheridan, I confess I should be indifferent on that point, provided he allowed as I think he must do, that, even in Mr Sheridan's opinion, Rolla best uttered the feelings and the sentiments of the English people.

Among his audience Sheridan had the honour to number Mr Pitt. The minister smiled significantly at the speech of Rolla; recognised some favourite figures that he had before admired at the trial of Mr Hastings; and pronounced Mr Kemble to be 'the *noblest* actor that he had ever seen'.

The press sent forth 30,000 copies of the play, which was read with the greatest avidity; and the author, after it had brought at least fifteen thousand pounds into the theatre in its first season, in a strain of marital gallantry not very usual among managers, declared that 'Mrs Sheridan's approbation and delight in its applause were to *him* the *highest* gratification its success had produced.'

James Boaden

17

G's Tragedy

William Godwin (1756–1836), whom Charles Lamb called 'the Professor', was the philosopher and novelist, author of *Political Justice*; Mary Wollstonecraft's husband, and the father-in-law of Shelley. John Philip Kemble and Sarah Siddons appeared at Drury Lane on 13 October 1800 in his unfortunate tragedy, *Antonio; or, The Soldier's Return.* Though Helen is betrothed to Rodrigo (who has been taken prisoner in battle), the King allows her to be married to Don Guzman. Her brother Antonio, returning from war and soliciting his friend's ransom at Court, finds that Rodrigo has lost his bride as well as his liberty. In the name of Spanish honour, Helen's two brothers bear her off to a convent where she is forced to take the vows. This revealed, the King orders her to be brought back and to remain with her husband. Whereupon Antonio stabs her to the heart.

In performance the play failed utterly. Lamb (1775–1834) had written the epilogue which began:

> Ladies, ye've seen how Guzman's consort died,
> Poor victim of a Spanish brother's pride,
> When Spanish honour through the world was blown,
> And Spanish beauty for the best was known.
> In that romantic, unenlighten'd time,
> A breach of honour was a sort of crime . . .

In the following essay, which once made part of that 'On the Artificial Comedy of the Last Century', as printed in *The London Magazine* (1822)—it was afterwards omitted—Lamb describes the dire occasion at Drury Lane. Godwin's friend ('old, steady, unalterable', as Lamb calls him in a letter to Thomas Manning) was named Marshall.

Godwin in 1807 published Charles and Mary Lamb's *Tales from Shakespeare.*

The story of his swallowing opium pills to keep him lively upon the first night of a certain tragedy, we may presume to be a piece of retaliatory pleasantry on the part of the suffering author. But, indeed, John had the art of diffusing a complacent, equable dulness (which you knew not where to quarrel with) over a piece which he did not like, beyond any of his contemporaries. John Kemble had made up his mind early that all the good tragedies that could be written had been written, and he resented any new attempt. His shelves were full. The old standards were scope enough for his ambition. He ranged in them absolute, and 'fair in Otway, full in Shakespeare shone'. He succeeded to the old lawful thrones, and did not care to adventure bottomry with a Sir Edward Mortimer or any casual speculator that offered.

I remember, too acutely for my peace, the deadly extinguisher which he put upon my friend G.'s *Antonio*. G., satiate with visions of political justice (possibly not to be realised in our times), or willing to let the sceptical worldling see that his anticipations of the future did not preclude a warm sympathy for men as they are and have been, wrote a tragedy. He chose a story, affecting, romantic, Spanish; the plot simple without being naked, the incidents uncommon without being overstrained. Antonio, who gives his name to the piece, is a sensitive young Castilian who in a fit of his country honour immolates his sister.

But I must not anticipate the catastrophe. The play, reader, is extant in choice English, and you will employ a spare half-crown not injudiciously in the quest of it.

The conception was bold, and the *dénouement*, the time and place in which the hero of it existed considered, not much out of keeping; yet it must be confessed that it required a delicacy of handling, both from the author and the performer, so as not much to shock the prejudices of a modern English audience. G., in my opinion, has done his part. John, who was in familiar habits with the philosopher, had undertaken to play Antonio. Great expectations were formed. A philosopher's first play was a new era. The night arrived. I was favoured with a seat in an advantageous box between the author and his friend M. G.

sat cheerful and confident. In his friend M.'s looks, who had perused the manuscript, I read some terror. Antonio, in the person of John Philip Kemble, at length appeared, starched out in a ruff which no one could dispute, and in most irreproachable mustachios. John always dressed most provokingly correct on these occasions. The first act swept by, solemn and silent. It went off, as G. assured M., exactly as the opening act of a piece —the *protasis*—should do. The cue of the spectators was to be mute. The characters were but in their introduction. The passions and the incidents would be developed hereafter. Applause hitherto would be impertinent. Silent attention was the effect all-desirable. Poor M. acquiesced, but in his honest, friendly face I could discern a working which told how much more acceptable the plaudit of a single hand (however misplaced) would have been than all this reasoning.

The second act (as in duty bound) rose a little in interest; but still John kept his forces under,—in policy, as G. would have it,—and the audience were most complacently attentive. The *protasis*, in fact, was scarcely unfolded. The interest would warm in the next act, against which a special incident was provided. M. wiped his cheek, flushed with a friendly perspiration,—'tis M.'s way of showing his zeal; 'from every pore of him a perfume falls'. I honour it above Alexander's. He had once or twice during this act joined his palms in a feeble endeavour to elicit a sound: there was no deep to answer to his deep. G. repeatedly begged him to be quiet. The third act at length brought on the scene which was to warm the piece progressively to the final flaming forth of the catastrophe. A philosophic calm settled upon the clear brow of G. as it approached. The lips of M. quivered. A challenge was held forth upon the stage, and there was a promise of a fight. The pit roused themselves on this extraordinary occasion, and, as their manner is, seemed disposed to make a ring; when suddenly Antonio, who was the challenged, turning the tables upon the hot challenger, Don Gusman (who, by the way, should have had his sister), balks his humour, and the pit's reasonable expectation at the same time, with some speeches out of the new philosophy against duelling.

The audience were here fairly caught; their courage was up and on the alert; a few blows *ding-dong*, as R——s, the dramatist, afterwards expressed it to me, might have done the business, —when their most exquisite moral sense was suddenly called in to assist in the mortifying negation of their own pleasure. They could not applaud for disappointment; they would not condemn for morality's sake. The interest stood stone-still, and John's manner was not at all calculated to unpetrify it. It was Christmas time, and the atmosphere furnished some pretext for asthmatic affections. One began to cough; his neighbour sympathised with him, and a cough became epidemical. But when, from being half-artificial in the pit, the cough got frightfully naturalised among the fictitious persons of the drama, and Antonio himself (albeit it was not set down in the stage directions) seemed more intent upon relieving his own lungs than the distresses of the author and his friends, then G. 'first knew fear', and, mildly turning to M., intimated that he had not been aware that Mr Kemble laboured under a cold, and that the performance might possibly have been postponed with advantage for some nights further,—still keeping the same serene countenance, while M. sweated like a bull.

It would be invidious to pursue the fates of this ill-starred evening. In vain did the plot thicken in the scenes that followed, in vain the dialogue was more passionate and stirring, and the progress of the sentiment point more and more clearly to the arduous development which impended. In vain the action was accelerated, while the acting stood still. From the beginning John had taken his stand,—had wound himself up to an even tenure of stately declamation, from which no exigence of dialogue or person could make him swerve for an instant. To dream of his rising with the scene (the common trick of tragedians) was preposterous; for from the onset he had planted himself, as upon a terrace, on an eminence vastly above the audience, and he kept that sublime level to the end. He looked from his throne of elevated sentiment upon the under-world of spectators with a most sovereign and becoming contempt. There was excellent pathos delivered out to them: an they would receive it, so; an they would not receive it, so. There was no offence against decorum in all this; nothing to condemn, to damn; not an irreverent symptom of a sound was to be heard. The procession of verbiage stalked on through four and five acts, no one venturing to predict what would come of it, when, towards the winding up of the latter, Antonio, with an irrelevancy that seemed to stagger Elvira herself,—for she had been coolly arguing the point of honour with him,—suddenly whips out a poniard and stabs his sister to the heart. The effect was as if a murder had been committed in cold blood. The whole house rose up in clamorous indignation, demanding justice. The feeling rose far above hisses. I believe at that instant, if they could have got him, they would have torn the unfortunate author to pieces. Not that the act itself was so exorbitant, or of a complexion different from what they themselves would have applauded on another occasion in a Brutus or an Appius; but for want of attending to Antonio's *words*, which palpably led to the expectation of no less dire an event, instead of being seduced by his *manner*, which seemed to promise a sleep of a less alarming nature than it was his cue to inflict upon Elvira, they found themselves betrayed into an accompliceship of murder, a perfect misprision of parricide, while they dreamed of nothing less.

M., I believe, was the only person who suffered acutely from the failure; for G. thenceforward, with a serenity unattainable but by the true philosophy, abandoning a precarious popularity, retired into his fasthold of speculation,—the drama in which the world was to be his tiring-room, and remote posterity his applauding spectators at once and actors.

Charles Lamb

THE LATE EDMUND KEAN,
AS GLOSTER, IN RICHARD 3RD

GLO: "Take up the sword again or take up me"
ACT 1, SC. 2.

18

Another Bottle

This extract is from *The Life of George Fred. Cooke* (*late of the Theatre Royal, Covent Garden*, 'composed principally from journals and other authentic documents left by Mr Cooke, and the personal knowledge of the author; comprising original anecdotes of his theatrical contemporaries, his opinions on various dramatic writings, &c.' Written by William Dunlap, the American dramatist, manager, and artist, it was published (*Memoirs of George Fred. Cooke, Esq.*) in 1813, and 'revised and improved', under the new title, two years later.

Its subject was the extraordinary George Frederick Cooke (1756–1812), an actor—admired by Edmund Kean—of an immense, rough power, a shaggy-pelted authority. But he ruined himself with audiences in London—where he first appeared when 44—by his preposterous intemperance. Though playgoers at Covent Garden knew what he could do as Richard III, Shylock, Iago, Sir Archy MacSarcasm (Macklin's *Love à la Mode*), and Sir Pertinax MacSycophant (Macklin's *The Man of the World*), they would not brook his habit of arriving on stage more or less drunk and incapable, and trying to pass it off as 'my old complaint', a plea for indulgence that became a dreary jest. In aspect he had a square, hook-nosed face, wide mouth, and dark, glinting eyes set wide apart; his voice was sharp and powerful. Leigh Hunt said glumly: 'He limited every character to its worst qualities; and had no idealism, no affections, no verse.' Eventually (1810) he was persuaded, with great difficulty, to leave for America where he acted for two years before dying of dropsy in September 1812.

Dunlap's book is rough-and-ready but extremely vivid, as we see from this description of a nightmare day in the life of that handsome and dignified actor, Thomas Abthorpe Cooper (1776–1849). Cooper, steadily befriended by the philosopher, William Godwin, and the dramatist, Thomas Holcroft, had played Hamlet and Macbeth at Covent Garden in 1795; in the next year he went to America and stayed there until 1803 when he came back to act at Drury Lane as Hamlet, Macbeth, and Richard III. He soon returned to America, becoming an important popular figure and actor-manager at the Park Theatre, New York. In 1810, while on a visit to England, he managed with the utmost trouble to get Cooke out of the country.

In this extract (May 1803) he and Cooke have just become friends. Drury Lane had treated Cooper rather shabbily, offering as payment for his work only a 'benefit' performance, on a poor date in June, which would hardly be worth taking, and a next season's engagement on unacceptable terms. Cooke said impulsively that he would act Iago to Cooper's Othello at the benefit if Thomas Harris, manager and chief proprietor of Covent Garden, would permit his appearance, for this occasion only, at the rival Theatre Royal. After a party at Cooper's lodgings one night in May, nothing remained but to get Harris's consent. There Cooper's trials begin.

When Cooke says he will 'return to London light as Gossamer', he is speaking of the character in Frederick Reynolds's comedy, *Laugh When You Can* (1798).

It was in the course of the evening fixed that Cooper should accept the 10th of June for his benefit night; that Othello should be the play, and that Cooke should play Iago to Cooper's Othello; all with the proviso that Mr Harris would consent to Cooke's playing one night at Drury Lane. Mr Godwin went home; Cooke stayed till six o'clock in the morning, in the interval having appointed Cooper to breakfast with him at ten, and then go down to Mr Harris's country seat, fifteen miles from London, at Uxbridge, to obtain the desired consent. At six he was carried home in a coach.

At the appointed hour, Cooper, with a post-chaise, called on Cooke, and found him in bed, and as wild as when he left him. As the post-chaise was ready, Cooper, after a time, persuaded him to get up and prepare to take an airing. Breakfast was ordered; Cooke having dressed, and taken a few dishes of *laced* tea, was all alive again. As they drove through the Park, Cooke asked the time. 'One.' 'One! Why we have time enough; I only play Sir Archy tonight; I don't go on till the after-piece, and am not wanted till nine; there's time enough to go down to Harris's; only fifteen miles.' Cooper gladly accepted the proposal, for he was extremely anxious that Cooke should be so employed during the day as to overcome the effects of the last night's excess. Accordingly about two they turned into the Uxbridge road, and in about two hours reached an inn near the country seat of the Great Man.

It was settled that while the horses were changing, Cooke should walk to Mr Harris's, and that Cooper, who did not wish to be seen in the business, should drive to the common, near the manager's house, and wait for him. Cooke accordingly went; Cooper, congratulating himself that the veteran would have no opportunity of renewing his excess, and might be carried to town, recovered and in prime order for playing, took some refreshment; and after allowing what he thought a reasonable time for settling the business, got into a post-chaise and drove to the common. No sign of Cooke. He drives round the common. A quarter—a half, three quarters of an hour pass, and no Cooke. Impatient and alarmed at the delay, the postillion is ordered to drive to Mr Harris's. The chaise arrives at the door, the bell is rung, and the porter appears.

'Is Mr Cooke here?'

'Yes, sir.'

'I want to see him.'

'Your name, sir?'

'Say a gentleman in a post-chaise waits to see Mr Cooke.'

The porter rings and a valet appears, receives the message, and returns with,

'Mr Cooke's compliments, and requests Mr Cooper to walk upstairs into the library.'

'Is Mr Harris with him?'—'No, sir.'

'Is anybody with him?'—'No, sir, he is alone. Mr Harris has a party to dine.'

'Has Mr Harris seen Mr Cooke?'—'No, sir. Mr Harris was walking with company in the grounds when Mr Cooke arrived, and desired that he might be shown into the library, ordering a dinner and a bottle of wine to be sent to Mr Cooke with his compliments. He would wait upon Mr Cooke when he had himself dined.'

'Has Mr Cooke dined?'—'No, sir, he is finishing his dinner and invites you to come and partake with him.'

Cooper's aversion to entering the house in this manner was great, but the image of Cooke with a bottle of wine before him, and the well-known consequences, and his own responsibility, overcame his reluctance. Alighting, he marched upstairs into Mr Harris's library. There sat the veteran, his bottle nearly empty, and as happy as though the manager had treated him with all the respect due to an equal, or superior.

'Come, my dear boy, sit down—excellent port—come, take a glass; you may as well take your dinner, since we must wait.' So he pours out two glasses of wine and empties the bottle. The valet, attentive to his master's good name for hospitality, flies and brings in a second bottle before Cooper has time to felicitate himself upon what he thought the end of the wine drinking. In this dilemma he saw no recourse but to drink as much as possible of the second bottle, and to aid him in this undertaking he must eat. He accordingly sat down to the remains of an excellent dinner, and poured out the wine by the tumbler-full as table liquor; expecting Harris every minute, and wishing to avoid him, and leave Cooke without wine. Cooper was extremely industrious, and soon reduced the bottle, then made a second appointment for the common, desiring Cooke to join him as soon as he had seen Harris. The post-chaise is again ordered to drive to the place of assignation.

About six o'clock the merry tragedian made his appearance at the place of appointment in high glee, and supported by a valet. What passed with Mr Harris in the absence of Mr Cooper was collected from Cooke's own account and other sources.

Mr Harris after dinner left his company, and came to Cooke, whose second bottle was nearly empty. 'Ah, Mr Cooke, how d'ye do?—glad to see you—well!—business, ha?—What is it?—left my company—what is it?—what is it?—what's the business?'

Cooke Sit down, and we'll take a glass of wine (*filling the glasses and emptying the bottle*). You look very well, sir. Here's to your health! (*drinks*)

Harris Thank you—your health, Cooke—well—what is it?—what is it?

Cooke You are my best friend, and I have come to ask you a particular favour.

Harris Well, well, well, what is it? what is it?

Cooke Money!—Money!—Money! (with his particular and inimitable expression of countenance, and a peculiar sharp emphatic tone which his mimics easily succeed in copying).

Harris Why—why, Cooke—what can you want of money, with your salary, and the benefits you have received?

Cooke All gone! I never could bear to lock up a guinea; I have too much love for my royal master to put even his image in confinement. 'Who rules over freemen should himself be free.' In serious earnest, sir, the end of the season is fast approaching with a long vacation, and it will find me without a shilling.

Harris Well—but—vacation?—you make as much money as you please in the summer.

Cooke But you know, sir, I must have something to start with. I know what harpies country managers are; I must not appear to want, and then I can make my bargain.

Harris Well, well, well—true enough—must not be bare—well, well—how much—how much?

Cooke Why, sir, fifty pounds will do to start with.

Harris Well, well—(*writes an order, and gives it to Cooke*), there—and now good-bye—good-bye.

Cooke My best friend—thank ye—thank you—and now—

Harris Company waits—good-bye—good-bye.

Cooke You are the best friend I ever had in the world. I must drink your health before you go . . . One glass more.

Harris rings and orders another bottle.

Cooke Your health, my best of friends . . . One thing more before you go.

Harris Well . . . Quick then!

Cooke Manchester. Ward and Bellamy. My good and fast friends in former days. Many's the slippery trick I've played them, and yet they never deserted me; and now that I am of some consequence, I would wish to show my gratitude. They want me to close their season. I'm not wanted here—let me go down and play for them a few nights before Covent Garden closes.

Harris Impossible, Cooke—bad example—give leave to you, all the rest ask it—then what becomes of the benefits—?

Cooke I'm not wanted after the 10th of June—all the remaining benefits are made out without me—I'm not to play again.

Harris You are sure of that?

Cooke Quite sure, or I would not think of such a thing.

Harris Well, well, go this time—good-bye.

Cooke My best of friends—your health—one thing more—Cooper.

Harris Well, sir, what is it?

Cooke Cooper! of Drury Lane—he has been very ill used, and he's a good fellow.

Harris What do you mean, sir?

Cooke Cooper—Holcroft's pupil; you know he played at our house some years ago; he played Hamlet in ninety-five.

Harris Aye-aye—remember—well, well, what of him?

Cooke Has his benefit at Drury Lane 10th of June, and wants me to play for him.

Harris No—no—no—no—

Cooke A good fellow, sir—and very ill used.

Harris No, Cooke—impossible—*You* play at Drury Lane! Quite out of the question—can't—won't—no, no, no!

Cooke The best creature in the world, sir—I know him well and love him much, sir—and can't bear to see him trampled on by those damned rascals at Drury Lane. Sheridan—to bring him from America where he was everything in his profession—bring him from his wife and family—promised him an engagement—here he has played part of the season, and the poor beggarly rogues won't give him a farthing, but offer him a benefit—like all the *tricks* and *shuffling* of their *pack*, every actor ought to *cut* them.

Harris Why, now you know, Cooke, that I would—but impossible—you know.

Cooke Offer him a benefit in the middle of June! poor dogs—*that* costs them nothing—a benefit!—he's a stranger—no friends—Lord Erskine's his friend, though—only think, sir, of the meanness of the rogues—the unfeeling scoundrels—

Harris Why—it is very bad treatment—but—

Cooke Sir, I knew you, and I knew that you would feel indignant at such treatment; and in my confidence—my certainty of your generosity, I pledged myself. I am in honour bound to play for him.

Harris Well—well, then, you must.

Cooke My dear—my best of friends—I must drink your health. You have granted me the three things I had most at heart—you have lifted a burthen—three burthens—from me—Money!—Manchester!—Cooper! I shall return to London light as Gossamer; I will first finish my wine, and then (*displaying the wine, and raising his voice from the low level tone in which he had been speaking, to its high sharp key*), my voice will be as clear as your liquor! I shall play in my best style tonight, I promise you!

Harris What! What's that? You play tonight!

Cooke I shall give it them in my best style. Aha! Aha!

Harris Play tonight!—and here at this time! and in this situation!—Thomas!—John! (*ringing the bell violently*), where's the carriage that brought Mr Cooke?

Servant On the common, sir.

Cooke Aha! Common! That's right, I'm to join Cooper on the common. But there's no hurry, let's have another bottle. Another bottle, my good friend!

Harris No, no, no. No more—go—go away—quick. Here, John, lead Mr Cooke.

Cooke Stand away, fellow! What do you mean, sir. Is this treatment for a gentleman? A gentleman, and the son of a gentleman, to be treated thus by the son of a soap-boiler! Pah! Fat! Is this the way you treat the man who has made your fortune?

Harris Well, my dear Cooke—go—consider—the audience—the time o'day—your friends—

Cooke suffered himself to be soothed and led away by the valet, leaving the astonished manager to anticipate the hisses and rioting of a disappointed public, and perhaps the discordant crashes of his lamps and chandeliers.

Having been helped into the post-chaise, Cooke, highly delighted with his success, exclaims, 'My dear boy, all's settled!' and tells what has past. The postillion, bribed to use the utmost speed of his horses, drives them furiously towards London. Cooke soon begins to complain of spasms, his 'old complaint', and must stop for brandy, but, by the address of his companion, the answer is uniformly at every public-house that they have nothing but beer. His spirits kept up till near London, and he frequently protested that he would play better that night than ever he had done; but when near the goal he began to be fretful, and curse the theatre; then resolving not to play that night, he gave way to drowsiness, and his companion began to despair of his doing anything on the stage, or even going to the house. Stimulated, however, by the knowledge that any failure would be attributed to him, he determined upon one effort more, and ordered the postillion to drive to Holcroft's; hoping that tea and the conversation of a man whose writings Cooke admired, but who was personally a stranger to him, and the desire to appear respectable in his eyes, would be a sufficient stimulus and save the impending disgrace . . .

Holcroft received them very cordially, and after the usual formalities, to Cooper's infinite mortification, instead of suffering Cooke to drink tea, ordered wine. Cooper took an opportunity, while Cooke was in conversation with Miss Holcroft, to tell her father what the situation was and the necessity of Cooke playing that evening. Holcroft, seeing Cooper's great anxiety, promised to second his intentions. Cooke, now thoroughly aroused, entered spiritedly into conversation, and being a sincere admirer of Holcroft's dramatic writings, made them his subject and eulogised the author unsparingly; he in his turn praised Mr Cooke's great histrionic talents, and the author and the actor, forgetting Cooper and all concerns of the present moment, went on with unceasing eloquence in each other's praise, to the great annoyance of at least one of the auditors. Cooper, seeing Cooke swallowing glass after glass and perceiving no end to the conversation, now applied to Miss Holcroft to remind her father of the situation. A pretence of household concerns gave the opportunity, and Holcroft, in compliance, pretending an engagement and saying, 'I should be more chagrined, but that I see by the bills you are to play Sir Archy tonight, and the time has come for you to go to the house,' the party broke up.

Cooper, who had sent for a hack, got Cooke into it, and driving with speed to Covent Garden Theatre, fairly delivered him into the hands of the dressers, but not before the managers, prompter, and all the company, were in consternation at his absence, and the audience impatiently waiting and expressing as usual their disapprobation. He played the first act tolerably, but the second was stopped by hisses . . . He walked up the stage, and was followed by Johnstone, who played Sir Callaghan. After a minute's pause, Johnstone came forward, and addressing the audience in full brogue, said: 'Ladies and Gentlemen—Mr Cooke *says* he *can't spake.*' This laconic apology was received with roars of laughter, and the curtain dropped amidst the most violent tokens of disapprobation levelled at Cooke.

William Dunlap

19

Critical Playgoing

[James Henry] Leigh Hunt (1784–1859) was one of the powerful early nineteenth-century drama critics (in effect, he was the first; principally on *The Examiner*, which he edited with his brother). He was a friend and associate of the Romantic poets; and he went to prison for two years (1813–15)—a sentence served in some comfort—for libelling the Prince Regent. As a critic he held up a clear looking-glass to his period; we feel that the reflection is unflawed. He could be also a wistful remembrancer. Dickens caricatured him unkindly as Horace Skimpole in *Bleak House*.

The dramatists mentioned are James Cobb (1756–1818), Samuel Birch (1757–1841), George Colman, Jr (1762–1836), and John O'Keeffe (1747–1833). Mrs (Mary—'Perdita') Robinson (1758–1800) was briefly an actress and mistress of the Prince Regent; and Michael Kelly (1762–1826), the singer and later musical director at Drury Lane. Kemble's parts: Penruddock in Richard Cumberland's *The Wheel of Fortune* (1795); Abbé de l'Epée in Thomas Holcroft's *Deaf and Dumb; or, The Orphan Protected* (1801) from the French of J. N. Bouilly.

That is a pleasant time of life, the playgoing time in youth, when the coach is packed full to go to the theatre, and brothers and sisters, parents and lovers (none of whom, perhaps, go very often) are all wafted together in a flurry of expectation; when the only wish as they go (except with the lovers) is to go as fast as possible, and no sound is so delightful as the cry of 'Bill of the Play'; when the smell of links in the darkest and muddiest winter's night is charming; and the steps of the coach are let down; and a roar of hoarse voices round the door, and *mud-shine* on the pavement, are accompanied with the sight of the warm-looking lobby which is about to be entered; and then enter, and pay, and ascend the pleasant stairs, and begin to hear the *silence* of the house, perhaps the first jingle of the music; and the box is entered amidst some little awkwardness in descending to their places, and being looked at; and at length they sit, and are become used to by their neighbours, and shawls and smiles are adjusted, and the play-bill is handed round or pinned to the cushion, and the gods are a little noisy, and the music veritably commences, and at length the curtain is drawn up and the first delightful syllables are heard:

'Ah, my dear Charles, when did you see the lovely Olivia?'

'Oh, my dear Sir George, talk not to me of Olivia. The cruel guardian,' etc.

Anon the favourite of the party makes his appearance, and then they are quite happy; and next day, besides his own merits, the points of the dialogue are attributed to him as if he were their inventor. It is not Sir Harry, or Old Dornton, or Dubster, who said this or that; but 'Lewis', 'Munden', or 'Keeley'. They seem to think the wit really originated with the man who uttered it so delightfully.

Critical playgoing is very inferior in its enjoyments to this. It must of necessity blame as well as praise; it becomes difficult to please; it is tempted to prove its own merits, instead of those of its entertainers; and the enjoyments of self-love, besides, perhaps being ill-founded, and subjecting it to the blame which it bestows, are sorry substitutes at the best for hearty delight in others. Never, after I had taken critical pen in hand, did I pass the thoroughly delightful evenings at the playhouse which I had done when I went only to laugh or be moved. I had the pleasure, it is true, of praising those whom I admired; but the retributive uneasiness of the very pleasure of blaming attended it; the consciousness of self, which on all occasions except loving ones contains a bitter in its sweet, puts its sorry obstacle in the way of an unembarrassed delight; and I found the days flown when I retained none but the good passages of plays and performers, and when I used to carry to my school-fellows rapturous accounts of the farces of Colman, and the good-natured comedies of O'Keeffe.

I speak of my own feelings, and at a particular time of life; but forty or fifty years ago people of all times of life were much greater playgoers than they are now. They dined earlier, they had not so many newspapers, clubs, and pianofortes; the French Revolution only tended at first to endear the nation to its own habits; it had not yet opened a thousand new channels of thought and interest; nor had railroads conspired to carry people, bodily as well as mentally, into as many analogous directions. Everything was more concentrated, and the various classes of society felt a greater concern in the same amusements. Nobility, gentry, citizens, princes,—all were frequenters of theatres, and even more or less acquainted personally with the performers. Nobility intermarried with them; gentry and citizens too, wrote for them; princes conversed and lived with them. Sheridan, and other Members of Parliament, were managers as well as dramatists. It was Lords Derby, Craven, and Thurlow that sought wives on the stage. Two of the most popular minor dramatists were Cobb, a clerk in the India House, and Birch, the pastry-cook. If Mrs Jordan lived with the Duke of Clarence (William IV) as his mistress, nobody doubts that she was as faithful to him as a wife. His brother, the Prince of Wales (George the Fourth), besides his intimacy with Sheridan and the younger Colman, and to say nothing of Mrs Robinson, took a pleasure in conversing with Kemble, and was the personal patron of O'Keeffe and of Kelly. The Kembles, indeed, as Garrick had been, were received everywhere among the truly best circles; that is to say, where intelligence was combined with high breeding; and they deserved it; for whatever difference of opinion may be entertained as to the amount of genius in the family, nobody who recollects them will dispute that they were a remarkable race, dignified and elegant in manners, with intellectual tendencies, and in point of aspect very like what has been called 'God Almighty's nobility'.

I remember once standing behind John Kemble and a noble lord at a sale. It was the celebrated book sale of the Duke of Roxburgh. The player and the nobleman were conversing, the former in his high, dignified tones, the latter in a voice which I heard but indistinctly. Presently, the actor turned his noble profile to his interlocutor, and on his moving it back again, the man of quality turned his. What a difference! and what a voice! Kemble's voice was none of the best; but, like his profile, it was nobleness itself compared with that of the noble lord . . .

I never denied the merits which that actor possessed. He had the look of a Roman; made a very good ideal, though not a very real Coriolanus, for his pride was not sufficiently blunt and unaffected: and in parts that suited his natural tendency, such as Penruddock and the Abbé de l'Epée, would have been altogether admirable and interesting, if you could have forgotten that their sensibility in his hands, was not so much repressed, as wanting. He was no more to be compared to his sister, than stone is to flesh and blood. There was much of the pedagogue in him. He made a fuss about trifles; was inflexible on a pedantic reading; in short, was rather a teacher of elocution than an actor; and not a good teacher, on that account. There was a merit in his idealism, as far as it went. He had, at least, faith in something classical and scholastic, and he made the town partake of it; but it was all on the surface—a hollow trophy: and I am persuaded, that he had no idea in his head but of a stage Roman, and the dignity he added to his profession . . .

One of the things on which I was always harping [as a young critic] was Kemble's vicious pronunciation. Kemble had a smattering of learning, and a great deal of obstinacy. He was a reader of old books; and having discovered that pronunciation had not always been what it was, and that in one or two instances the older was metrically better than the new (as in the case of the word *aches*, which was originally a dissylable—*aitches*), he took upon him to reform it in a variety of cases, where propriety was as much against him as custom. Thus the vowel *e* in the word 'merchant', in defiance of its Latin etymology, he insisted upon pronouncing according to its French derivative, *marchant*. 'Innocent' he called *innocint*; conscience (in defiance even of his friend Chaucer), *conshince*; 'virtue', in proper slip-slop, *varchue*; 'fierce', *furse*; 'beard', *bird*; 'thy', *thĕ* (because we generally call 'my', *mĕ*); and 'odious', 'hideous', and 'perfidious', became *ojus*, *hijjus*, and *perfijjus*.

Nor were these all. The following banter, in the shape of an imaginary bit of conversation between an officer and his friend, was, literally, no caricature:

> *A* Ha! captain! how dost? Thĕ appearance would be much improved by a little more attention to the bird.
>
> *B* Why, so I think: there's no sentimint in a bird. But then it serves to distinguish a soldier, and there is no doubt much military varchue in looking furful.
>
> *A* But the girls, Jack, the girls! Why, thĕ mouth is enough to banish kissing from the airth etairnally.
>
> *B* In maircy, no more of that! Zounds, but the shop-keepers and the marchants will get the better of us with the dear souls! However, as it is now against military law to have a tender countenance, and as some birds, I thank heaven, are of a tolerable qual-ity,* I must make a varchue of necessity; and as I can't look soft for the love of my girl, I must e'en look hijjus for the love of my country.

Leigh Hunt

* quality (with the *a* as in *universality*).

William Charles Macready

20

Roman Matron

Charles Mayne Young (1777–1856), was an actor whom everyone except, oddly, John Keats ('ranting, coxcombical, tasteless') seemed to admire both on and off the stage. Urbane and generous, he had one of the finest voices in the theatre ('damned musical' said Edmund Kean), appeared with the other leaders of the time—John Philip Kemble, Mrs Siddons, Kean, Macready—and in his day acted Hamlet and Macbeth. In 1832 he began a long retirement. His son, Julian Charles Young, wrote, as a Warwickshire parson, a *Memoir of Charles Mayne Young, Esq., Tragedian, with Extracts from his Son's Journal.* The memoir is brief, the journal cheerfully discursive. My copy (1871; second edition) was the author's gift to Dean Ramsay: it came into the hands of E. V. Lucas, who endorsed the fly-leaf in 1917, 'This is one of the best "bed books" ever written.' Here Julian Young describes Mrs Siddons as Volumnia, in *Coriolanus,* which she was playing for her brother, John Philip Kemble.

In the second scene of the second act of *Coriolanus*, after the victory of the battle of Corioli, an ovation in honour of the victor was introduced with great and imposing effect by John Kemble. On reference to the stage directions of my father's interleaved copy, I find that no fewer than 240 persons marched, in stately procession across the stage. In addition to the recognised dramatis personae, 35 in number, there were vestals, and lictors with their fasces, and soldiers with the *spolia opima*, and sword-bearers, and standard-bearers, and cup-bearers, and senators, and silver eagle-bearers, with the S.P.Q.R. upon them, and trumpeters, and drummers, and priests, and dancing-girls, &c., &c.

Now, in this procession, and as one of the central figures in it, Mrs Siddons had to walk. Had she been content to follow in the beaten track of her predecessors in the part, she would have marched across the stage, from right to left, with the solemn, stately, funeral step conventional. But, at the time, as she often did, she forgot her own identity. She was no longer Sarah Siddons, tied down to the directions of the prompter's book—or trammelled by old traditions—she was Volumnia, the proud mother of a proud son and conquering hero. So that, when it was time for her to come on, instead of dropping each foot at equi-distance in its place, with mechanical exactitude, and in cadence subservient to the orchestra; deaf to the guidance of her woman's ear, but sensitive to the throbbings of her haughty mother's heart, with flashing eye and proudest smile, and head erect, and hands pressed firmly on her bosom, as if to repress by manual force its triumphant swellings, she towered above all around, and rolled, and almost reeled across the stage; her very soul, as it were, dilating, and rioting in its exultation; until her action lost all grace, and yet, became so true to nature, so picturesque, and so descriptive that pit and gallery sprang to their feet electrified by the transcendent execution of an original conception.

Julian Charles Young

21

Mrs Siddons Returns

William Hazlitt (1778–1830), firmest and most searchingly fastidious writer in the early nineteenth-century efflorescence of drama criticism. It has been said of him that he invented Edmund Kean (whom certainly he did much to establish). The following review of the return of Sarah Siddons, as Lady Macbeth, is from *The Examiner*, 16 June 1816. He wrote, too, for several other journals; a famous book is *A View of the English Stage* (1818).

Though Sarah Siddons had formally retired, also in the part of Lady Macbeth, in 1812, she gave various other performances—returning, for example to Covent Garden (June 1816) at the desire of Princess Charlotte and her husband, Prince Leopold of Saxe-Coburg, who had never known the Siddons in the theatre. It was this performance that Hazlitt reviewed. Horace Twiss, who was the actress's nephew, wrote in 1812 a farewell speech that ended with the words:

> Judges and Friends! to whom the magic strain
> Of Nature's feeling never spoke in vain,
> Perhaps your hearts, when years have glided by,
> And past emotions wake a fleeting sigh,
> May think on her whose lips have poured so long
> The charmed sorrows of your Shakespeare's song—
> On her who, parting to return no more,
> Is now the mourner she but seem'd before;
> Herself subdued, resigns the melting spell,
> And breathes, with swelling heart, her long,
> Her last Farewell!

Sarah Siddons spoke these lines herself after the Sleepwalking scene when the audience refused to hear the end of the tragedy once Lady Macbeth had left the stage. There was no similar demonstration in 1816.

Players should be immortal, of their own wishes or ours could make them so; but they are not. They not only die like other people, but like other people they cease to be young, and are no longer themselves, even while living. Their health, strength, beauty, voice, fails them; nor can they, without these advantages, perform the same feats, or command the same applause that they did when possessed of them. It is the common lot: players only are *not* exempt from it. Mrs Siddons retired once from the stage: why should she return to it again? She cannot retire from it twice with dignity; and yet it is to be wished that she should do all things with dignity. Any loss of reputation to her, is a loss to the world. Has she not had enough of glory? The homage she has received is greater than that which is paid to Queens. The enthusiasm she excited had something idolatrous about it; she was regarded less with admiration than with wonder, as if a being of a superior order had dropped from another sphere to awe the world with the majesty of her appearance. She raised Tragedy to the skies, or brought it down from thence. It was something above nature. We can conceive of nothing grander. She embodied to our imagination the fables of mythology, of the heroic and deified mortals of elder time. She was not less than a goddess, or than a prophetess inspired by the gods. Power was seated on her brow, passion emanated from her breast as from a shrine. She was Tragedy personified. She was the stateliest ornament of the public mind. She was not only the idol of the people, she not only hushed the tumultuous shouts of the pit in breathless expectation, and quenched the blaze of surrounding beauty in silent tears, but to the retired and lonely student, through long years of solitude, her face has shone as if an eye had appeared from heaven; her name has been as if a voice had opened the chambers of the human heart, or as if a trumpet had awakened the sleeping and the dead. To have seen Mrs Siddons was an event in every one's life; and does she think we have forgot her? Or would she remind us of herself by showing us what *she was not*? Or is she to continue on the stage to the very last, till all her grace and all her grandeur gone, shall leave behind them only a melancholy blank? Or is she merely to be played off as 'the baby of a girl' for a few nights . . .

It is said that the Princess Charlotte has expressed a desire to see Mrs Siddons in her best parts, and this, it is said, is a thing highly desirable. We do not know that the Princess has expressed any such wish, and we shall suppose that she has not because we do not think it altogether a reasonable one. If the Princess Charlotte had expressed a wish to see Mr Garrick, this would have been a thing highly desirable, but it would have been impossible; or if she had desired to see Mrs Siddons *in her best days*, it would have been equally so; and yet without this, we do not think it desirable that she should see her at all. It is said to be desirable that a Princess should have a taste for the Fine Arts, and that this is best promoted by seeing the highest models of perfection. But it is of the first importance for Princes to acquire a taste for what is reasonable; and the second thing which it is desirable they should acquire, is a deference to public opinion; and we think neither of these objects likely to be promoted in the way proposed. If it was reasonable that Mrs Siddons should retire from the stage three years ago, certainly these reasons have not diminished since, nor do we think Mrs Siddons would consult what is due to her powers or her fame, in commencing a new career. If it is only intended that she should act a few nights in the presence of a particular person, this might be done as well in private. To all other applications she should answer—'Leave me to my repose'.

Mrs Siddons always spoke as slow as she ought; she now speaks slower than she did. 'The line too labours, and the words move slow.' The machinery of the voice seems too ponderous for the power that wields it. There is too long a pause between each sentence, and between each word in each sentence. There is too much preparation. The stage waits for her. In the sleeping scene, she produced a different impression from what we expected. It was more laboured, and less natural. In coming on formerly, her eyes were open, but the sense was shut. She was like a person bewildered, and unconscious of what she did. She moved her lips involuntarily; all her gestures were involuntary and mechanical. At present she acts the part more with a view to effect.

She repeats the action when she says, 'I tell you he cannot rise from his grave', with both hands sawing the air, in the style of parliamentary oratory, the worst of all others. There was none of this weight or energy in the way she did the scene the first time we saw her, twenty years ago. She glided on and off the stage, almost like an apparition. In the close of the banquet scene, Mrs Siddons condescended to an imitation which we were sorry for. She said, 'go, go', in the hurried familiar tone of common life, in the manner of Mr Kean, and without any of that sustained and graceful spirit of conciliation towards her guests, which used to characterise her mode of doing it. Lastly, if Mrs Siddons has to leave the stage again, Mr Horace Twiss will write another farewell address for her: if she continues on it, we shall have to criticise her performance. We know which of these two evils we shall think the greater.

Too much praise cannot be given to Mr Kemble's performance of Macbeth. He was 'himself again', and much more than himself. His action was decided, his voice audible. His tones had occasionally indeed a learned quaintness, like the colouring of Poussin; but the effect of the whole was fine. His action in delivering the speech, 'Tomorrow and tomorrow', was particularly striking and expressive, as if he had stumbled by an accident on fate, and was baffled by the impenetrable obscurity of the future. In that prodigious prosing paper, *The Times*, which seems to be written as well as printed by a steam-engine, Mr Kemble is compared to the ruin of a magnificent temple in which the divinity still resides. This is not the case. The temple is unimpaired; but the divinity is sometimes from home.

William Hazlitt

22

Enter Macready

This is a great actor's narrative of the night on which he reached the London stage, in the vast Covent Garden Theatre. He was William Charles Macready, who was born in London on 3 March 1793, and who died at Cheltenham, after long retirement, just over eighty years later. Son of an actor-manager and an actress, he was of Irish descent on his father's side. He had not wished to go on the stage—indeed he had thought of the Bar—but his father's pressing money troubles made it inevitable; William left Rugby School prematurely and became at length a savagely hard worker, bound to the wheel of the stock companies; in 1812, at Newcastle, he acted with the visiting Sarah Siddons in Edward Moore's *The Gamester* and John Home's *Douglas*. His provincial fame developed; in 1816 he received a contract to appear at Covent Garden (£16 a week for the first two years, £17 for the next two, and £18 in the fifth); and on the night of 16 September 1816, aged 23, he appeared as Orestes in Ambrose Philips's *The Distrest Mother* (1712), a very poor version of Racine's *Andromaque*, with the indifferent support of Mrs (Julia) Glover as Andromache, Mrs Egerton (in Eliza O'Neill's absence) as Hermione, and William Abbott as Pylades. Edmund Kean was in the audience that saw the young actor make his entrance in the Covent Garden idea of a chlamys, and with an auburn wig curling to his shoulders. The early speech for which he was applauded ran:

. . . Hermione is my life,
My soul, my rapture! I'll no longer curb
The strong desire that hurries me to madness:
I'll give a loose to love; I'll bear her hence;
I'll tear her from his arms; I'll—Oh, ye gods!
Give me Hermione, or let me die! . . .

And his final speech:

> Who talks of reason? Better to have none,
> Than not enough. Run, someone, tell my Greeks
> I will not have them touch the king. Now, now!
> I blaze again! See there—look where they come—
> A shoal of furies! How they swarm about me!
> My terror—hide me—Oh! their snaky locks—
> Hark, how they hiss—see, see their flaming brands!
> Now they let drive at me! How they grin,
> And shake their iron whips! My ears—what yelling!—
> And see, Hermione she sets them on.
> Thrust not your scorpions thus into my bosom!
> Oh! I am stung to death! Despatch me soon!
> There—take my heart, Hermione! tear it out!
> Disjoint me! kill me! Oh! my tortur'd soul!

That night was the beginning of a London career in which, after Edmund Kean's death in 1833, Macready led the stage. Often unpopular with his colleagues, he had no time for the 'Bohemian', for players who did not mind whether their calling was despised. Deeply sensitive, he hid nothing from his journals, the most honest and absorbing self-revelation. He was devoted to his art; and he was never far from the top, whereas the sometimes magnificent Kean's career was a fever-chart with impenetrable depths. Macready's fame has suffered because a man who could be called 'moral, grave, sublime' (Tennyson's unguarded phrase in the farewell ode) must always be less cherished than the legends of romantic profligacy. As Hilton Brown wrote once in another context, 'We are a great people for labels, and we furnish them with well-nigh imperishable gum.'

Macready, as I have said, was a man of many paradoxes: humble and vain, choleric and gentle, impatient and numbingly shy, bitter and loving, a despot and a republican. In the theatre he was an exciting Shakespearian (particularly as Macbeth and Lear) and a man who could ennoble the mediocre drama of the time in such parts as Knowles's Virginius, Bulwer's Richelieu, and Byron's Werner. He managed Drury Lane and Covent Garden in celebrated seasons.

Five feet ten in height, Macready had a flat, high-cheekboned face, an irregular nose, burning blue eyes, and a violoncello-voice of astonishing range. There were physical and vocal mannerisms, but he had, too, the most intense pathos and humanity. We shall meet him again in this book. The following extract is from the *Reminiscences*, begun during the 1850s and unfinished; Sir Frederick Pollock edited them in 1875.

Arrived in London, and temporarily quartered at my former hotel, the old Slaughter Coffee House, I lost no time in presenting myself to the Covent Garden managers. Mr Henry Harris, Reynolds, the dramatic author, reader, and adviser, and Fawcett formed 'the cabinet' of the theatre, and I was made a party to their consultations on the still perplexing subject of my opening play. They had a heavy stake in their venture with me, and were in a proportionate degree cautious of risking comparisons that might prove detrimental to it. A club much talked of at the time, that bore the name of 'The Wolves', was said to be banded together to put down anyone appearing in Kean's characters. I believed the report not to have been founded in strict fact; but it was currently received, and had its influence on the Covent Garden deliberations. Orestes was the part finally resolved on, as least likely to provoke party criticism; Charles Kemble would be all that could be desired in the dignified declamation of Pyrrhus, but for Hermione and Andromache, two first-rate tragic characters—where was the passion and pathos to give effect to them, and how to fill them? The plea of necessity at length bore down all previous objections, and the part of Hermione was cast to Mrs Egerton, whose merits were confined to melodrama, whilst a special engagement was made with Mrs Glover, the best comic actress then upon the stage, to appear as the weeping widowed Andromache. A play so mounted—to borrow the French expression—was not very encouraging in the prospect of its attracting; but I had only to hold steadily to my purpose, and 'do my best'. Monday, September 16th, was fixed for my appearance. The interim was employed in settling myself in lodgings at 64, Frith Street, Soho, attending rehearsals, giving directions in the wardrobe for my dress, and thinking night and day upon the trial that was before me.

With most of us the course of life is uneven, and there are doubtless few who cannot recall periods of difficulty, of hazard and danger, where it was needful to string up every nerve to the utmost degree of tension in striving against the enfeebling discouragement of doubt. Several times in my life it has fallen to my lot to encounter a crisis of this sort, where all seemed at stake, and of them all this was one of the most formidable; but the day arrived and the venture must be made. Unaccustomed to the vast size of these large theatres, it was with a feeling like dismay that I entered on the stage; but to all appearance I managed to keep under control the flutter of my spirits, went through my rehearsal, inspected my room, and gave all directions necessary. Every courtesy was shown to me, and, as an ordinary civility to a *débutant*, whatever 'orders' or free admissions I might wish for my friends were liberally set at my disposal by the managers; but I had then no friends, not even an acquaintance that I could call upon.

After my early dinner I lay down, endeavouring to compose myself, till the hour appointed for my setting out to the theatre. The hackney-coach—a conveyance happily, in the advance of civilisation, 'mingled with the things o'erpast'—was called, and I can almost fancy in recollecting it that I feel every disquieting jolt of the rumbling vehicle as it slowly performed the office of a hurdle in conveying me to the place of execution. The silent process of dressing was only interrupted by the callboy Parsloe's voice, 'Overture on, sir!' which sent a chill to my heart. The official rap at the door soon followed, and the summons, 'Mr Macready', made me instantly rally all my energies, and with a firm step I went forward to my trial. But the appearance of resolute composure assumed by the player at this turning-point of his life belies the internal struggles he endures. These eventful trials, in respect to the state of mind and body in which they are encountered, so resemble each other that one described describes all. The same agitation and effort to master it, the dazzled vision, the short quick breath, the dry palate, the throbbing of the heart—all, however painfully felt, must be effectually disguised in the character the actor strives to place before his audience.

Abbott, as Pylades, was waiting for me at the side-scene, and when the curtain had risen, grasping his hand almost convulsively, I dashed upon the stage, exclaiming as in a transport of the highest joy, 'Oh, Pylades! what's life without a friend!' The welcome of applause that greeted my entrance (always so liberally bestowed by a London public on every new performer) was all I could have desired; but it was not until the long and loud plaudits following the vehement burst of passion in the line, 'Oh, ye Gods! give me Hermione or let me die!' that I gained any degree of self-possession. As the play proceeded I became more and more animated under the conflicting emotions of the distracted lover, and at the close, as I sank, '*furiis agitatus Orestes*', into the arms of Pylades, the prolonged cheers of my auditors satisfied me of my success. The custom of 'calling for' the player had not then been introduced into our English theatres; but it was considered a sufficient testimony of a triumphant issue to give out the play for repetition on the Friday and Monday following. Congratulations were profusely tendered me by the various members of the Covent Garden company, who stopped me in passing from the stage to my dressing-room; and when summoned to the manager's room, Mr Harris, in his peculiar way, observed, 'Well, my boy, you have done capitally; and if you could carry a play along with such a cast, I don't know what you cannot do!' I was to dine with him next day to settle further proceedings, and I returned to my lodgings in a state of mind like one not fully awake from a disturbing dream, grateful for my escape, yet almost questioning the reality of what had passed.

In the attendance of that evening it was observed that the members of the *corps dramatique* mustered in unusual force, among whom Kean, conspicuous in a private box, was very liberal of his applause . . .

William Charles Macready

ADELPHI THEATRE

STRAND.

BY AUTHORITY OF THE] *[LORD CHAMBERLAIN.*

DOCTOR FAUSTUS and the BLACK DEMON, which is acknowledged to be the Best and most Successful Pantomime produced this Season, will be repeated every Evening.

☞ *St. RONAN'S WELL still increasing in Attraction, and being received with reiterated Shouts of Applause, by crowded and fashionable Audiences, will be repeated every Evening till further Notice.*

MONDAY, February 2, 1824, and During the Week,

Will be presented, for the 18th Time, a New Serious MELO-DRAME, entitled and founded on the Language, Incidents, &c. of the popular New Scotch Novel

St. Ronan's Well.

The NEW MUSIC by Mr. G. B. HERBERT. The DRESSES by Mr. & Miss GODBEE. The SCENERY by Mr. FRANKLIN.

Lord Etherington, Mr. POWER. Tyrrell, Mr. BURROUGHS.
Sir Bingo Binks, Mr. SALTER. Mowbray of St. Ronan's, Mr. ELLIOTT. Capt. Jekyl, Mr. CHAPMAN
Captain Hector O'Turk, *an Irish Officer on Half Pay*, Mr. LEE Mr. Quackleben, Mr. PROUD.
Mr. Micclewhame, Mr. DALY. Mr. Winterblossom, Mr. W. REEVES.
Mr. Bindloose, Mr. MEREDITH. Mr. Touchwood, Mr WILKINSON.
Patrick, *Servant to Mowbray*, Mr. GAY. Anthony, *Postilion at the Old Clickhum Inn*, Mr. COOPER.
Solmes, *Valet to Lord Etherington*, Mr. PHILLIPS. Servant, Mr. MILLER.
Lady Penelope Penfeather, Mrs. BRYAN. Lady Binks, Miss BROWN. Clara Mowbray, Mrs. WAYLETT.
Miss Digges, Miss CARR. Mrs. Dodds, Mrs. DALY.
Kesie Chambermaid, Jenny Anderson, } *Servants at the Clickhum Inn*, { Miss GASCIANI. Miss VIDAL.

After which, for the 32nd Time, an entirely new Grand and Magnificent CHRISTMAS PANTOMIME, with New Scenery, Machinery, Tricks, Properties, Dresses, and Decorations, that has been the whole Summer in Preparation, and on which no Labour or Expence has been spared in the Production, entitled

Doctor Faustus

AND THE

BLACK DEMON;

OR

Harlequin & the Seven Fairies of the Grotto.

The SCENERY of the Pantomime painted by Messrs FRANKLIN, KIRBY, MORRIS and numerous Assistants. The PANORAMIC VIEW of the BOMBARDMENT of ALGIERS, by Mr. WILSON. The ALLEGORICAL LAST SCENE designed and painted by an eminent Artist, assisted by Mr. WILSON The DRESSES by Mr. and Miss GODBEE and Assistants. The MACHINERY executed by Mr R. DENNIS and Mr. KEYS. The PROPERTIES by Mr. DIX. The DANCES by Mr. W. KIRBY. The New GRAND OVERTURE, and the Whole of the MUSIC composed by Mr. G. B. HERBERT.

Scene 1. **Magician's Study, with distant View by Moonlight.** *(Franklin)*
Doctor Faustus, *a Rosicrusian Cabalist*, Mr. ELLIOTT, *(afterwards Pantaloon)* Mr. JONAS,
Long Chow Chot, *his Chinese Slave, (afterwards* Clown*)* **Mr. KIRBY.**
The Black Demon, Mr. SMITH. Mephostophiles, *favorite Imp of the Black Demon*, Master PHILLIPS.
Chorus of Demons, by Messrs. MOORE, PROUD, CAHILL, PADBURY, &c. &c.

Scene 2. ***Silver Palace of the Golden Isles*** *(Franklin*
Ringfangfunnibus, *King of the Golden Isles*, Mr. J. SHAW.
Ortangus, *Prince of the Ruby Lips, (afterwards Harlequin)* Mr. W. KIRBY.
High Priest of the Golden Altar, Mr. W. REEVES. Attendants on the High Priest, Messrs. WALLACE and RUMBLE.
Ringtanghunnibus, *Queen of the Golden Isles*, Mr. COOPER.
Alzalla, *Princess of the Diamond Eyes, (afterwards Columbine)* Mrs. SEARLE.
Grotesque Procession of Courtiers, by Messrs. GAY, RIGNOLD, PHILLIPS, MILLER, PAYNE, and FOSTER.
Ladies of the Court, Misses GAY, BROWN, GILES, GASCIAN, ARNOLD, and GASKIN.
Bearers of the Jewel Banners, Messrs. GLOVER and SHEPPERD Love Step Bearers, Messrs. COMEQUICK and HIGHMINDED.

Scene 3. **BASALTIC CAVE AND POISONED SPRING,**
With Magic Change. *(Kirby)*

Scene 4. **Coral Grotto of the Seven Fairies.** *(Kirby)*
Silverspray, *Queen of the Fairies*, Miss CHIVERS.
Her Six Attendant Fairies, Misses WALBOURN, BILLINGS, PHILLIPS, WILKINSON, BLAIR, BLOOMFIELD.

Scene 5. **GREY VALLEY BY MOONLIGHT.** *(Morris)*
Characters as before.

Scene 6. **View of the New Chain Pier at Brighton.** *(Morris)*
Scull, Oar, Stern, & Stem, Mess. WRIGHT, FEARLESS, GUNNER, & STEERWELL. Searchem & Graball, *Exciseman*, Mess. WAKE & FLY.
Baby of a Year Old, Master SMALLBOY. Fishwoman, Mrs. DENNIS.

Scene 7. **INTERIOR OF A LODGING HOUSE.**
Landlady, Mr. MILLER. Lover. Mr. SANDERS. Black Boy, Master WHITE.

Scene 8. ***Richardson and Goodluck's Lottery Office.*** *(Morris)*
Mr. Goodluck, Mr. PHILLIPS. Glover, Mr. PAYNE Baker, Mr. DOUGH.
Man with Lottery Board, Mr. CAHILL. Clerk of the Lottery Office, Mr. WALLACE. Butcher, Mr. RIGNOLD. Greenwoman, Miss IRELAND.

Scene 9. INTERIOR OF *(Kirby)*
Jonathan Warren's Blacking Warehouse, Hungerford Stairs.
Shopman, Mr. TOTTER, Dandy, Mr. SHAW. Customer, Miss GASCIANI.

Scene 10. **Saracen's Head, Aldgate.** *(Morris)*
Alderman Gobblegoose, Mr. K. COOPER. John, *his Servant*, Mr. SAD. Pudding Man, Mr. HUMBLE. Painter, Mr. LESS.
Lady Gobblegoose, Mrs. PLEASURE. Dolly, Miss BROWN. Laundry Maid, Miss CARR.
A Broad Sword HORNPIPE, by Mr. W. KIRBY and Mrs. SEARLE.

Scene 11. **KITCHEN of the SARACEN's HEAD.** *(Kirby)*
Cook, Mr. DENNIS. Waiter, Mr. MILLER.

Scene 12. **SPARROW'S TEA WAREHOUSE.** *(Morris)*
Military Officer, Mr. BRAGG. Grocer, Mr. FIG. Waiter, Mr. CUMMING. Flying Pieman, Mr. SMITH,
Mud and Slush, *two Scavengers*, Mr. THICK and Mr. THIN. Officer's Lady, Miss STIFF. Alderman Butbelly, Mr. GAY,
Milliner, Mrs. BUCKRAM.

Scene 13. **Deck of the QUEEN CHARLOTTE Man of War,**
ON HER VOYAGE TO ALGIERS. *(Franklin)*

Scene 14. **A Grand Marine Moving Panorama**
Of the BOMBARDMENT of ALGIERS! *(Wilson)*

Illustrative of the most interesting Events of that victorious Enterprize, so Glorious in itself, and so Important in its Consequences to the Interests of GREAT BRITAIN, and the Maritime World at large.

The PANORAMA commences with a View of the City of Algiers, with the Emperor's Fort on the left, as it appeared from the Bay, prior to the Battle, displaying the Mole, the Forts, the Batteries, Light House, &c. As the View proceeds, the British Fleet is seen approaching the Bay of Algiers, when the Firing commences, and gradually increases, till the Bombardment is at its hottest Period—Evening—At the Entrance of the Mole, in the most conspicuous Part of the View, and close upon the City, is the Queen Charlotte, (Admiral Lord Exmouth) bring a Broadside against the Battery of the Mole, opposite her, and in the Entrance of the Mole, is an Algerine Frigate on [illegible] illuminating the Town and every Object near it. Near the Queen Charlotte, are the Leander and the Severn, partly enveloped in Smoke, their Masts, Yards, [illegible] cut up; they received the greatest Damage from the European Fort. Between them and the Queen Charlotte, is the Flotilla of Gun, Mortar, and Rocket [illegible] in the act of discharging Showers of Rockets into the Town. In the Front of the Mole, are seen the Granicus Frigate, the Superb 74, the Minden, the [illegible] Fury, the Impregnable [illegible], and the Beelzebub Bomb Vessels, &c. In the Foreground, is a Boat sailing from the Queen Charlotte to the Hebrus, to order [illegible] Assistance of the Leander. The Town is also on Fire in several Places. The Cry of Victory is heard from the British Vessels, and the View changes [illegible] City of Algiers, displaying its ruinous Appearance the Day after the Battle. The Christian Slaves coming off in Boats, shouting and waving their Caps [illegible]
Whole concludes with

AN ALLEGORICAL REPRESENTATION OF

Neptune presenting the Crown of the Ocean to Britannia,

At the Feet of Britannia, the British Lion is seen growling and trampling on Turbans, Chains, Fetters, and other Symbols of Slavery, while Fame is seen hovering above, sounding her Trumpet in praise of this last and glorious Act of

BRITISH BRAVERY.

BOXES, 4s. PIT, 2s. GAL. 1s. Doors open [illegible], and commence at a Quarter before 7. HALF PRICE at Half-past 8. [illegible] open from [illegible] till 4, where Places may be taken, and a Private Box had Nightly, of Mr. CALLAN. Children in Arms cannot be admitted. No Money returned. Printed by W. GLINDON, Rupert Street, Haymarket.

23

Kean as Timon

Timon of Athens, nowadays among the least popular of Shakespeare's plays in the theatre, is often disliked simply because people will not listen to it, preferring an incantation of the familiar. The tragedy is a shout against ingratitude. In its first half the prodigal patrician, rapt in a kind of philanthropic euphoria, must learn that there is deepest winter in his purse; that though 'to Lacedaemon did my land extend', he is deserted by the whole race of toadies. In the second half—'I am Misanthropos, and hate mankind'—he summons the lightning in a fury of invective when the play seems to recoil upon itself. This second part contains most of the phrases we think of: the sudden exquisite flush of eight words, 'embalms and spices to the April day again'; Apemantus's 'Will these mossed trees That have outlived the eagle, page thy heels?'; Timon's 'Lie where the light foam of the sea may beat Thy gravestone daily'; and the magnificent 'beachéd verge of the salt flood, Who once a day with his embosséd froth The turbulent surge shall cover'.

Samuel Phelps was the most notable nineteenth-century Timon. In our day Ralph Richardson (Old Vic, 1956) and, particularly, Paul Scofield (Stratford-upon-Avon, 1965) have played the part better than any other actors; there has been little competition.

The tragedy had to endure versions by Shadwell (who added a love interest to *The History of Timon of Athens, the Man-Hater*), Cumberland, and Hall. Edmund Kean (*c*1790–1833) appeared as Timon (28 October 1816) in the first major production since 1786, the text adapted now by the Hon George Lamb in an effort 'to restore Shakespeare to the stage, with no other omissions such as the refinement of manners has rendered necessary'. This meant the loss of the courtesans, Phrynia and Timandra, and, more sadly, some of the great verse. There were only seven Drury Lane performances. Leigh Hunt's notice appeared in *The Examiner* on 4 November 1816.

The tragedy of *Timon of Athens*, after a lapse of several years, was revived at this theatre [Drury Lane] on Monday. The Managers, we suppose, were led to their choice of it, not only by their general desire to bring forward what is good, but by the great success of Mr Kean in characters of a certain caustic interest; yet, although the selection is honourable to both parties, and the performance was received and given out for repetition with great applause, we doubted and still doubt whether it will have what is called a run. If it has, we shall save our self-love by attributing a part of it to the present times, which are certainly favourable ones for giving effect to representations of pecuniary difficulty, and of friendship put to the test. But the parts of the tragedy which contain the dramatic interest are comparatively few; the moral, though strong, is obvious, and in fact too easily anticipated; and when Timon has once fallen from his fortunes, there is little to excite further attention in the spectator. The *reader* is still delighted, but he would be still more so in his closet, where he could weigh every precious sentence at leisure, and lose none of the text either by the freaks of adapters or the failure of actors' voices . . .

The whole play . . . abounds in masterly delineations of character, and in passages equally poetical and profound; though the latter unfortunately reduced the adapter of the piece to an awkward dilemma; for they constitute its main beauty, and yet he seems to have felt himself obliged to cut them short, either for fear of making it drag with the spectators, or in compliance with a sophisticated decorum. Thus many of the most striking pieces of satire are left out; and we see nothing of the two females who come in upon Timon's retreat with Alcibiades . . .

The play, upon the whole, was well performed. Mr Kean, as usual, gave touches of natural excellence, such as no other living actor could produce. [But] Timon will not rank as one of his first performances; it wants sufficient variety and flexibility of passion for him. Neither do we think that he succeeded in the first part of the play, where Timon is prosperous and indulges his credulous generosity. He was too stately and tragic. It is true this may appear reconcilable with the ostentation which is charged Timon; but . . . the charge appears to us to be unfounded, as far as the leading passion is concerned; and Timon is a man of ardent animal spirits whose great enjoyment is the sense of a certain glorious fellowship upon which he thinks he could equally reckon in a time of adversity, and the disappointment of which drives him, in a manner, distracted. He smiles at first, when his steward talks to him of cold friends; finds a reason for the first disappointment he encounters from the senators in the cold-bloodedness of their time of life; and, during the banquet in the second scene, the fullness of his trusting heart fairly runs over into tears of delight. From all this, it appears to us that the actor's representation of him in his prosperity should be more easy and cordial, and that he should receive and entertain his visitors, not like a prince with a diadem, but like a companion who has the happy art of being heartily though gracefully one's equal. If Timon had been only ostentatious, he would hardly have been so willing to borrow, and to think all his friends as generous as himself: he would have run mad for pride; whereas his misanthropy is really owing, as in almost all instances, to an unexpected and extreme conviction of the hollowness of the human heart.

We think Mr Kean also had too great a tendency in some parts to be violent, or rather to carry the paroxysms of Timon to a pitch beyond true rage, and too often to mistake vehemence for intenseness. Timon's curses in general should have been 'not loud but deep': and where Mr Kean's acting was of this description, it certainly had the greatest effect out of the pale of the galleries, though some of his passionate starts were deservedly admired also. The finest scene in the whole performance was the one with Alcibiades. We never remember the force of contrast to have been more truly pathetic. Timon, digging in the woods with his spade, hears the approach of military music . . . Kean started, listened, and leaned in a fixed and angry manner on his spade, with frowning eyes, and lips full of the truest feeling, compressed but not too much so; he seemed not to be deceived, even by the charm of a thing inanimate; the audience were silent; the march threw forth its gallant note nearer and nearer; the Athenian standards appear, then the soldiers come treading on the scene with that air of confident progress which is produced by the accompaniment of music; and at last, while the squalid misanthrope still maintains his posture and keeps his back to the strangers, in steps the young and splendid Alcibiades, in the flush of victorious expectation. It is the encounter of hope with despair.

Alcibiades luckily had a representative in Mr Wallack who, besides performing the rest of his part with good credit, dressed and looked it uncommonly well. He seemed to have been studying the bust of his hero as well as the costume of the Greek soldier. Mr Bengough, in Apemantus, made as good a Cynic philosopher as we wished to see; he did not look quite so shrewd or beggarly as Diogenes, but he was wise enough for the part. As for Mr Holland in the kind and lamenting Steward, he seemed quite inspired. We do not know that we ever saw him in so much advantage; but Mr Kean's acting, we suspect, has given a great fillip to all the minor performers nowadays.

With respect to the scenery and other mechanical matters, the piece was excellently got up. One of the scenes was a striking view of Athens, composed, perhaps, from the picture in *Hobhouse's Travels*. Timon's solitude was also very leafy and to the purpose; and the splendour of the banquet scene obtained great applause. We must protest, however, against the dance of young Amazons clashing their swords and shields. Shakespeare, we allow, has specified Amazons for the occasion; but if Amazons there must be, they should at least have had lutes in their hands, which he has specified also, instead of weapons. We are at a loss to conjecture why Shakspeare introduced Amazons at all, which seem to be no more to his taste in general than they were to old Homer's; but did he find, anywhere, that an Amazon with a lute was Timon's device? We have not the commentators at hand to refer to; but Timon in thanking the dancers, tells them that they have entertained him with his 'own device'; and devices of this kind were common from time immemorial. A dramatic mask, it is true, was called a device; but the host in the present instance seems to have been taken unawares, and could hardly have spoken as he did, had he himself invented the subject of the dance. We should like to have as little of these unfeminine feminines as possible: lutes would make them more human, and might act as a sort of compliment to Alcibiades, who is one of the guests, or to the spirit of sociality in general, as much as to say—a spirit of harmony corrects what is barbarous. We doubt also the propriety of the diadem and fillet worn by Mr Kean, as well as the want of another sort of wreath to the heads of him and his guests during the banquets. They should undoubtedly, as was the custom, wear roses, myrtles, or other flowers mentioned by Anacreon and Plutarch, which besides being proper, would also have a pleasing effect and contribute to the luxury of the scene: not that all this is necessary to Shakspeare, or demanded by him, but that it is as well to complete the costume, in all instances, where it is undertaken in most.

We thank the Managers for *Timon*, which for our part we could see over again, were it only for the fine scene before mentioned: though we are afraid they have miscalculated the chances of its long run. We hope their next representation will be equally creditable to their taste, and more likely to reward it.

Leigh Hunt

24

Exit Kemble

John Philip Kemble acted for the last time in the Theatre Royal, Covent Garden, on 23 June 1817. His part was Coriolanus. On Friday, 27 June, he was entertained at a farewell banquet in the Freemasons' Tavern, Great Queen Street.

The Ode, read by Charles Mayne Young, was by the poet Thomas Campbell. (Walter Scott had written for Kemble a farewell address on his last Edinburgh night, 29 March, which contained the lines, 'My life's brief act in public service flown, The last, the closing scene, must be my own'.) John Fawcett (1768–1837), Young (1777–1856), and Charles Mathews Sr (1776–1835) were actors. The Frenchman who 'spoke, in English, a compliment not ill-turned', was none other than the tragedian François-Joseph Talma (1763–1826), who had been playing at Covent Garden, with Mlle George, in extracts from his major parts. Only three weeks before, Talma had himself been entertained at the Clarendon Hotel, Bond Street, by the actors of Covent Garden (among them the young Macready, who was away in the provinces at the time of the Kemble banquet). The Clarendon bill began with 'Dinner, dessert, wax lights, beer, etc. for 22 Gents—£23.2.0', and proceeded, through a variety of wines—particularly twenty bottles of claret—to tea and coffee (£1 1s 0d), sandwiches (1s), and 'Broken glass' (12s): total, £54 6s 0d.

But here is Kemble's own banquet as recorded by James Boaden—who does not give the menu—in *Memoirs of the Life of John Philip Kemble, Esq.*, 1825.

At seven o'clock dinner was announced in the grand room of the Freemasons' Tavern. Mr Kemble and the noble president, Lord Holland, were preceded from the drawing-room by the committee, the band playing the march from the occasional overture. Mr Kemble sat on the right hand of the chairman, and his Grace the Duke of Bedford on the left. Selections from Handel were performed during the dinner by the band, and on the removal of the cloth, the matchless *Non Nobis* was given in all its thrilling awe by the best singers of it that I have ever heard, Leete, Nield, Terrail, Master Turle, and others.

After the usual toasts, Mr Rae and Mr Mathews handed to Lord Holland the cast and drawing of the Vase, which was to be presented to Mr Kemble. His Lordship immediately rose and addressed the company . . . Mr Young then recited an Ode written for the occasion by Mr Campbell, of which one stanza so utterly distances the rest, that I beg to keep it, like Paulina's statue of Hermione, 'lovely, apart':

His was the spell o'er hearts
That only Acting lends,
The youngest of the sister arts,
Where all their beauty blends.
For Poetry can ill express
Full many a tone of thought sublime;
And Painting, mute and motionless,
Steals but one partial glance from Time.
But by the mighty Actor brought,
Illusion's wedded triumphs come,
Verse ceases to be airy thought,
And Sculpture to be dumb . . .

Mr Kemble seems to have been rather chilled and checked by the unavoidable attention to his own praises. He perhaps, with some other persons present, thought of the way in which he had *rushed* from such a hearing in Coriolanus; but he did the best that could be done in the circumstances: something of *disclaimer*, something of *pride*, mixed up gracefully with sincere *thanks*; and he saw the '*pleasures of hope*', neatly enough, at the bottom of his glass.

Fawcett made him his *General*, in a warm and affectionate speech; Mathews, his dramatic King. Talma spoke, in English, a compliment not ill-turned; and Young expressed his conviction that 'lasting reputation was only to be obtained at the price which Mr Kemble had paid for it'.

The last toast given was *the Ladies*; and a little before twelve o'clock, the noble chairman and his guest rose to depart. As Mr Kemble passed slowly down the room, the company pressed upon him to grasp his hand; and, when he retired, they merely drank one bumper to his future health and enjoyment, and immediately quitted the scene of perfectly rational and ennobling hospitality. Such was, I rejoice to say, 'the grac'd respect that claim'd him to the last'.

James Boaden

Theatre Royal, Covent-Garden
This present WEDNESDAY, Jan. 7, 1829.
Will be acted, (3d time) FARQUHAR's Comedy of The

Beaux Stratagem

Aimwell, Mr. WARDE, Archer, Mr. C. KEMBLE,
Sullen, Mr. BLANCHARD, Freeman, Mr. RAYMOND,
Foigard, Mr. POWER, Gibbet, Mr. O. SMITH,
Boniface, Mr. BARTLEY, Scrub, Mr. KEELEY,
Hounslow Mr. ATKINS, Bagshot Mr. FULLER, Tapster Mr. HEATH,
Lady Bountiful, Mrs. DAVENPORT, Dorinda, Mrs. CHATTERLEY,
Mrs. Sullen, Miss CHESTER,
Cherry, Miss FORDE, Gipsey, Mrs. DALY.

After which, *for the 11th time*, a New Comic Pantomime, *(founded on a Fairy Tale)* called

HARLEQUIN
AND
Little Red Riding Hood;
OR, THE
Wizard and the Wolf.

The OVERTURE, & MUSIC of first Five Scenes, by Mr. WATSON—the remainder composed and selected by Mr. WODARCH
The Scenery by Mess. GRIEVE, T.GRIEVE, W.GRIEVE, FINLEY, ROY, MORRIS & ROBERTS
The MACHINERY and CHANGES Mr. E. SAUL. The Properties and Decorations by Mess. KELLY, REED, &c.
The DRESSES by Mr. HEAD, and Miss ABBOTT.
THE WHOLE ARRANGED AND PRODUCED BY Mr. FARLEY.

The WIZARD, *(or Brown Man of the Hill,)* Mr. EVANS,
HUMPO, his Son, *(changed to the Wolf*, afterwards *Blanche-Noir, Rival to Harlequin)* Mr. E. J. PARSLOE
BARLEY-DUST, the Miller, (afterwards *Pantaloon*) Mr. T. BLANCHARD,
COLIN, the Miller's Apprentice,..(afterwards *Harlequin*).. Mr. ELLAR
GRANNY ROSE,....(afterwards *Clown*)....Mr. J. S. GRIMALDI,
Millers, Mess. Tinney, Miller, Shegog, Tett, S. Tett, Irwin,
Bucheron (the Woodcutter) Mr HENRY, Driver of the Diligence, Mr. COLLETT,
Dr. Nostrum, Mr. TURNOUR, Endall, (the Undertaker) Mr. SIMPSON, Brown Stout, (Landlord of the Constitution) Mr. PLATT
Cobler, Mr. MILLER. Fat Beadle, Mr. CHAPLIN, Mons. Fit'emtight, (fashionable Tailor) Mr. GRIFFITHS,
THE YACHT CLUB, Mess. d'Albert, Austin, Collet, J. Cooper, Heath, Sutton,
AND A HORNPIPE, BY MISS FANNY MARSHALL,
ROSE,..(called ROSE D'AMOUR,)......afterwards *Colombine*...... Miss EGAN,
The Genius of the Rose, *(Protectress of Rose)* Miss WATSON,
Old Nurse, Miss SHIVERS, French Flower Girls, Mrs. BROWN and Mrs. FENWICK.

The following is the Order of the Scenery:

1. **CHAOTIC DWELLING** of the Wizard, which disappears & shews the City of *Rouen, Normandy.* Grieve
2. **ROUEN CATHEDRAL** from the Faubourg St. Sever, with the Bridge of Boats, Miller's House & Mill. W.Grieve
3. The FOREST of NOUVELLES, with GRANNY ROSE's COTTAGE, by Sunset. Grieve
4. INSIDE of GRANNY ROSE's COTTAGE. T. Grieve
5. ***THE ROSY BOWER.*** T.Grieve
6. OUTSIDE of the MESSAGERIES ROYALES—Diligence ready to start for Le Havre. Morris
7. Distant View of the ISLE of WIGHT, at the time of **THE REGATTA at COWES.** T Grieve
8. ST. JOHN'S GATE, SOUTHAMPTON. W.Grieve
9. **THE NEW POST-OFFICE IN LONDON.** T.Grieve
10. **DOCTOR'S SHOP**......and his Neighbour .....**THE UNDERTAKER'S.** Finley
11. THE OPENING OF THE **St. Katharine's Docks,** With the Vessels—THE PRINCE REGENT—THE ELIZABETH—THE MARY—&c. &c. Coming into the Inner Basin; *as they appeared on the 25th of October*, 1828. W.Grieve
12. Outside of SADLER's REPOSITORY. Finley
13. St. Dunstan's Church—Temple-Bar—and Fleet-Street—by MOONLIGHT. W.Grieve
14. WATERLOO-BRIDGE, at a distance—by Night. Grieve
15. THE NURSERY GROUND. Grieve. 16 A CAVERN. Finley
17

ROBERTS'
MOVING
PANORAMA

Of the GRAND RUSSIAN ARMY'S MARCH to TURKEY.
Comprehending the following Scenery:——
ST. PETERSBURGH at the time of a **GRAND FESTIVAL,**
MOUNTAINS and FORTRESSES.
THE NIGHT WATCH——SOLDIERS BIVOUACING, &c.
AMBUSCADE and BATTLE,
THE HALT OF A CARAVAN IN THE DESERT, AT SUNSET;
The FLEET, the DARDANELLES, the CASTLE of the SEVEN TOWERS,——and the
GENERAL VIEW OF CONSTANTINOPLE.

18 SPAR CAVERNS on the COAST of AFRICA. GRIEVE
19 **THE PALACE OF ROSES.** W.Grieve

BOOKS of the Pantomime, &c. with a Lithographic of the Panorama to be had at the Theatre, and of Mr. MILLER, No. 40, Pall-Mall, Price Tenpence.

Printed by W. Reynolds, 9, Denmark-Court, Strand.

A play-bill for *Beaux Stratagem* at Covent Garden during the management of Charles Kemble

25

No 'Mere Poetry'

Percy Bysshe Shelley (1792–1822) wrote *The Cenci* in the summer of 1819, at Rome, when he was 26; it was published with an affectionate dedication to Leigh Hunt. Astonishing tragedy though it is—even if we know too well, in the Murder scene, that Shelley had been reading *Macbeth*—its themes of incest and parricide kept it from the stage. Shelley, who was quite prepared to use a pseudonym, had hoped that it might be acted with Edmund Kean as the Count and the young Eliza O'Neill as Beatrice.

Macready, as late as December 1847, wrote in his journal: 'Looked through *The Cenci* . . . The *idea* of acting such a monstrous crime, beautiful as the work is!' Finally, as we shall see later, the newly formed Shelley Society staged a single 'private' performance in the early summer of 1886.

The extract is from Shelley's Preface. 'The story is,' he said, 'that an old man, having spent his life in debauchery and wickedness, conceived at length an implacable hatred towards his children; which showed itself towards one daughter under the form of an incestuous passion, aggravated by every circumstance of cruelty and violence. This daughter, after long and vain attempts to escape from what she considered a perpetual contamination both of body and mind, at length plotted with her mother-in-law and brother to murder their common tyrant. The young maiden, who was urged to this tremendous deed by an impulse which overpowered its horror, was evidently a most gentle and amiable being, a creature formed to adorn and be admired, and thus violently thwarted from her nature by the necessity of circumstance and opinion. The deed was quickly discovered, and, in spite of the most earnest prayers made to the Pope by the highest persons in Rome, the criminals were put to death.'

This is the passage, noted by Shelley, on the chasm. Beatrice speaks:

> But I remember
> Two miles on this side of the fort, the road
> Crosses a deep ravine; 'tis rough and narrow,
> And winds with short turns down the precipice;
> And in its depth there is a mighty rock,
> Which has, from unimaginable years,
> Sustained itself with terror and with toil
> Over a gulf, and with the agony
> With which it clings seems slowly coming down;
> Even as a wretched soul hour after hour,
> Clings to the mass of life; yet clinging, leans;
> And, leaning, makes more dark the dread abyss
> In which it fears to fall; beneath this crag
> Huge as despair, as if in weariness,
> The melancholy mountain yawns; below,
> You hear but see not an impetuous torrent
> Raging among the chasms, and a bridge
> Crosses the chasm; and high above there grow
> With intersecting trunks, from crag to crag,
> Cedars, and yews, and pines; whose tangled hair
> Is matted in one solid roof of shade
> By the dark ivy's twine. At noonday here
> 'Tis twilight, and at sunset blackest night.

This story of the Cenci is indeed eminently fearful and monstrous; anything like a dry exhibition of it on the stage would be insupportable. The person who would treat such a subject must increase the ideal and diminish the actual horror of the events, so that the pleasure which arises from the poetry which exists in these tempestuous sufferings and crimes may mitigate the pain of the contemplation of the moral deformity from which they spring. There must also be nothing attempted to make the exhibition subservient to what is vulgarly termed a moral purpose. The highest moral purpose aimed at in the highest species of the drama, is the teaching the human heart, through its sympathies and antipathies, the knowledge of itself; in proportion to the possession of which knowledge, every human being is wise, just, sincere, tolerant, and kind. If dogmas can do more, it is well: but a drama is no fit place for the enforcement of them. Undoubtedly, no person can be truly dishonoured by the act of another; and the fit return to make to the most enormous injuries is kindness and forbearance and a resolution to convert the injurer from his dark passions by peace and love. Revenge, reconciliation, atonement, are pernicious mistakes. If Beatrice had thought in this manner she would have been wiser and better; but she would never have been a tragic character. The few whom such an exhibition would have interested, could never have been sufficiently interested for a dramatic purpose, from the want of finding sympathy in their interest among the mass who surround them. It is in the restless and anatomising casuistry with which men seek the justification of Beatrice, yet feel that she has done what needs justification; it is in the superstitious horror with which they contemplate alike her wrongs and their revenge,—that the dramatic character of what she did and suffered, consists . . .

I have avoided with great care in writing this play the introduction of what is commonly called mere poetry, and I imagine there will scarcely be found a detached simile or a single isolated description, unless Beatrice's description of the chasm appointed for her father's murder should be judged to be of that nature.

In a dramatic composition the imagery and the passion should interpenetrate one another, the former being reserved simply for the full development and illustration of the latter. Imagination is as the immortal God which should assume flesh for the redemption of mortal passion. It is thus that the most remote and the most familiar imagery may alike be fit for dramatic purposes when employed in the illustration of strong feeling, which raises what is low, and levels to the apprehension that which is lofty, casting over all the shadow of its own greatness. In other respects, I have written more carelessly; that is, without an over-learned and fastidious choice of words. In this respect I entirely agree with those modern critics who assert that in order to move men to true sympathy we must use the familiar language of men, and that our great ancestors, the ancient English poets, are the writers, a study of whom might incite us to do that for our own age which they have done for theirs. But it must be the real language of men in general and not that of any particular class to whose society the writer happens to belong. So much for what I have attempted; I need not be assured that success is a very different matter; particularly for one whose attention has but newly been awakened to the study of dramatic literature.

Percy Bysshe Shelley

26

Robson Remembers

William Robson (*c*1785–1864), writer and schoolmaster, is remembered for what he called, in a dedication to the actor Charles Kemble, a 'retrospective review of bygone excellence', *The Old Play-goer* (1846). It is an acute and affectionate record of the theatre of his early playgoing days which he found more exciting than the present: he deeply regretted the diffusion of talent after the two great Patent houses, Covent Garden and Drury Lane, had lost their monopoly.

In the following extracts the character of Sir Giles Overreach is from Philip Massinger's *A New Way to Pay Old Debts* (1625); Kitely from Ben Jonson's *Every Man in His Humour* (1598); Glenalvon from John Home's *Douglas* (1756); and King John from Shakespeare's tragedy. John Henderson (1747–85) was an actor applauded for a number of parts that included Shylock and Falstaff.

Behold George Cooke. With a person fully up to the middle size and rather stout, a good stage face, that is, prominent nose, sharp keen eyes, and expressive mouth, but all affected a little by the stamp of habitual intemperance, he was well qualified for the walk in tragedy he generally took; his principal drawbacks being a somewhat harsh voice, particularly short arms, and a not too graceful carriage. But mind . . . when I hint that George Cooke wanted grace, his motions were the steps of an Apollo when compared with the wriggle of a Kean. The part of Peregrine [George Colman's comedy, *John Bull*] was hardly worthy of Cooke, but he threw a respectability into it—he spoke the sometimes nervous and frequently sentimental speeches with such propriety as to keep them free from the charge of mawkishness, which, perhaps, a less judicious actor would not have been able to do. Poor George! he is before me now, in his blue coat, pantaloons, and hessian boots, with Job Thornberry's box of treasure under one arm, and Dennis's mug of sour beer in the hand of the other! . . .

I dearly loved Cooke, though he was my idol's rival, and in some parts a successful one. But the scenes and actors are now so far removed that I view them with the same feeling that the historian surveys the events which have now no bearing upon existing party. I now see that the energy and decided genius of Cooke placed him at least upon an equality with Kemble in Shylock, Richard, Sir Giles Overreach, Kitely, John, Glenalvon, and all characters whose villainy was meant to create disgust; but in the noble walk, where pity was to be stirred, deep grief was to soften, elegance to charm, or lofty bearing to impose, then Cooke was very, very far below Kemble. The power of fancy cannot make me mix up the idea of Lear, Hamlet, Coriolanus, Brutus, Cato, or even Timon, with George Cooke, though he was much admired in the last named. But his Scotchmen, in my opinion, were his masterpieces. I never, of course, saw Macklin, but he *must* have been like Cooke. Oh! to hear Sir Pertinax [in Macklin's *The Man of the World*] describe his wooing at the conventicle; his 'booing and booing'; and to listen to the harsh tones of his powerful voice, the effect heightened by his prominent features, when with a catching kind of fury of utterance, he exclaimed, 'Y're a dommed black sheep, Sir! Y're a dommed black sheep!'

In your stage recollections, do there not exist some little pictures, whereon a gathering of talent stamped such an interest that the parts all remain vivid and perfect in your mind? Such a one recurs to me now in connexion with Cooke. In Macklin's farce of *Love à la Mode*, the four rivals are at once trying to make an impression upon their common mistress. Cooke was Sir Archy MacSarcasm: Johnstone, Sir Callaghan O'Brallaghan; Gentleman Lewis, Squire Groom; and little Simmons, Beau Mordecai. To see four such actors stimulated to the very top of their bent, giving absolute *life* to the scene; their spirits carrying them away so that they appeared to forget they had an audience, and were only playing up to one another, is a dramatic treat few can boast of having seen equalled, none of having seen excelled! The dry, sarcastic mirth, the perfect concentration of self-good opinion, the inward triumphant chuckle, and sneering *Scotch* laugh of Cooke, were beyond belief fine. The twirl with his finger and thumb, with which he put Beau Mordecai forth, with 'Walk aboot, and shew y're shapes, mon', was just as if he had been shewing out the tricks of a dancing dog or monkey.

Poor George! the drink! the drink! I do not think he would have excelled what he did, if he had been a teetotaller, but he might have continued to do it, and have been always hailed with applause instead of sometimes being greeted with hisses. He went as high as nature intended him to go. I remember being struck, on witnessing one of his receptions, with the impunity with which a good actor may offend. He had, for several nights, displeased and disappointed his admirers by appearing intoxicated and marring his parts. I went to see him in John—he was sober, and in excellent vein—what had we to do with sins committed against others? Here was the man we came to see, and as we wished to see him. There was one attempt at a hiss, but it could not have been more eagerly silenced if it had proceeded from a serpent. His bright eye, albeit a little swimming, flashed proudly on those who came to be delighted, and on he went, amidst shouts and bravos.

On Edmund Kean

Nature must do much for a tragedian, or the call will be far greater upon himself: that is, if in personal appearance he be not the hero or the prince, it will require a great deal more mental dignity and grace to make the picture at all passable. Kean's person was mean. Garrick was short, but his person was not mean. Kean was famous, I believe, for activity and *tours de force*; it might be so, but no man, on the stage, was more ungraceful: if his part afforded him cloak or coat-tail, its perpetual wiggle-waggle was quite amusing. That which his admirers most praised in him was his energy and natural acting in parts of strong feeling. Of the latter of these I have spoken, as a fallacy, in a former letter. Of all moods, the energetic is the least imposing for a real play-goer. He sits down with Shakespeare's incomparable direction in this respect, in his head and heart—he may be, at first, startled by vehemence and gesticulation, but he refers back, he begins with the master's precept, he is not like yonder agitated, lovely girl in the boxes, who sees the play for the first time; he has seen, perhaps, Henderson, Kemble, Cooke, and Young in the part, he knows nothing is good or great but by comparison, he examines into the bottom of all this; and Mr Kean's acting proves to be 'sound and fury, signifying nothing'.

He wanted finish, he wanted study; his mind was not cultivated. I don't think he ever sat half an hour, comfortably to himself, in the presence of an educated gentleman, in his life. From the moment of his attaining to celebrity, and, with it, obtaining money, who were his associates? What were his amusements? Were his companions such as would keep his mind in tone, for the delineation of the heart-breaking of the noble Moor? I say, *no*; in spite of all who may contradict me, I say, No! I have absolutely *studied* his famous Othello, to try to like him; but his person and carriage in it were mean and contemptible, his judgment was poor, his pathos weak, his passion violent, extravagant, and unnatural: he was not Othello! *Who* was? I admit in my time Echo has still answered, *Who*?

William Robson

Theatre Royal, Drury Lane.

This Evening, FRIDAY May, 2, 1828

His Majesty's Servants will perform the Tragedy of

VIRGINIUS.

Virginius, ... Mr. MACREADY,
Icilius, ... Mr. WALLACK,
Siccius Dentatus, ... Mr. COOPER,
Appius Claudius, Mr. MUDE, Numitorius, Mr. THOMPSON,
Spurius Oppius, Mr. HOWELL, Lucius, Mr. YOUNGE,
Vibulanus, Mr. E. VINING, Honorius, Mr. GREGORY, Valerius, Mr. DARNLEY,
Caius Claudius, Mr. WEBSTER, Marcus Mr. C JONES, Publius, Mr. HONNOR,
Titus, Mr. YARNOLD, Servius Mr. WAKEFIELD, Cneius, Mr. FENTON,
Virginia, ... Miss FOOTE,
Servia, Mrs. KNIGHT, Slave, Mrs. WILLMOTT.

After which, with Alterations, and compressed into two Acts,

ALADDIN.

Schah of Persia, Mr YOUNGE, Grand Vizier, Mr. FENTON,
Aladdin (*4th time*) Miss FOOTE.
Haggi, (*a Barber*) Mr. WEBSTER, Hassan (*a Coppersmith*) Mr GATTIE,
Mourad, (*an Enchanter*) Mr. COOPER, Genius of the Lamp, Miss VINCENT.
Nourmahal, (*Daughter to the Schah*) Miss I PATON,
Zeenab, (*Mother to Aladdin*) Mrs. C. JONES, Unda, (*Genius of the Ring*) Miss A. TREE;
Zuleika, Miss NICOL, Leila, Miss WILLMOTT.
Soldiers, Peasants, Huntsmen, Slaves, Boys, &c. &c.

SCENERY.

STREET AND CITY OF ISPAHAN.
SUBTERRANEAN PASSAGE of the ROCKS.
Gardens of the Genii of the Lamp. Royal Baths.
Aladdin's Magic Palace
AFRICAN DESERT, with DESCENT of the MAGIC PALACE.
Hall in Schah's Palace.

To conclude with (*21st time*) an entirely New Melo-Dramatic Entertainment, with New Music, Scenery, Machinery, &c. called, The

Dumb Savoyard,

AND HIS MONKEY.

The Action arranged by Mr. W BARRYMORE.

Count Giovanni Maldicini, Mr. YOUNGE, Florio, Miss LANE, Sturmwald, Mr. WEBSTER,
Herr Vatchvell, Mr. BROWNE, Pipino, Mrs. BARRYMORE, Marmazette, Master WIELAND,
Spielsburgh, Mr. C. JONES, Leopoldstadt, Mr. YARNOLD,
Rapinstein, Mr. HOWELL, Fiercenfold, Mr. BARNES, Riflestaff, Mr. BARTLETT,
Celestina, Countess Maldicini, Mrs. W. WEST, Teresa Vanepa, Mrs. FIELD.
Principal Dancers......Mr. NOBLE, and Mrs. NOBLE,

The PASSAGE of the RHINE.
Represented by a Series of
PANORAMIC VIEWS;
[*The whole painted by* STANFIELD.]

ALADDIN,
Having been greeted with universal Applause, will be repeated every Evening, Tomorrow excepted.

The Comedy of Roses and Thorns,
With a New INTERLUDE, to be called,
The School for Gallantry,
Will be produced To-morrow Evening, for the First Time.

The Poor Gentleman
will be acted every TUESDAY Evening.

The Dumb Savoyard and his Monkey,
Increasing nightly in attraction and approbation, will be repeated every Evening.

To-morrow, the Comedy of **Roses and Thorns.**
The principal Characters by
Mr. Mathews, Mr. Liston, Mr. Cooper, Mr. W. Bennett. Miss E. Tree, Mrs. Orger. After which,
The School for Gallantry.
The Characters by—Mr. Jones. Miss E. Tree and Miss Love, *with Songs.*
And KILLING NO MURDER. Mr. Apollo Belvi, Mr. Liston, Buskin, Mr. Mathews.
On Monday, **Macbeth.** Macbeth, Mr. Macready, Macduff, Mr. Wallack.
With The DUMB SAVOYARD and his MONKEY. And other Entertainments.
On Tuesday, **The Poor Gentleman.** With the DUMB SAVOYARD.
And other Entertainments.
On Wednesday, A favourite OPERA.

VIVAT REX. J. Tabby, Printer, Theatre Royal Drury Lane

27

From the Gods

John William Cole, who wrote *The Life and Theatrical Times of Charles Kean, F.S.A.* (1859), from which this extract is taken, was previously an actor under the name of Calcraft and, for a quarter of a century, a Dublin theatre manager. Later, he became Kean's secretary: his book is scarcely remarkable for its objectivity. He died in 1870.

Among those named here are Tyrone Power (1795–1841), Irish actor, drowned in the sinking of the SS *President* while on a return voyage from America; James Sheridan Knowles (1784–1862), Irish actor and dramatist who wrote, for example, *Virginius* and *The Hunchback*, and who became late in life a Baptist preacher; Thomas Cobham (1779–1842), melodramatic actor described as 'the Kemble of the minor theatres'. 'The Victoria, formerly the Coburg', is the Old Vic; from 1963 to 1975 it was the home of the National Theatre Company.

On the 20th of April, 1828, Charles Kean presented himself to his warm-hearted countrymen, in Dublin, as Young Norval, and met with the cordial reception which might have been anticipated. His father had ever been one of their especial favourites; and they remembered, with gratitude, how in 1822 he had given the proceeds of his benefit to relieve their starving peasantry. The humour of the Dublin gallery has long been proverbial; but latterly it has received heavy checks from the 'exodus' and the temperance movement. To fun succeeded propriety, the police, politics, and poverty—poverty of wit engendered by vacuity of purse. Nothing checks the play of imagination more effectually than empty pockets. In 1827 there was yet fun enough left among the merry Olympians of the Irish capital, to astonish and amuse a stranger. No sooner had the play terminated, on Charles Kean's opening night, than he was unanimously demanded; and having, under similar circumstances in London, merely made a silent bow and retired, he naturally thought the same pantomimic acknowledgement would pass muster elsewhere. Most unexpectedly, he was greeted by a general demand for 'a speech'. Completely taken by surprise, he hummed and hawed for a moment or two; then endeavoured to look grateful, placed his hand on his breast, and stammered out a few incoherent sentences, nearly as intelligible as the following: 'Ladies and Gentlemen, I am deeply sensible of your being quite unprepared—no, I don't mean that—I mean, of my being quite unprepared—overwhelming kindness—incapable of thanks —totally unmerited—never to be effaced—when time shall be no more.' Here a friendly auditor cried out, 'That will do, Charley; go home to your mother'; which produced a universal burst of approbation, during which he bowed himself off. As he disappeared at the wing, and the applause was dying away, a stentorian shout arose of 'Three cheers for Charles Kean's speech!' which was taken up with overpowering effect.

A volume might be filled with characteristic anecdotes of the Dublin gallery. On an occasion when the gods were overcrowded on a benefit night, a loud clamour rose for relief, or more accommodation. After becoming diplomatic delay, the tardy manager appeared, and addressed them with the usual formula, 'What is your pleasure?' 'None at all!' roared out a dozen or more; 'but a d——d sight of pain, for we're all smothering here.'

A new piece by Power had not made a very successful impression; however, as usual, he was vociferously called for at the close and announced it for repetition with the customary plaudits. As he was retiring, an anxious admirer in the gallery called out, in a confidential tone, 'Tyrone, a word in private—don't take that for your benefit!'

There was an old actor at the Dublin Theatre, still living in 1825, named Michael Fullam, who died on the stage during the following year. He had outlived his powers, and was on very familiar terms with the galleries who, knowing the tetchiness of his temper, perpetually tried to excite him by shouting 'Speak up!' a favourite practice of theirs from time imemorial, and a natural one enough when people have paid their money to hear, and the actors are mysterious. 'Arrah, then, Mick Fullam, the divil a word can we hear! Speak up, old boy!' The first time he would reply, sharply, but without halting in the scene, 'I can't.' If the call was repeated a second time, 'I won't,' angrily. If a third time, 'Be quiet, fools!' in a burst of indignant reproof. Then ensued a roar of laughter in which the whole house joined; and, by-and-by, a *da capo* of the same composition.

On the first night of a new play by Sheridan Knowles, not many seasons ago, a heavy explanatory scene was 'dragging its slow length along' between two still heavier actors, who had no effects to produce, and were unable to elicit them if they had. The audience were evidently tired, though patient from respect to the name of the author, and now and then relieved themselves by an expressive yawn. There happened to be a momentary pause, when a voice from one of the gallery benches called out, in parliamentary cadence, 'I move that this debate be adjourned to this day six months.' This sally woke up the house and prepared them to enjoy the more telling scenes which were about to follow.

A troublesome customer in a thin pit once adopted a strange mode of vindicating independent opinion. He amused himself and disturbed the rest of the audience by lying nearly at full length and hissing and applauding every speech from every actor at the same time. After a desperate struggle he was removed to the police office, and when interrogated by the local authorities as to why he had thus interrupted the performance, he said 'he didn't know, he meant no offence; but he had always understood that anyone who paid his money in a theatre had a right to hiss or applaud according as he pleased; and he thought the fairest way of exercising his privilege was to keep on doing both together.'

It is amazing what the public will sometimes endure, without anger, from favourite performers, when they are either taken by surprise, or the good-humoured vein predominates. George Frederick Cooke told the people of Liverpool to their teeth that they were a disgrace to humanity, and that every stone in their city was cemented by human blood—a figurative mode of conveying that their commercial prosperity sprang from encouraging the slave trade. They saw that he laboured under his 'old complaint', and forgave the actor while they pitied the man. At Washington, in America, when the President had come expressly to see him in *Richard III*, he flatly refused to commence his character, or act before the 'King of the Yankee Doodles', as he called him, until the band had played 'God save the King', in addition to their own national air. And in this extravagance the stiff republicans actually indulged him.

During Elliston's management of the Surrey Theatre, a very poor play was one night unequivocally condemned. He rushed from his dressing-room on the stage, under a tempest of disapprobation, and when silence was with difficulty restored, exclaimed with a face of bewildered astonishment, 'I thought I heard a hiss—unusual sound! Ladies and gentlemen, you are under a very lamentable mistake here. I can assure you (and I think you will allow my opinion is worth something) this is a most excellent piece, and so you will find out when you exercise your unbiassed judgment and have seen it three or four times. A British audience invariably gives fair play. With your kind permission, therefore, I shall announce the new drama for every evening, until further notice.' This address was received without a dissentient voice, and procured for the doomed play a long and successful run.

But the climax of public endurance occurred with Edmund Kean at the Victoria, formerly the Cobourg, on the Surrey side of the water. He had been tempted into the engagement by the large terms of £50 per night. He opened in *Richard III* to an enormous house; and all passed off with great effect. On the second night he appeared as Othello, on which occasion Iago was personated by Cobham, a prodigious Victoria favourite. The house was crowded as before, but noisy and inattentive. There were nearly twelve hundred persons in a gallery measured for about half the number. The best speeches in the most striking scenes were marred by such unclassical expletives and interruptions as a Cobourg audience was given to dispense with more freedom than politeness—by the incessant popping of ginger-beer bottles, and by yells of 'Bravo, Cobham!' whenever Kean elicited his most brilliant points. The great tragedian felt disconcerted, and by the time the curtain fell he overflowed with indignation, a little heightened by copious libations of brandy and water. He was then loudly called for, and after a considerable delay came forward, enveloped in his cloak, his face still smirched, not more than half cleansed from the dingy complexion of the Moor, and his eyes emitting flashes as bright and deadly as forked lightning. He planted himself in the centre of the stage, near the footlights, and demanded, with laconic abruptness, 'What do you want?' There was a moment's interval of surprise when 'You! you!' was reiterated from many voices. 'Well then, I am here.' Another short pause, and he proceeded: 'I have acted in every theatre in the United Kingdom of Great Britain and Ireland, I have acted in all the principal theatres throughout the United States of America, but in my life I never acted to such a set of ignorant, unmitigated brutes as I now see before me.' So saying, he folded his mantle majestically, made a slight, contemptuous obeisance, and stalked off with the dignity of an offended lion. The actors, carpenters, and property men who listened to this harangue, stood aghast, evidently expecting that the house would be torn down. An awful silence ensued for a moment or two, when suddenly a thought of deadly retaliation suggested itself, and pent-up vengeance burst out in one simultaneous shout of 'Cobham! Cobham!' Cobham, who was evidently in waiting at the wing, rushed forth at once, bowed reverentially, placed his hand on his heart again and again, and pantomimed emotion and gratitude after the prescribed rules. When the thunders of applause subsided, he delivered himself as follows: 'Ladies and gentlemen, this is unquestionably the proudest moment of my life. I cannot give utterance to my feelings; but to the latest hour of my existence I shall cherish the remembrance of the honour conferred upon me by one of the most distinguished, liberal, and enlightened audiences I ever had the pleasure of addressing.'

John William Cole

28

Bad House

Here is William Charles Macready, seen through a group of entries in his journal. He is writing while on tour in Lincolnshire, and at Sheffield and Nottingham, in the winter of 1834. William Robertson, who ran the Lincoln circuit, was father of a large family of which T. W. (Tom) Robertson, the dramatist (1829–71) was the eldest (of twenty-two) and Margaret Shafto Robertson (Dame Madge Kendal, 1848–1935) the youngest. The play on 10 and 12 December was *William Tell* (1825) by Sheridan Knowles, and on 11 December, Byron's *Werner* (first acted 1830, Drury Lane).

Louth, November 27 1834. Arrived at Louth, which seems a miserable little place. After dinner (too good a one!) lounged away some time over old magazines—accounts of young Betty's first appearance—much violent abuse of Napoleon as the 'Corsican assassin', and of Josephine as the most notorious strumpet. Things have mended, judging both from the prose and poetry, which is horrid stuff.

Louth, November 29. Walked with Mr Robertson to the post office and to the theatre, which answers also the double purpose of a Sessions House; it is not the worst I have seen. Went to the theatre—dressed in magistrates' room—'quite convenient'. When ready to go on the stage, Mr Robertson appeared with a face full of dismay; he began to apologise, and I guessed the remainder. 'Bad house?' 'Bad? Sir, there's no one!' 'What? nobody at all?' 'Not a soul, sir—except the Warden's party in the boxes.' 'What the d——l! not one person in the pit or gallery?' 'Oh yes, there are one or two.' 'Are there five?' 'Oh yes, five.' 'Then go on; we have no right to give ourselves airs, if the public do not choose to come and see us; go on at once!' Mr Robertson was astonished at what he thought my philosophy, being accustomed, as he said, to be 'blown up' by his *Stars*, when the houses were bad. I never acted Virginius better in all my life—good taste and earnestness. Smyth, who was contemporary with me at Rugby and has a living in this neighbourhood, came in and sat with me, and saw the play with which he was greatly pleased.

November 30. Read the newspaper in which my abhorrence of that wretch Cobbett and his beastly faction was kindled anew. Note came from Mrs Robertson, inviting me to tea, which I accepted. Went there, and was much amused by Mr W. Robertson's account of the extremities of ludicrous distress—though sometimes it was no laughing matter—to which he was reduced in his vagabondizing tours of Scotland and Cumberland.

December 1. Walked out with Mr Robertson; posted my letters, and then walked two miles on the Horncastle road. He related to me two anecdotes of Kean, to which he was witness; once of his having, on coming off the stage in Othello, thrashed a man of the name of Williams, whom I remember well, for distressing him by being imperfect in Iago! and another—a pure specimen of his charlatanry. A vagabond who lived upon petitioning companies and drank their charity, applied for the third or fourth time while Kean was with Mr Robertson. Mr Robertson represented to Kean that he was a worthless, drunken man, and lived upon this practice. Mr K—— (there were several present) said: 'You dined very well yesterday, sir, and you will have a good dinner today; why should you wish to prevent this poor man from doing the same?' And this Kean left his wife without one shilling for herself and son; the woman that lived with him having taken the comparatively small residue left of his disgusting and reckless dissoluteness!! Enjoyed my walk very much; wrote directions for my luggage. Dozed from fatigue after dinner, wrote a letter to Kenneth, made my toilet, and went to theatre. Felt that the house was not very good; but determined to make a study of the night, which I did, and certainly acted great part of Hamlet in a very true and impressive manner. I hit upon the exact feeling in the passage which I have often thought on: 'He was a man', etc.; my intercourse with Horatio, Rosencrantz, Guildenstern, etc. was earnest and real—*ad homines*. Indeed, it was a good performance. Smyth came into my room after the play and talked of my speaking the closet scene at Rugby. He also told me of endeavouring to commit a poacher. He is a clergyman! . . .

Sheffield, December 10. Went to the theatre, where I acted William Tell only tolerably; was a good deal distressed by the actors, imperfect and innattentive, and once or twice rather angry with them, but very kind to the poor child who acted with me, though several times disconcerted by her, but this is from having children of my own, the dear ones. My dresser is a Benedictine monk on leave from the convent in Ireland on account of derangement; his trade is a tailor.

December 11. Went to theatre, where I acted very ill, but should not have been so bad but for the shamefully neglectful and imperfect state of the play. Idenstein, Josephine, and Guba were all more or less imperfect; Ulric did not know two consecutive lines of the last three acts. I sat down at last attempting nothing. I never was so completely *terrassé* in my life. But I was rude and uncivil to no one.

Nottingham, December 12. Went to theatre, and found a horrid fellow in the part of Gessler, whom I had met at Richmond—it was enough! Rehearsed, dressed, and acted William Tell to a very good house in a creditable manner, but was very cross with the little dull boy whom they had placed in Albert, and fined myself half-a-crown, which I paid him for my ill-behaviour.

William Charles Macready

29

Manager

Alfred Bunn (1798–1860), English theatrical manager, was a floridly genial personage and unabashed showman; he would present anything from Shakespeare to performing animals, and did. He managed both Drury Lane and Covent Garden—at one point, and unsuccessfully, together ('the Grand Junction'); and he tried to humiliate Macready, with whom he was at deadly war, by presenting him in a truncated version of *Richard III*—the first three acts only—as a secondary piece. Whereupon, on an evening in April 1836, Macready, having come from the stage, entered Bunn's Drury Lane office and knocked him down.

Known as 'Poet' Bunn, he wrote various libretti, including *The Bohemian Girl* ('I dreamt that I dwelt in marble halls'). His racily malicious memoir, *The Stage: Both Before and Behind the Curtain*, from which we quote, appeared in 1840. His wife was the actress Margaret Somerville (1799–1873). He figures in Thackeray's *Pendennis* as 'the famous London impresario, Dolphin': 'a tall and portly gentleman with a hooked nose and a profusion of curling brown hair and whiskers; his coat was covered with the richest frogs, braidings, and velvets. He had under-waistcoats, many splendid rings, jewelled pins, and neck-chains.'

Macready, who usually referred to him as 'scoundrel', 'this reptile', or words to that effect, would not have agreed with an obituary notice after Bunn's death of apoplexy at Boulogne. This said: 'He was universally admitted by all who knew him to be a kind, staunch friend, an inexpressibly amusing acquaintance . . . and an intelligent, active, and enterprising public man.'

In these extracts there are references to:

Personages

Stephen Price (1783–1840), American theatre manager who controlled the Park, New York, and who, for a time (1826–30), leased Drury Lane in London; he often engaged English actors for New York. John Cooper, actor (1790–1870), 'about as much like a real first-rate actor,' said Oxberry, 'as a fine statue is to a living being'; J. Powell, actor (d1836, aged 82); Robert William Elliston (1774–1831), actor and theatrical manager; John Liston (1776–1846), idiosyncratic comedian, much admired by Charles Lamb; John Braham (1774–1846), vocalist and actor, 'a beast of an actor,' said Walter Scott, 'though an angel of a singer'; Thomas Morton (*c*1764–1838), dramatist, in whose *Speed the Plough* (1796) occurs the reference to an unseen 'Mrs Grundy'.

Plays

Simpson and Company, comedy (1823) by J. Poole; *The Duenna*, comic opera (1775) by R. B. Sheridan; *My Neighbour's Wife*, farce from the French (1833) by Alfred Bunn; *Turning the Tables*, farce (1830) by Poole.

In his capacity of proprietor of the Park Theatre, New York, he [Mr Price] has lured away to the shores of America every performer of any distinction (and what is of equal importance—utility) whom gold could tempt or speculation seduce. He is perfectly right in so doing, and any man far less gifted than he is would have done the same; but that does not alter the fact.

None but those who have experienced it can tell the inconvenience theatres of this magnitude [Drury Lane; Covent Garden] suffer by the abduction of performers apparently of an inferior grade, who have enacted a given line of business for a series of years, and have thereby become the very movers of the machine. Accustomed to play nightly in every piece, and playing many parts in most of them, they are the chief reliance of a theatre in any of the numerous dilemmas in which circumstances involve it. In the same ratio they must be of the utmost importance to the transatlantic stage, and are worth any reasonable sum that can be given for them. It may appear ridiculous, on the first mention of it, but the secession of such utilitarians as John Cooper, or the late octogenarian Powell, caused incalculable trouble for the time to the theatre in which they were engaged. From being habituated all their lives to the performance of the entire range of the drama, and being equally good, or bad as it may be, in one part as another, they might be applied to in all times of difficulty; and from having a quick study in learning, and laying claim to the almost greater advantage of not forgetting, they might at all times be depended upon. Powell's faculty of retention in particular characters was so great, that all the blunders of those with whom he happened to perform, could never cause him to make a blunder himself. Whether he received a right cue from the speaker to whom he had to reply, or not, was to him a matter of perfect indifference—he would give the answer set down in the text, without deviating to the right, or to the left.

A curious instance of this occurred some years ago, at the termination of the tragedy of *Richard III.* Mr Elliston was enacting the part of Richmond; and having during the evening disobeyed the injunction which the King of Denmark lays down to his Queen, 'Gertrude, do not drink', he accosted Mr Powell, who was personating Lord Stanley (for the safety of whose son Richmond is naturally anxious) thus, on his entry after the issue of the battle:

Elliston (*as Richmond*) Your son, George Stanley, is he dead?
Powell (*as Lord Stanley*) He is, my Lord, and *safe in Leicester town*!
Elliston (*as Richmond*) I mean—ah!—is he missing?
Powell (*as Lord Stanley*) He is, my Lord, and *safe in Leicester town*!

And it is but justice to the memory of this punctilious veteran to say that he would have made the same reply to any question which could at that particular moment have been put to him.

This is carrying utility to a great extreme, no doubt, but it exemplifies how far the force of habit will go. Such men as these we cannot afford to lose; and when, in addition to many of that class, Mr Price has from time to time transported nearly all the leading performers of the day, the usual difficulties attendant upon management at home have become thereby materially increased . . .

His Majesty's Servants

Their Majesties [King William IV and Queen Adelaide] were graciously pleased to signify, through their Chamberlain, that Drury Lane theatre would be honoured with a state visit on the 24th April, and Covent Garden theatre with one on 1st of May [1834].

Have I not, reader, already told you that 'there is no tyrant like a player-king'? I will now prove it to you. The actual monarch of the British Empire condescendingly commanded the supposed monarch of the British drama to command 'His Majesty's servants', to play *The School for Scandal* and *Simpson and Co.* at the one house, and *The Duenna*, *My Neighbour's Wife*, and *Turning the Tables* at the other. With the view of representing the best modern comedy of which the stage is in possession, in the best possible manner, all the leading performers of the two theatres were cast in it, and, with one exception, they all played in it. That exception was Mr Macready, whom no argument nor request could prevail upon to appear in Joseph Surface, though he had so often performed the character before. A journal of the morning following the Royal visit, thus alludes to this subject:

> We cannot avoid mentioning a point which was the general subject of conversation last evening, *viz.* that Braham volunteered his gratuitous services, and that Macready declined to play Joseph Surface in *The School for Scandal* before his Sovereign. That is what we call 'sovereign contempt'. But the onus falls on the mimic, and not on the Monarch. What sad nonsense this is. With all the respect we can possibly have for the art and artist, it is a fact requiring no comment, that as they both depend on the breath of the King, his very breath should summon them into action. We do not absolutely think a tragedian should be required to dance on the tight-rope, or a singer to warble with a worsted stocking in his mouth; but beyond those peculiarities, we think they are bound to do anything in their power to contribute to the amusement of the King by whom they live, and move, and have their being.

Beyond these observations little need or indeed can be said.

In the other instance, the entertainments were announced precisely in the order commanded by His Majesty, by a letter from the Vice-Chamberlain now in my possession; and, without direction from the Court, I dared not alter the arranged routine of the performances. With a thorough contempt, it would seem, for either the authority of the real monarch, or the duty of the assumed one, this letter was addressed to me:

> Monday, April 28, 1834.
>
> Dear Sir,
>
> I perceive by the advertisements that *Turning the Tables* is to be performed as the last piece on Thursday next; this I trust will not be persisted in, otherwise I must decline the honour of appearing before His Majesty so late in the evening.
>
> Yours, &c.
>
> J. LISTON
>
> To A. Bunn, Esq.

Now pray who is the King in all this business? Mr Liston had £20 for playing in *Turning the Tables*, commanded by His Majesty to be the last entertainment of the evening; and Mr Liston says 'if his Majesty (for his letter implies as much) persists in it, I decline the honour of appearing before him so late in the evening'. It is not 'too late in the evening' for the King of England to sit in his private box, but it *is* 'too late' for one of 'His Majesty's servants' to appear on the stage to amuse him! Surely this is carrying out the Wolseyan doctrine of '*Ego et rex meus*' a little too far. I say nothing about the unhappy wretch of a manager, and his £20—they are not worth bestowing a thought upon; but it *is* a question whether such monstrous consequence as this should be assumed, in opposition to the pleasure of a crowned head. It is almost needless to observe that, on stating as delicately as possible the subject to the Lord Chamberlain, the nonsensical alteration was made; but it is as well to let the reader into the secret of the whole business. The letter may convey the idea of its writer not being strong enough in health to be out so late at night, or that he was engaged at home, or elsewhere; but the actual meaning of it is, 'Don't you think that I'm coming on the stage at half-past eleven o'clock at night, when His Majesty, who has been so heartily laughing at the two preceding pieces, will not have a titter left for me.' Talk for a thousand years, and the latent meaning will be found to be this, and nothing else.

Bunn added a footnote: On the occasion of this visit, Mr Liston and myself were conversing in the ante-room of the Royal box, with a nobleman attached to the Household, when one of the pages, passing by and not seeing his lordship, slapped the comedian on the back, ejaculating, 'D'ye think you'll make him laugh to-night? He was devilish stupid at dinner.' I cannot now determine which created the greater roar, the face of Mr Liston, or that of the lacquey on perceiving the noble lord before whom he had so committed himself, respecting his illustrious master. If the reader never saw the face of a dignified performer, when reminded that he was nothing more *than* a performer, he has a treat to come.

Reader's Report

A slight summary of pieces sent to the management of a London theatre for examination, and in the hopes of approval, will give my present reader some rough idea of what a past reader of mine had to wade through. I refer to . . . poor Morton, who returned me, after a careful examination of their pretensions, a packet of manuscripts with his remarks attached. Thus:

Paired Off—The plan, characters, and dialogue of this piece are by no means objectionable, but I fear it is not up to the mark for the breadth necessary for a one-act piece. The part intended for Mrs Glover is tame, and what she *could* or *would* do nothing with.

Nicholas Pedrossa—Sad stuff—to be returned.

The Adventurers—Not worth adventuring—sure to be damned . . .

The Chimney-piece—Is a fair farce, and smartly written; the only danger in the piece is the far too frequent mention of Mrs Horn. A certain author says, 'Push the duke as far as he'll go'; Mrs Horn is pushed too far, and verifies Sheridan's words, 'When these fellows get hold of a good thing, they never know when they've had enough of it.' I have pencilled at the end a finishing speech which, if the author pleases, is at his service. [*Bunn's note:* This was by Rodwell, and was played with much success.]

The Way To Get Mad—May be returned to Mr Heaven-know-who, for I can't even make out the author's name, but his address is——

The Iron Shroud—Avoid it.

Panthea—Read the last page! [*Bunn's note:* I did so, and found that six people stabbed themselves in less than six minutes, and four of them were eunuchs.]

Edelbert—Respectably written—but of what use to Drury Lane would a respectable Saxon tragedy be? Certainly none.

Imbio or *The Requital*—Nonsense.

The Two Catherines—The perusal took me more time to understand than half-a-dozen better ones; and, after all, the riddle was not worth finding out. It cannot be used.

One Fool Makes Many—The author, I am sorry to say, is one of 'the many'.

The Dead Alice—Quite hopeless.

Murtoch M'Griffin and O'Dogharty in Spain—The merit this piece has consists in an intimate knowledge of the manners, localities, and habits of the Spaniards—warlike and domestic—but the essentials of passion and dramatic interest are not in sufficient force. I think the author overrates his Irish hero. He has called on me, telling me Power has reduced the piece from five to two acts 'at one fell swoop'; it might not be condemned, but could not be attractive.

Swamp Hall—This piece I have either read or seen, as all the circumstances are familiar to me. Won't do at all.

The Baby—Hasty and trivial—the inviting thing is the title, which I think a good one; but the business is commonplace.

Women As They Are—Are very bad.

It may readily be believed that where some hundreds of pieces of the quality herein described are submitted to the decision of the manager of a theatre, the task of deciding, to say nothing of reading, is quite harassing enough.

Alfred Bunn

30

Vagabonds

Old Drury Lane is a poor title for the rambling book Edward Stirling (1807–94) published in 1881. Its second title, *Fifty Years' Recollections of Actor, Author, and Manager*, is more reasonable. Stirling, who went on the stage at fourteen—his real name was Edward Lambert—was a vigorous theatre-man as strolling actor, highly professional hack dramatist of some 200 plays, and London manager, Drury Lane included. His wife was the celebrated Victorian actress, Mrs Stirling (Fanny Clifton, who had been born Mary Ann Hehl; in 1894, at the age of 81, she was married for a second time—to Sir Charles Gregory—but died a year later).

The ensuing passages are about Stirling in the provinces during the 1830s (dates do not worry him). Some of the references are to:

Personages

Frederick Yates (1795–1842), actor-manager, notably at the Adelphi Theatre; father of Edmund Yates, writer, editor, and dramatist. William Creswick (1813–88) became a distinguished London actor (he was with Phelps at Sadler's Wells) and managed the transpontine Surrey Theatre. Andrew Ducrow (1773–1842), equestrian and theatrical manager, became joint proprietor of Astley's Amphitheatre in London.

Plays

The Shipwreck of the Medusa; or, The Fatal Raft (1820) by W. T. Moncrieff. *Mazeppa*: probably *Mazeppa; or, The Wild Horse of Tartary* (1831) by H. M. Milner.

White Lion, Kidderminster—Mrs Waylett, Wright, Bedford, Lee, and myself played to good audiences in the assembly room. One night, after the performance, an alarm of fire awoke the Lion and its cubs, bringing all the terrified inmates out in their night-gear—men, women, and children. Paul Bedford rushed out with a water-bottle; Wright tumbled literally downstairs; Mrs Waylett fainted in Lee's arms; her old aunt tried to perform the same experiment in mine, but I ungallantly let her drop. The confusion and terror reached fever heat. What was it all about? Nothing. It proved to be after all a false alarm. The night porter had dropped asleep; one of the commercial gents, finding himself shut out, very naturally knocked and rang to obtain admission, and failing in this he tried crying 'Fire!' at the top of his voice, and so succeeded at last in rousing the porter and the house.

Warwick—Race Week. A seedy, neglected theatre, evidently seldom used. With our entertainments, it proved attractive. A silly fracas was caused by Mrs Waylett's name not being printed large enough in the bills. I was the culprit, and Lee, her champion, challenged me to fight a duel. By Wright's persuasion I accepted the challenge. Paul Bedford was Lee's second, and Wright mine. Pistols were borrowed, but not loaded. Paul asked Lee to make his will before he went to the ground—a marshy field in the outskirts of the town. We met at six o'clock in the morning. The ground having been measured and our places taken, Wright gave the signal to fire. Bang went the powder—down fell both our seconds as if mortally wounded. This caused a hearty laugh, a general shaking of hands, immediate return to Warwick, and a jolly breakfast at the combatants' expense.

Worcester—Manager Bennett. This versatile man did everything himself, assisted by an old party styled Mrs Gummage, never seen in summer or winter without pattens. Bennett commenced theatrical life with a puppet-show; saved upon that, started a theatre, acted all the best parts himself, in Worcester, Coventry, Shrewsbury, etc., and prospered. His travelling-boxes formed city and castle walls (painted stone); chairs became stools by removing their backs; helmets, canvas folded up, and a cork put in the crown for feathers to stick in. Every property corresponded in its double or treble utility. If by chance Bennett employed a scene-painter (a rare chance it was), he filled up the artist's leisure hours at his own dwelling. Tables were transmogrified into highly-coloured flower-beds; cupboards, cornices, etc., by the painter's skill became iron safes or jewelled caskets, and ceilings azure blue covered with roses. Illustrations from Shakespeare, history, and the *Pilgrim's Progress*, adorned the walls of every chamber. But his kitchen was the masterpiece of artful deception—sides of bacon, hams, hung beef dangled, garnishing the walls. One room, sacred to privacy, he named Temple of Venus. Two old ladies (the Misses James) presided over this pictorial abode, utilising their evenings by taking money at the theatre; Mrs Gummage attending to the lights (oil-lamps), and keeping an eye on noisy half-price boys. In the daytime she cooked and cleaned up at home. Old 'Gummy' was a special favourite with gallery customers. Bennett's band: a leader, violin, French horn, drum, all the rest young shopmen leaving early to play. This naturally produced discord; they never played at follow my leader. Bennett dressed splendidly by day, workman-like by night, always avoiding the principal streets on his way to the theatre. He died a churchwarden, respected and rich.

Romford, Essex—Applied to a local magistrate for permission to perform a few nights in the Town Hall during a London vacation. The ruling Dogberry met my humble request in this fashion:

'What, sir! bring your beggarly actors into this town to demoralise the people? No, sir; I'll have no such profligacy in Romford; poor people shall not be wheedled out of their money by your tomfooleries. The first player that comes here I'll clap him in the stocks as a rogue and vagabond. Good-morning, sir,' motioning his servant to show me out.

Liverpool Amphitheatre (*late 1830s*)—Playing a popular drama entitled *El Hyder, Chief of the Gaunt Mountains*, a famous old Cobourg favourite, written by W. Barrymore; my role a British tar, one of the old school, who had only to look at a Frenchman on the stage to frighten him into fits. Turks collapsed at the very sound of his 'Shiver my timbers!' 'Britons never will be slaves!' or 'Come on, you lubbers!' Tom encounters a party of the enemy in a rocky defile; nothing daunted, at them he goes; a desperate combat of eight—seven to one; awful struggle; yet, strange to relate, no one appeared killed or wounded. During the mêlée, a real sailor, half-seas over, slid down the gallery and box pillars, jumped into the circus, climbing over double-basses, fiddlers, French horns, and reached the scene of action on the stage, placing himself by my side. Throwing down his jacket, he called out, 'Messmate, I'll stand by you; seven to one ain't fair noways. Pour a broadside into the blackamoor lubbers. Hurrah!' He knocked two down, the others wisely taking to their heels. Cheered by the house, Jack Tar No 1 left the boards, with Jack Tar No 2 glad to get rid of him.

Exeter—Huntley May, an Hibernian of the first water—a Tipperary boy. This man was the incarnation of deception; part of his daily occupation was to issue bills of large dimensions, with most attractive pieces never to be performed. At last the people became restive, demanding their money back. One night they threatened to pull up the benches; May, quite equal to the emergency, rushed on the stage in his shirt-sleeves:

'What's up now, boys?'

'Money, money, swindle!'

'Hark at 'em now! Murder and Moses, there's broth of boys for ye!—money's just what I want myself!' (*Mournfully*) 'Think of your cathedral ground: who lies in it? My sainted wife, Norah; poor sould! She loved Exeter so that she would come here to be buried among ye. We all love ye, myself, and little Pat. Aisy now, I'll give you a trate! Tomorrow night's my benefit—make me a thumping house; Norah won't forget you in heaven. Behave like gentlemen—come early tomorrow night, good-luck to ye!' Exit manager; re-enters, carrying a towel. 'Boys, don't cry after poor Norah; enjoy yourselves; leave all the crying to myself—Och a hone a ree!'

Swansea—An old actor in our company, Jock Wilson, whose memory was much impaired, had a small part in a new melodrama allotted to him. The few lines he had to speak ought to have been spoken at the opening of the third act. He is discovered tied to a barrel, floating on the sea; his words run thus:

> 'For fifteen hours I have been floating on this dreadful sea, tossed to and fro.'
>
> Poor old man, his memory failed him (as it will fail us all sooner or later); music, thunder and lightning, calm.
>
> Victim on the Barrel: 'For fifteen years I've been tied to this tub, tossed up and down by the relentless waves.'
>
> A Voice from Gallery: 'Stop, stop, Mr Wilson, look you; tap the tub, and let's have a drink.'

This decided the career of our unfortunate drama, *The Shipwreck of the Medusa*. Poor Wilson had repeated the speech of Reginald, an ancient prisoner in Earl Osmond's dungeons in 'Monk' Lewis's *Castle Spectre*, a popular drama once in town and country.

Gloucester, 1835—We were acting in Cheltenham and tried a night with the Adelphi company in this fine old city. Much to our manager's chagrin, it failed; this annoyed him, but still more so at not being acknowledged when he came on the stage. Advancing towards the footlights, he addressed his auditors as follows: 'Ladies and gentlemen, I am Frederick Yates. Possibly I may be unknown to you; in town, at my own theatre, they do recognise me; applause always accompanies my acting, in fact it would be dull and vapid without; it is like salt to meat to an actor. The house tonight is badly supported. I am a loser. Let me ask you to applaud, and I will act, thus accommodating each other.' They clapped their hands at everyone and everything after this appeal.

Hull—Yates and his company. The venture proved a decided failure. Driven to his wit's end, he sent for me to come to London to give him a helping hand in his trouble. My first idea was to hit upon a piece that had been popular in the town. All spoke of *Mazeppa*. They, the townsfolk, had seen it produced by Ducrow with great splendour and real horses. 'You shall see it without,' said I. A wild horse of the Ukraine, made of pasteboard to gallop over rocks, deep ravines, and roaring torrents, with poor Creswick (Mazeppa in effigy, pasteboard again). A cab horse—hired nightly—dashed on the stage from the wings with the real Creswick tied to him. This cunning device completely bewildered crowded audiences. They came in shoals, neglecting really good acting and legitimate plays for paste board.

Edward Stirling

31

Massacre

John Forster (1812–76), at the time of this notice, was drama critic of *The Examiner* in London. Edwin Forrest (1806–72) was a hurricane of an actor, physically superb, intellectually less so, a raging patriot who saw no reason why a leading American actor should not stir the London stage as he had stirred his own theatres. He came over in 1836, under Bunn's management at Drury Lane; and again in 1845–6, now at the Princess's and on a long series of provincial engagements. His first visit was much more comfortable than the second, but John Forster, a firm dogmatist, was steadily unmoved by Forrest's work in such classical parts as Othello, Lear, Macbeth, and Richard III. Because he was a close and rash friend of Macready (who, though worried enough about Forrest in his journal, had asked Forster in 1836 to 'deal liberally and gently'), Forrest suspected Macready's influence. When the English tragedian visited America in 1843 he faced much prejudice. Nearly three years later, in Edinburgh (March 1846) there was an explosion when Forrest—who had come to the city during a free week—hissed Macready's Hamlet in an extravagant handkerchief-waving passage before the Play scene; it had been called the *pas de mouchoir*. Macready was bitterly hurt. When during 1848–9 he acted in America again, partisanship was intense; he did his best to sustain his dignity in the most trying circumstances. All ended with the frightening anti-British riot in and round the Astor Place Opera House, New York, on 10 May 1849; in firing by soldiers outside the theatre thirty-one people in the mob were killed. Macready spent some hours in a friend's house, got away early next morning in a covered carriage, and eventually sailed from Boston on 23 May.

Here, from twelve years before, is Forster's review of Forrest's Richard III (*The Examiner*, 25 March 1837). William Archer, considering it more than half a century later, judged it to be absolutely sincere; but he noted, as thoroughly tasteless, the offhand contempt of paragraphs on Forrest's acting that appeared in *The Examiner* during 1845. (Forster, ill about the time, may not have written them.)

James William Wallack (1791–1864), who is mentioned, was a most capable actor who divided his work between England and the United States; he had played Richmond to the Richard of Edmund Kean.

Mr Forrest's Richard the Third forms no exception to those murderous attacks upon Shakespeare which this gentleman has so ruthlessly made since his arrival among us. Since the time of that elder Forrest, who had such a hand in the murder of the princes of the Tower, we may not inappropriately take this last execution of Richard at Drury Lane to be

> The most arch deed of piteous massacre
> That ever yet this land was guilty of.

We have tried very hard, since witnessing the performance, to discover the principle or intention of it; but to no effect. We remember some expressions, however, in an old comedy of Greene's, which may possibly suggest something to the purpose. 'How,' says Bubble, on finding himself dressed out very flauntingly indeed, 'how apparel makes a man respected! The very children in the street do adore me!' In almost every scene Mr Forrest blazed forth a new and most oppressively gilded dress, for which he received precisely the kind of adoration that the simple Bubble adverts to. Richard the Third may have been a great dandy, we dare say; but it is giving too literal a meaning to the expressions of his wit and humour, to seek to drive the audience into a belief of his actually entertaining a score or two of tailors to study fashions to adorn his body. Yet, after all, this is to be forgiven where no other resources present themselves; provided only it 'shakes the pit and makes the boxes stare'. When we cannot have strokes of passion or niceties of character, we may be dazzled by layers of tinsel gilt.

Colley Cibber's 'acting version' of Shakespeare's tragedy of *Richard the Third* is one of the severest reproaches that could possibly be passed upon the profession of the stage, considered as an intellectual art. Great actors, however, have been able, by the variety and brilliancy of their resources, in some sort to neutralise the reproach. The performance of the late Mr Kean was an eminent instance of this. The thorough decision and self-possession which he threw into it was not to be surpassed. The apparent intellectual vigour surmounted the moral depravity and blunted the edge even of Cibber's vulgar scenes.

When will the deep and eloquent thoughtfulness, the silent and piercing looks, the matchless grace and persuasiveness of manner and tone, which distinguished that fine actor in this part, be forgotten by those who witnessed them? These characteristics, far beyond the resistless fire and rapidity of his style in the later scenes, stamped Mr Kean's reputation in Richard the Third. But these, or even a remote glimpse of them, are not accessible to an imitator.

We say this because it was clear to us that Mr Forrest was only thinking, all the while he played in the tragedy, of Mr Kean and Mr James Wallack, and of his own tremendous power of lungs. Now it was curious to see how ineffective those resources were, and chiefly the last. The noise of artillery could scarcely be more ear-stunning than his voice; but it was voice and nothing else. A more striking example could scarcely be given of the incapacity of an actor. Such, on the other hand, was Mr Kean's exquisite art, that a manifest defect of voice in these scenes was converted, in his case, into the means of giving stronger and more piercing expression to them. The surgy sound that tore upwards from his throat when he animated his soldiers to the charge, or vented his own despair, brought us at once upon the scene. We felt ourselves under the open air of Bosworth Field.

It should be said that Mr Forrest in some sort reconciles us to the worst of his imitations when he ventures on an 'original' point. When the confident and sarcastic Richard, as his eye falls on the bloodstained blade which he has just withdrawn from Henry's death-wound, sports with his crime and makes it the toy of his fancy—

> See how my sword weeps for the poor king's death!
> O, may such purple tears be always shed
> From those that wish the downfall of our house—

Mr Forrest gave a vulgar and absurd expression to the lines by shaking his sword violently while he uttered them, as if it were necessary so to assure the audience that blood continued to 'drip, drip, drip' (as Mr Coleridge says in one of his tragedies) from off the blade.

Shakespeare in this passage adverted to the blood upon Glo'ster's sword, simply that he might resort to the play of fancy that rose out of it; the actor insisted on the blood alone, and threw a heap of rubbish over the fancy. It is always thus with the poet, and his merciless translator into prose. A matter of fact is insisted on, in the one case, for the beauty and grandeur that accompanies it; in the other, it is insisted upon because it is a matter of fact, while the beauty or grandeur is thrust out of sight. We could illustrate this by a dozen other passages from this very performance.

Mr Forrest's ideas of heroism, and of the passion of courage or despair, appear to have been gathered among the wilds of his native country. This we have had occasion to remark before. Through the fourth and fifth acts of the tragedy he carried these notions to their extreme; and truly, if hideous looks and furious gestures, ear-splitting shouts and stage-devouring strides, could be supposed to embody a princely dignity, a courageous gallantry, or a terrible despair, why then Mr Forrest was Richard indeed. One of the most wretched and melodramatic tricks of the profession closed the performance. While Richard fought with Richmond he had provided himself with long and heavy strips of black hair, which were fixed in such a way that they came tumbling over his forehead, eyes, and face, with every barbarous turn and gesture. The princely Plantagenet—he

> who was born so high
> His aery buildeth in the cedar's top,
> And dallies with the wind and scorns the sun—

was thus accomplished by Mr Forrest in all the points of a savage newly caught from out of the American backwoods.

John Forster

THEATRE, SHEFFIELD.

FOURTH APPEARANCE OF

MR. G. V.

BROOKE,

ENGAGED

FOR TEN NIGHTS ONLY,

WHOSE PROVINCIAL CELEBRITY RANKS HIM AMONGST THE BEST TRAGEDIANS OF THE DAY.

Fourth, and Last Appearance but One,

OF THAT CELEBRATED AND FAVOURITE ACTOR,

MR. RAYNER,

(Of the Theatres Royal Covent Garden and Drury Lane.)

This present Thursday, Feb. 2, 1837,

Will be performed Shakspeare's Tragedy of

OTHELLO:

The Moor of Venice.

Othello, - - - - - - - - - - - - - - - - Mr. G. V. BROOKE.

Iago	Mr HAMILTON	Roderigo	Mr ATTWOOD
Cassio	Mr GLOVER	Montano	Mr STOKER
Duke of Venice	Mr G. COOKE	Giovanni	Mr CHICHELEY
Brabantio	Mr A. YOUNGE	Julio	Mr RIVERS
Gratiano	Mr THOMPSON		
Lodovico	Mr MUIR	Desdemona	Miss JULIA NICOL
Paulo	Mr SEARLE	Emelia	Mrs WATKINS

AT THE END OF THE PLAY,

MASTER RIVERS,

ONLY FIVE YEARS OF AGE!

WHO, IN HIS REPRESENTATION OF THE

INFANT HERCULES!

Excited such universal astonishment and admiration, will again repeat the

COMIC MEDLEY DANCE!

From Tom and Jerry, which was received with continued shouts of Laughter and Applause

To conclude with a Domestic Drama, of powerful interest, written expressly for the peculiar talent of Mr. RAYNER, entitled

LOVE'S FRAILTIES:

Or, Passion and Repentence.

Lubin, - - - - - - - - - - - - Mr. RAYNER.

As originally acted by him upwards of 200 nights in London.

Squire Belgrade (in love with Susan) .... Mr STOKER | Exquisite (his Valet) .... Mr SKERRETT

Old Greenwell .... Mr THOMPSON

Michael .... | Irish Labourers. | Mr G. COOKE

Patrick .... | | Mr CHICHELEY

Ralph .... Mr SEARLE | James .... Mr MUIR

Susan Greenwell .... Miss JULIA NICOL | Jenny (in love with Lubin) .... Miss MERCER

Betty .... Mrs H. HALL

TO-MORROW, (FRIDAY)

TOWN AND COUNTRY

Reuben Glenroy - - - - - - Mr. G. V. BROOKE.

Hawbuck - - - - Mr. RAYNER.

THE MERRY MOURNERS.

Joey - - - - - - - - - - - - Mr. RAYNER.

AND

ELLA ROSENBERG.

Rosenberg, - - - - - - - - - - Mr. G. V. BROOKE.

Storm, - - - - - Mr. RAYNER.

For the BENEFIT OF MR. RAYNER,

And positively the Last Night of his Appearance.

SERJEANT TALFOURD'S NEW AND POPULAR TRAGEDY OF "ION" IS IN PREPARATION.

NOTICE.—Mr. W. J. Hammond requests Tradesmen and others to observe, that he will not be accountable for articles of any description obtained, without his signature, or that of Mr. W. R. Copeland, being attached to a Written Order.

Acting Manager, Mr. W. R. COPELAND.

Boxes 4s., Pit 2s., Gal. 1s.—Second Price—Boxes 2s., Pit 1s., Gal. 6d.

The Second Price will be taken at the termination of an Act, which will be so arranged as never to exceed Nine o'clock, but more generally at a Quarter before that Hour.

The Doors will be opened at Six o'clock, and the Performance to commence at Seven precisely.

Tickets and Places for the BOXES may be had of Mr. CARMAN, at the Box Office, from Eleven till Two o'Clock each Day

N.B.—A Female Attendant will be placed to take charge of Ladies' Cloaks, Bonnets, &c.

PRINTED BY WHITAKER & Co., IRIS OFFICE, 18, FARGATE, SHEFFIELD

32

The True Lear

Jettisoning Tate at last, William Charles Macready restored *King Lear* to the stage at Covent Garden on 25 January 1838. He had been strongly concerned about it; and indeed, at a first rehearsal, he had feared that the inclusion of the Fool might be a failure. Then, next day, as he noted in his journal on 5 January, when he described the 'sort of fragile, hectic, beautiful-faced, half-idiot-looking boy that it should be, and stated my belief that it never could be acted', the experienced George Bartley observed that a woman should play it. 'I caught at the idea, and instantly exclaimed: "Miss P. Horton is the very person." I was delighted at the thought.'

After the performance on 25 January—when Helen Faucit was Cordelia and Bartley the Kent—Macready wrote: 'I scarcely know how I acted the part. I did not satisfy myself . . . Was occasionally pretty good, but I was not what I wished to have been.' Still, the result was a triumph. Charles Dickens, who was deeply attached to Macready and who was then 25, wrote in *The Examiner* of 4 February the review that follows. At the time Priscilla Horton, the Fool, was an impish girl of 19; in later life she became Mrs German Reed of the 'Entertainment' that was a part of London life for four decades. She retired from it in 1879 and died in March 1895.

What we ventured to anticipate when Mr Macready assumed the management of Covent Garden Theatre, has been every way realised. But the last of his well-directed efforts to vindicate the higher objects and uses of the drama has proved the most brilliant and the most successful. He has restored to the stage Shakespeare's true *Lear*, banished from it, by impudent ignorance, for upwards of a hundred and fifty years.

A person of the name of Boteler has the infamous repute of having recommended to a notorious poet-laureate, Mr Nahum Tate, the 'new modelling' of *Lear*. 'I found the whole', quoth Mr Tate, addressing the aforesaid Boteler in his dedication, 'to answer your account of it; a heap of jewels unstrung and unpolished, yet so dazzling in their disorder that I soon perceived I had seized a treasure'. And accordingly to work set Nahum very busily indeed: strung the jewels and polished them with a vengeance; omitted the grandest things, the Fool among them; polished all that remained into commonplace; interlarded love-scenes; sent Cordelia into a comfortable cave with her lover, to dry her clothes and get warm, while her distracted and homeless old father was still left wandering without, amid all the pelting of the pitiless storm; and finally, rewarded the poor old man in his turn, and repaid him for all his suffering, by giving him back again his gilt robes and tinsel sceptre!

Betterton was the last great actor who played Lear before the commission of this outrage. His performances of it between the years 1663 and 1671 are recorded to have been the greatest efforts of his genius. Ten years after the latter date, Mr Tate published his disgusting version, and this was adopted successively by [Anthony] Boheme, Quin, Booth, Barry, Garrick, Henderson, Kemble, Kean. Mr Macready has now, to his lasting honour, restored the text of Shakespeare, and we shall be glad to hear of the actor foolhardy enough to attempt another restoration of the text of Mr Tate! Mr Macready's success has banished that disgrace from the stage for ever.

The Fool in the tragedy of *Lear* is one of the most wonderful creations of Shakespeare's genius. The picture of his quick and pregnant sarcasm, of his loving devotion, of his acute sensibility, of his despairing mirth, of his heartbroken silence—contrasted with the rigid sublimity of Lear's suffering, with the huge desolation of Lear's sorrow, with the vast and outraged image of Lear's madness—is the noblest thought that ever entered into the heart and mind of man. Nor is it a noble thought alone. Three crowded houses in Covent Garden Theatre have now proved by something better than even the deepest attention that it is for action, for representation; that it is necessary to an audience as tears are to an overcharged heart; and necessary to Lear himself as the recollections of his kingdom, or as the worn and faded garments of his power. We predicted some years since that this would be felt, and we have the better right to repeat it now. We take leave again to say that Shakespeare would have as soon consented to the banishment of Lear from the tragedy as to the banishment of his Fool. We may fancy him, while planning his immortal work, feeling suddenly, with an instinct of divinest genius, that its gigantic sorrows could never be presented on the stage without a suffering too frightful, a sublimity too remote, a grandeur too terrible—unless relieved by quiet pathos, and in some way brought home to the apprehensions of the audience by homely and familiar illustration. At such a moment that Fool rose to his mind, and not till then could he have contemplated his marvellous work in the greatness and beauty of its final completion.

The Fool in *Lear* is the solitary instance of such a character, in all the writings of Shakespeare, being identified with the pathos and passion of the scene. He is interwoven with Lear, he is the link that still associates him with Cordelia's love, and the presence of the regal estate he has surrendered. The rage of the wolf Goneril is first stirred by a report that her favourite gentleman had been struck by her father for 'chiding of his fool',—and the first impatient questions we hear from the dethroned old man are: 'Where's my knave—my fool? Go you and call my fool hither.'—'Where's my fool? Ho! I think the world's asleep.'—'But where's my fool? I have not seen him these two days.'—'Go you and call hither my fool',—all which prepare us for that affecting answer stammered forth at last by the knight in attendance: 'Since my young lady's going into France, sir, the fool hath much pined away.' Mr Macready's manner of turning off at this with an expression of half impatience, half ill-repressed emotion—'No more of that, *I have noted it well*'—was inexpressibly touching. We saw him, in the secret corner of his heart, still clinging to the memory of her who was used to be his best object, the argument of his praise, balm of his age, 'most best, most dearest'. And in the same noble and affecting spirit was his manner of fondling the Fool when he sees him first, and asks him with earnest care, 'How now, my pretty knave? *How dost thou?*' Can there be a doubt, after this, that his love for the Fool is associated with Cordelia, who had been kind to the poor boy, and for the loss of whom he pines away? And are we not even then prepared for the sublime pathos of the close when Lear, bending over the dead body of all he had left to love upon the earth, connects with her the memory of that other gentle, faithful, and loving being who had passed from his side—unites, in that moment of final agony, the two hearts that had been broken in his service, and exclaims, 'And my poor fool is hanged!'

Mr Macready's Lear, remarkable before for a masterly completeness of conception, is heightened by this introduction of the Fool to a surprising degree. It accords exactly with the view he seeks to present of Lear's character. The passages we have named, for instance, had even received illustration in the first scene, where something beyond the turbulent greatness or royal impatience of Lear had been presented—something to redeem him from his treatment of Cordelia. The bewildered pause after giving his 'father's heart' away—the hurry yet hesitation of his manner as he orders France to be called—'Who stirs? Call Burgundy'—had told us at once how much consideration he needed, how much pity, of how little of himself he was indeed the master, how crushing and irrepressible was the strength of his sharp impatience. We saw no material change in his style of playing the first great scene with Goneril, which fills the stage with true and appalling touches of nature. In that scene he ascends indeed with the heights of Lear's passion; through all its changes of agony, of anger, of impatience, of turbulent assertion, of despair, and mighty grief, till on his knees, with arms upraised and head thrown back, the tremendous Curse bursts from him amid heaving and reluctant throes of suffering and anguish. The great scene of the second act had also its passages of power and beauty: his self-persuading utterance of 'hysterias passio'—his anxious and fearful tenderness to Regan—the elevated grandeur of his appeal to the heavens—his terrible suppressed efforts, his pauses, his reluctant pangs of passion, in the speech, 'I will not trouble thee, my child'—and surpassing the whole, as we think, in deep simplicity as well as agony of pathos, that noble conception of shame as he *hides his face* on the arm of Goneril and says—

> 'I'll go with thee;
> Thy fifty yet doth double five and twenty,
> And thou art twice her love.'

The Fool's presence then enabled him to give an effect, unattempted before, to those little words that close the scene when, in the effort of bewildering passion with which he strives to burst through the phalanx of amazed horrors that have closed him round, he feels that his intellect is shaking, and suddenly exclaims, 'O Fool! I shall go mad!' This is better than hitting the forehead and ranting out a self-reproach.

But the presence of the Fool in the storm-scene! The reader must witness this to judge its power and observe the deep impression with which it affects the audience. Every resource that the art of the painter and the mechanist can afford is called in aid of this scene—every illustration is thrown on it of which the great actor of Lear is capable, but these are nothing to that simple presence of the Fool. He has changed his character there. So long as hope existed he had sought by his hectic merriment and sarcasms to win Lear back to love and reason, but that half of his work is now over, and all that remains for him is to soothe and lessen the certainty of the worst. Kent asks who is with Lear in the storm, and is answered—

> 'None but the Fool who labours to outjest
> His heart-struck injuries.'

When all his attempts have failed, either to soothe or to outjest these injuries, he sings, in the shivering cold, about the necessity of 'going to bed at noon'. He leaves the stage to die in his youth, and we hear of him no more till we hear the sublime touch of pathos over the dead body of the hanged Cordelia.

The finest passage of Mr Macready's scenes upon the heath is his remembrance of the 'poor naked wretches', wherein a new world seems indeed to have broken upon his mind. Other parts of these scenes wanted more of a tumultuous extravagance, more of a preternatural wildness. We should always be made to feel something beyond physical distress predominant here. His colloquy with Mad Tom, however, was touching in the last degree, and so were the two last scenes, the recognition of Cordelia and the death which elicited from the audience the truest and best of all tributes to their beauty and pathos. Mr Macready's representation of the father at the end, broken down to his last despairing struggle, his heart swelling gradually upwards till it bursts in its closing sigh, completed the only perfect picture that we have had of Lear since the age of Betterton.

Charles Dickens

33

Scaffolders

George Vandenhoff (1813–85) gave up a legal career to go on the stage where he proved to be capable and vigorous in an ample range of parts. His father, John Vandenhoff, had been a London actor with a special provincial reputation; George began in 1839 as Mercutio at Covent Garden. The Blackburn engagement he describes was in the winter of 1840; he went back to Covent Garden in 1841, and in the following year began a long American stay. On his return to England in 1856 he practically (though not entirely) retired from the stage and was presently called to the Bar; his final appearance was as far ahead as 1878.

The part of Rolla is in *Pizarro* (Kotzebue-Sheridan). *The Players* magazine, newly started in 1860, did not much like Vandenhoff: 'The self-conceit displayed throughout this book [*Dramatic Reminiscences*, from which we quote] is almost unparalleled. It has rarely been our lot to read anything like it, and we hope to Heaven it never will again.' What, I wonder, could have happened there?

I had just finished breakfast at the hotel in Bolton, a small town in Lancashire where I was playing a short engagement, when the waiter told me that a gentleman wanted to speak to me. 'He's rather a strange-looking gentleman, sir.'

'How strange?'

'Well, sir, I can't exactly say; I think he must be one of the actor-chaps, or else a gipsy.'

'Oh,' said I—a highly complimentary alternative, I thought to myself.

'Well,' I added, 'let me see this strange gentleman.'

A queer-looking chap he was indeed. A tall, gaunt, high-shouldered, raw-boned, bossy-faced, hook-nosed, sunburnt, and hollow-cheeked individual, with a pair of keen, restless black eyes, deep set, under shaggy overhanging eyebrows; dressed in a faded frock-coat which had once been brown but was now of no positive colour, and which—having formed part of the wardrobe of a smaller man than its present wearer, to whom by some freak of fortune it had lapsed—being too short for him in every way, showed his bare, bony wrists, innocent of wristbands; a dark double-breasted waistcoat, buttoned close across his chest, to conceal, perhaps, his bosom's secret (a scarcity of linen), a pair of trousers that, having probably been derived from the same source as the coat, presented the same exiguousness of length, and displayed the tops of a pair of very seedy and travel-worn high-lows; a fuzzy head of hair, so promiscuous and so indistinct of tint, from dryness, age, and the dust of the roads, that it was impossible to guess at its original shade: such were the principal features of the strange-looking gentleman who now, with a rusty, battered hat in his large, muscular hands, presented himself, bowing, to my notice.

His name was Hall, or Hill (I forget which), he said in a husky, hoarse, foggy voice; such as one hears so often on a London cabstand, indicative of Old-Tom propensities, or a weakness for Geneva—perhaps in this case, poor fellow, of a consumption.

'You seem tired,' I said; 'pray sit down.'

He did so, thanking me; and, after a preliminary cough,

by way of clearing his throat, he began, in a somewhat less thick utterance—and in a style semi-oratorical, semi-theatrical: the style, in fact, adopted usually by the presenters of snuff-boxes, pieces of plate, gold watches, and testimonials generally, to the happy recipient (to use the set phraseology) who has paid the day before, through his agent, the full price of the article to be presented to him.

'I am commissioned, sir,' he said, 'by Mr Parish, the manager of the Blackburn Theatre, to ask if your engagements will allow you to give us the aid of your splendid talents for a few, say three or more, nights; and if so, on what terms you would consent to visit us.'

Now there was nothing in this address particularly *outre* in itself; it was the grandiloquent ambassadorial style of the man, coupled with his mean and wild appearance, that made it ludicrous. He had all the burlesque dignity and self-importance of a ragged plenipotentiary from Otaheite.

'I have not the pleasure, Mr Hall,' I said, 'of being acquainted with Mr Parish.'

'A highly respectable and responsible man, I assure you, sir; the soul of honour, sir,' quickly replied the ambassador, laying his hand on his breast.

'What plays are your company capable of performing, Mr Hall?'

'Any, sir, and all,' he answered with a flourish: 'We are *up* in all the stock tragedies, and have an efficient company.'

'A good leading actress, Mr Hall?'

'An angel, sir. Young, perfect, talented, and *amenable*.' He laid particular stress on the last epithet.

'A rare assemblage of qualities,' I said; 'but let me order you some breakfast, Mr Hall; you seem fatigued. How did you come?'

'Walked, sir.'

'Walked!' I repeated; 'why, it's twelve miles.'

'I know it, sir,' he replied, 'but exercise is good for me, and I preferred it to the coach; it will do me good.'

A good breakfast, thought I, would do you more good; and—

the waiter just then coming into the room with a letter for me—'Order a beefsteak for this gentleman,' I said. 'Tea or coffee, Mr Hall?'

'Why,' said that gentleman, 'you're very good, sir; but if you'll allow me, I'll take a little ale.'

'Bring some ale, waiter,' I said.

'Ale, sir? yes, sir'; and, with a look of unconcealed wonder, the waiter left the room.

As soon as he had closed the door, my new friend wished to resume the subject of his mission; but I stopped him by saying: 'Wait till you've had something to eat, Mr Hall, and then we'll attend to that little matter. Meanwhile there's the *Times*; excuse my reading and answering a letter.'

In a few minutes the steak and ale were brought in. The strange gentleman fell to without ceremony, despatched them in a few minutes more, and gave me notice, as I continued my writing, that he had finished, with a satisfied explosion of breath, something between a yawn and 'a paviour's sigh'.

I turned towards him, as he rubbed his hands together; and he said in a theatrical way, quoting from *The Merchant of Venice*: 'Well, sir, shall I have your answer? Will you pleasure us?'

'Well, Mr Hall,' I replied, 'I am in your neighbourhood. I have three vacant nights next week, and I will come to you Monday, Wednesday, and Friday, for a clear half of the receipts each night.'

'Those are very high terms, sir,' he replied, raising his eyebrows and screwing up his mouth. 'I am commissioned to offer you a clear third, and half a benefit. My power extends no further.'

'The value of a thing,' I answered, 'is that which it will bring, you know, Mr Hall. Allow me to ask how much money you play to ordinarily. What were the receipts of the house last night, for example? I trust to your honour.'

'Well, sir, last night was a bad night. We had not a great house last night.'

'Come now; had you thirty shillings?'

'Oh yes, sir; we had thirty shillings.'

'Not much more, eh?'

'No, not much more,' he said, with a comic smile.

'Well, suppose I play to an average of twenty pounds nightly, and you pay me half of it, if your ordinary business does not produce more than two pounds, you'll be a considerable gainer by the transaction.'

'Yes,' said he, 'if that were certain——.'

'Nothing is certain,' I replied, 'in theatrical matters; but I have every right to expect it; and it is only on the terms I have mentioned that I can consent to visit you.'

'Well, sir,' said he, 'my instructions are to secure your services, and therefore I must accept your terms.'

A scratch of a pen on a sheet of paper settled the agreement; and Mr Hall, with a profusion of bows and thanks for what he was pleased to call my 'hospitable treatment', took up his hat to depart. There was a farmer's light taxed-cart at the door, and finding its owner was going as far as Blackburn, I gave him half-a-crown to take my strange-looking friend to his destination.

The next week, on Monday, I reached Blackburn early in the morning, and about half-past ten o'clock, my strange negotiator was ushered into my room, accompanied by another spirit almost as strange as himself: a very swarthy, powerful man, considerably over six feet high, with jet-black glossy hair that hung on the sides of his cheeks in short ringlets. He was dressed in a velveteen suit, and had altogether a regular gipsy look and air. The last stranger was duly presented to me as 'Mr Gould; our stage manager, sir.'

They had called to show me to the theatre; and I got up and followed them to the rather dingy back street in which it was situated. The company was assembled, and we began the rehearsal of *Othello*. The tall Gould was the Iago, and my Desdemona was the 'angel' aforesaid, a well-looking young woman who, without seeming particularly to understand them, was very perfect in the words of the text. My new friend, the stage manager, barring occasional extraordinary and hitherto undreamt-of readings, was pretty safe; and though there was a general air of seediness about the *corps dramatique*, they were all evidently desirous of doing their best, and we got through the rehearsal tolerably satisfactorily. The Emilia, it is true, did not seem to have any innate reverence for Shakespeare, or any intimate acquaintance with her share of the dialogue, or her connection with the plot; and Roderigo, a very melancholy-looking youth, with a very tallowy complexion, and very thin legs and a squeaky voice, seemed particularly innocent of everything connected with the play, especially as to who he was, what he was, and where he was, and *why* he was what he was, who he was, and where he was. However, as I had little to do with these individuals, their malfeasances did not much trouble me.

In the evening I went rather early to the theatre, and was agreeably surprised by finding that a very good-sized room had been fitted up as my dressing-room, cleaned, carpeted, sofa'd, well lit, with extra lights, and in every way made snug. This attention to my private comfort gave me better hopes of the appointments for the stage about which I confess I had my doubts. But when we came to the Senate scene, I was pleased to find a respectable array of properties, with a Duke who, though he had the snuffles in his utterance, was well-dressed, and correct in the text. Barring a few little contretemps which did not seem to affect the enjoyment of the audience, if they did not even increase it (certainly they gave uproarious tokens of delight at the burlesque and *Bombastes Furioso* death of Roderigo, who, in his agony, kept his leg shaking and quivering in the air as if he were galvanised, while Iago kept sticking his sword into him, and at every stick a fresh kick)—except this and one or two other rather striking effects, the play went off with immense applause, and the actors were evidently highly satisfied with their own efforts in the Shakespearian Drama.

The house, as I had prophesied, was well filled; and after the performance I had my first interview and settlement with the manager; and a strange settlement it was.

He walked into my room as I had just finished my change of dress, and washed off the last tint of Othello's swarthy hue; and said, with a strong Lancashire accent: 'Moy name's Parish, sir. A'm th'manager o'this cuncearn, and aw've coomb to settle.'

'Good evening, Mr Parish; I hope you're pleased with the house tonight.'

'It's a foine house, sir; yaw've doon well; and every neet I expect yaw'll do better. Yaw've got th'stoof in yaw, and th'chaps loike you.'

I bowed. He went on: 'A'don't know haw much is in th' 'ouse; A' haven't counted th'brass; but I took it all mysen', and so there's no cheating here.'

With that he turned his back to my dressing-table, and emptied out of his coat pockets as I looked on with wonder, a large quantity of silver and copper. Having turned his coat pockets thoroughly out, he next put his hand into his waistcoat pocket and fished out a five-pound note which he laid down on the table; and lastly, he pulled from the pockets of his pants a couple of sovereigns; those also he deposited with the rest of the current coin of the realm, saying:

'Theere! theere it awe is, just as A tuk it. Now th'bargain is auf and afe; pretty stiff terms, maister, but yaw've airn't it; so count away; and yaw take and A'll tak afe; and then all'll be straight 'twixt you and me.'

So down we sat to 'count the brass'; the five-pound note, with the two sovereigns upon it, were placed in isolated dignity, as became their aristocratic value and denomination, at one side; the copper we piled into shilling heaps of twelve pennies, and the silver into heaps of twenty shillings, or more frequently of forty sixpences (the price of the gallery being sixpence), representing the pound sterling.

During this interesting 'financial operation', not a word was spoken on either side; the piles being duly made up, it appeared on counting them, that there were twenty pounds ten shillings in silver, and two pounds and sixpence in copper; which, with the five-pound note and the two pounds in gold, amounted to twenty-nine pounds, ten shillings, and sixpence; large receipts for a small country theatre, I can tell you (I have seen less in a very large one, with a good company, and two or three London actors in the cast).

Mr Parish was evidently no Michael Cassio, no great arithmetician; but after some little difficulty, after a good deal of puzzling and scratching of his head (there was no pen, pencil, or paper in the room), he gradually satisfied himself that the half of £29 10s 6d was £14 15s 3d; whereupon, making an exact division, he said: 'Theere! theere's thy share, and here's moine. A've given thee th' gowd and th' flimsy 'cause A s'pose yaw won't be wanting to carry the copper; and A can pay it away to moy fawks at onest. So that's settled.'

'And a very simple and straightforward settlement, too, Mr Parish.'

'Whoy, yaw see, sir,' he replied, 'Ah'm not much i'th'littery loine; moine's mostly headwork. A don't do mooch wi'pen an'ink. Ah'm a scaffolder, Oi am.'

'A scaffolder, Mr Parish!'

'Aye; we're open-air chaps, we are; we play under canvas i'th' summer, and i'th' winter A'm forced to go into th'regular business, in walls; and it welly ruins me. But yaw see, I mun keep my people together again th'summer time, or A should lose 'em. However, yaw'll find me aw reet, upreet an' downreet. And now, sir, we mun hae a glass togither, if yaw please, just to wet th' first neet, and for luck for th'others.'

With that he pulled a bottle of brandy out of a capacious side-pocket (I had observed the neck of it sticking out, and guessed its purpose), poured me out a rather stiff allowance in the one glass which was in the room, assuring me that it was 'the reet sort'. I added some water which he declared would 'spile it', and drank to his health.

He then poured himself out about half a tumbler, and without running the risk of spoiling it by any elemental addition, shook hands with me in the most cordial manner, wished me luck, and drank it off.

This was the system of settlement he followed every night; and, looking back on the many theatres I have played in since, and the many managers that have settled with me, I am inclined to think that, though it was not the most formal or high-Roman fashion of settlement, it was perhaps the fairest and honestest that I have ever been favoured with.

The company was in fact, a *Show*-company—scaffolders—that played in booths in summer, and in winter betook themselves to small theatres, doing the best they could and sharing the profits—if there were any.

My other two nights (Rolla and Hamlet) produced two excellent houses, and I took away from this petty place, as my share, about £40. I went thence to Liverpool for twelve nights, and did not do better in that large city, though Mr Elton (a London actor of fair standing) played with me. I received £15 a week and a clear half-benefit; my benefit was about £90, so that the two weeks gave me about £75.

George Vandenhoff

THEATRE. DURHAM.

THE

Greatest Novelty

AND MOST

Splendid Spectacle ever offered to the Durham Theatrical Public,

A GRAND MOVING DIORAMA,

BY MR W. BEVERLY.

This present TUESDAY, 12th April, 1842,

Will be produced, for the second time, a Nautical Turkish Spectacle, written expressly for these Theatres, called the

FALL of ACRE;

Or, the Perils of British Sailors.

The Scenery by **MR W. BEVERLY.**

Mr B. TANNETT and Assistants. Machienery by Mr Sarkeld. The Music by Mr Stoker.
The Properties by Mr Smith. The Dresses by Mr Benson. The whole produced
under the direction of Mr Robert Roxby.

Captain Mandeville H. M. S. Dart....Mr C. H. SIMMS—Lieut. Morden... Mr B. TANNETT
Lieut. Harcourt, his rival....Mr FLORINGTON—Ben Brace, a British Sailor....Mr ROBERT ROXBY
Harry Lanyard, Mate of the Dart Mr MARTIN—Jack Ratlin Mr VINCENT
Stubby, Landlord of the Jolly Sailor....Mr DUVAL—1st Marine ...Mr BENSON—2nd do......Mr KISH
Simon Simple, an unwilling volunteer in search of Naval promotion......Mr ROXBY
Muly Ishmael, commander of the Fort Saint Jean d'Acre Mr MASTERMAN
Fahardin, his second in command.... Mr DUVAL
Emma Mandeville, beloved by Harcourt and Morden..Miss MORVEN—Katty Mooney..Mr DOWNEY
Zulmeda, sister of Muly Ishmael .... Miss LEWIS—Sue......Miss BENSON—Polly......Mrs VINCENT

LIST OF THE SPLENDID NEW SCENERY. ACT I.

Scene 1. **View of Portsmouth Harbour from the Platform, with exterior of the Jolly Sailor..........W. Beverly.**

In this Scene a Characteristic Nautical Ballet by the Characters.

2. Captain's cabin in the Dart....................B. Tannett.

3. Between Decks of the Dart.................... Ditto.

Tempest and striking of the Vessel.

4. The Ocean, with the Crew assembled on the FATAL RAFT. Horrible treachery of Harcourt, who abandons the Crew of the Raft to all the

HORRORS OF STARVATION.

Act 2. Scene 1. A distant View of Acre from the Road to Jerusalem. . . . . . W. Beverly.

Scene 2nd. The OCEAN, as before.

THE MUTINY AND LOTTERY OF DEATH.

Scene 3rd. A View near Acre. . . . W. Beverly.

Scene 4th. The FATAL RAFT, as before.

LAST EXTREMITY—Crew of the Fatal Raft saved by Harcourt.

Scene 5th. A View near Acre, as before.

Scene 6th. Magnificent Tent of Muly Ishmael, with View of Acre by Sunset . . . W. Beverly.

Act 3. Scene 1. Apartment in the Fortress........................B. Tannett.

THE VISION.

A GRAND MOVING

DIORAMA

Extending over a space of 2000 square feet of Canvas.
embracing the following Views:--

1 PORTSMOUTH with MEN OF WAR & EMBARKATION OF TROOPS.
2 Rigging Hulk at Portsmouth
3 The Ocean with men of War
4 View of the Rock of Gibralter with Fishing Boats
5 Rocky View in Syria
6 The City of Berout and distant View of Mount Liban
7 The Walls of Acre

8 The Siege of Acre by the combined FLEET
By Mr W. BEVERLY

Scene 9. A Dungeon in the Fortress. Scene 10. Muly's Apartment in the Fortress immediately after the FATAL EXPLOSION.

MAGNIFICENT PANORAMIC VIEW OF ACRE,

And Triumph of British Bravery.

After which

A Dance by Miss Benson.

The whole to conclude with the laughable Farce of

Fortune's Frolic;

Or, the Ploughman turned Lord.

Old Snacks....Mr C. H. SIMMS—Mr Frank..Mr VINCENT—Rattle....Mr MASTERMAN
Clown........Mr DOWNEY————Joe......Mr MARTIN ————Bobby........Mr DUVAL
Robin Roughhead.................. ....Mr ROXBY
Miss Nancy......Miss E. BLAND——Margery......Mrs JEPHSON——Dolly......Mrs VINCENT

Doors open at half-past Six, and the performance to commence at Seven o'Clock.
Boxes 3s.— Pit 2s.— Gallery 1s.— Second Price at half-past Eight. Boxes 2s.— Pit 1s.— Gallery— 6d.
Children in arms cannot be admitted. No admittance behind the scenes.
Acting Manager, Mr Samuel Roxby. Stage Manager, Mr Robert Roxby.

W. AINSLEY, PRINTER, SADLER STREET, DURHAM.

An evening's entertainment in a provincial theatre, Durham, 1842

34

Honest John

John Coleman, in his seventies when he died in 1904, was everything a flamboyantly professional 'dear old' actor—as imagined in Dickens's Crummles and Pinero's Telfer—is popularly supposed to have been. His acting experience, in and out of London, was as strenuous as his memory, in old age, would be faulty, though he continued to know the intricacies of stock melodrama. A good-hearted romantic, booming like a full tide on the rocks, he seemed to be on Christian-name terms with his entire world. He has left his impression on Stratford-upon-Avon history in a ludicrous version of *Pericles*, staged there in 1900 with himself as the Prince. During his later years he wrote relishingly and at length; and in the following extract from a two-volume autobiography, *Fifty Years of an Actor's Life* (1904), he is remembering his early acting days in the provinces (late 1840s).

He mentions these plays: *Blue Devils* (1798), one-act comic drama by George Colman, Jr, from the French; *High Life Below Stairs* (1759) by James Townley; *Eugene Aram*, probably W. T. Moncrieff's version (1832) of the Lytton novel; *The Miller and His Men* (1813) by Isaac Pocock; *The Hunchback* (1832) by James Sheridan Knowles; *The Gladiator* (1831) by Robert M. Bird, in which Forrest played Spartacus; *Ruy Blas* (1860) by Edmund Falconer from the French of Victor Hugo.

People

J. Bennett, manager of the Worcester theatre; Tom Mead (1821–89), actor; Fanny (Frances Anne) Kemble (1809–93), actress, daughter of Charles Kemble, niece of John Philip Kemble and Sarah Siddons; Gustavus Vaughan Brooke (1818–66), Irish-born actor, drowned in the wreck of the steamship *London*, bound for Australia; Edwin Forrest, actor—see Number 31 (*Massacre*).

At Shrewsbury we played only three nights a week, which afforded us time for rehearsals and study; hence our pieces (standard works and popular dramas of the day, *Green Bushes*, etc.) were done with great propriety to good, frequently overflowing houses. The Shrewsbury folk were kind beyond my deserts, and crowded the theatre upon my benefit night, on which occasion the programme consisted of *The Lady of Lyons* (then at the height of its popularity), *Blue Devils* (selected especially for Terry O'Rourke, who was not in the first piece), and *High Life Below Stairs*. All the seats were taken at the box office. Thus assured of a good house, I needed little persuasion to provide a hot supper and copious libations instead of the customary bread, fowl, and toast and water for the supper scene [in *High Life*]. The repast, which was provided at my hotel, consisted of soup, a cod's head and shoulders, a saddle of mutton, and an apple tart. Such a sight had never been seen in the Shrewsbury Theatre before, and in all probability has never been seen since. When the savoury odours exuding from these delectable viands ascended into the front of the house, they created the sensation of the evening, and the applause was almost deafening.

It was an inflexible rule (and a very good one too) that the performance should terminate at eleven o'clock. Now just as Lady Charlotte, His Grace the Duke, Sir Harry, and their aristocratic friends sat down to supper, the clock struck the fatal hour. Whether our worthy manager considered the loud and long-continued applause a reproach to his parsimony, or whether he was influenced by a mere ebullition of temper, I can't tell; whatever the cause he rang down the curtain, and amidst a violent outburst of disapproval from the audience, ordered the band to play 'God save the Queen', and put out the lights. It was in vain that I appealed to him for permission to finish our repast on the stage. I met with nothing but a curt and decided negative, and an intimation that we must clear out in a quarter of an hour. I was, however, equal to the occasion. The banquet was removed to the hotel, where we adjourned and 'shut up in measureless content'.

O'Rourke told me that this peremptory managerial *coup* was nothing compared to what had occurred at Worcester during the previous season on the occasion of his benefit. The after-piece was *Eugene Aram*. Terry had a special weakness for his death scenes, and he never 'shuffled off this mortal coil' in less than a quarter of an hour. Provided with his quietus in the shape of a phial of poison, he leisurely commenced operations, when, lo! the clock struck eleven. At that moment on came the bold Bennett with a black coat thrown over his every-day costume.

'Ah! my dear Aram,' he exclaimed in his airiest tones, 'don't trouble to poison yourself! The Home Secretary has sent a reprieve, and Madeleine is waiting to be married. Edwards! [to leader of orchestra] 'strike up "Troubles o'er, Joys in Store". Ring down!' And down came the curtain, to the disgust of Aram and delight of the audience.

From Shrewsbury we went to Coventry, where we opened at Christmas to a house crowded to overflowing with girls from the ribbon factories. As our pieces were all, or nearly all, 'up', we had an easy time. Our treasury was a primitive but pleasant function. Punctually as the clock struck twelve every Saturday, our manager turned up with a bag, the contents of which he emptied on the prompt-table. They consisted of a number of little packages (gold and silver), each carefully sealed and labelled with the name of the recipient. The ladies came first, the men next, each answering to his or her name, as Mr Bennett presented to each 'the reward of merit'. The whole business was over in five minutes . . .

My stay here was of short duration. I had been there barely a month when I received an offer for the juvenile business at an increased salary, from Mr Mercer Simpson, for the Theatre Royal, Liverpool. On my arrival I found two gentlemen (Mr James Rodgers and Mr G. K. Dickenson) already engaged for my line of business. Nor was this all; on entering the green-room, to my intense mortification I found myself cast for a series of subordinate parts in Mr Vandenhoff's pieces. Boiling with indignation, I sought Mr Robert Roxby (Mr Simpson's representative), and intimated, without circumlocution, that I didn't intend to play anything out of my line of business. He was insolent; I was defiant. One word led to another; he 'pooh-pooh'd' and 'boy-boy'd' me. Beyond myself with anger, I returned to the green-room, and to the astonishment and almost to the consternation of everybody, tore down the casts and flung them on the fire.

Harry Nye (afterwards the well-known Brighton manager) was the only soul I knew in that large company, and he inquired, 'What in the name of fate do you mean?'

'Mean!' I replied. 'That ginger-headed cad with the peacock's voice has insulted me by casting me a heap of utility parts, and when I remonstrated, he cheeked me and called me a boy.'

'Boy! By G——, sir, you're a man, every inch of you!' exclaimed Tom Mead, introducing himself in this unconventional manner, and thus commencing an acquaintance which continued up to the day of the dear old chap's death.

This little explosion cleared the air, and Roxby not only cast me no more 'utility' parts, but actually came and apologised for his 'mistake'. As, however, three of us were engaged for the same parts, I only got an occasional look-in, which proved a blessing in disguise, as it afforded me ample time for study and elaboration.

Our company was a very strong one, [but] there were one or two rather pretentious 'swells' who made themselves perpetual laughing-stocks through their ignorance and incapacity. One imposing personage, a fine-looking wig-block (whom I remember to have seen shortly afterwards as a leading actor at a fashionable West End theatre), was a never-failing source of amusement. However hard he tried, the poor wretch never could acquire the words. Pat Corri laboured under the same misfortune, with this additional disadvantage, that when he broke down he burst forth in his native Irish.

In *Hamlet* the 'swell' was the Player King, while Pat was the Second Player. The 'swell' managed to get through his first speech without breaking down, but when he came to the next:

Anon he finds him
Striking too short at Greeks . . .

he portentously exclaimed:

Anon he finds him
Striking at two short Greeks.

To cover up this slip, Vandenhoff came to the rescue. 'Tis well!' quoth he, 'I'll have thee speak out the rest of this soon.' Whereupon an unsympathetic brute in the pit sarcastically interjected, 'God forbid! We've had enough already!' The roar which arose so disconcerted the poor swell that he bolted off the stage, and left them to finish the scene as well as they could without him.

All this, however, was as nothing to Pat Corri's experience, who, when he essayed to poison the Player King, rendered the text thus:

Thoughts black, hands apt!
Midnight weeds collected and rejected
By Hecate, thrice blast her, bad luck to her!
I, yes, I—by Jabers! I'll pour it into the owld Geeser's ear,
And polish him off at onst!

Not another word could be heard. Yell followed yell, and there was nothing for it but to drop the curtain.

'Good heavens!' exclaimed Vandenhoff, 'has the little bog-trotter taken leave of his senses? What does this mean, Mr Corri?'

'Mane, sir, mane? It manes chaps do becoddin' me till I dun know whether I'm on my head or my heels.'

Corri was not alone in his infirmity. To his dying day Tom Mead could never hammer the words accurately into his head. Although he made the oddest blunders, he laughed them off so genially that one was never sure whether he was in jest or earnest. One night I heard him inquire, as Grindoff (*Miller and his Men*), '*Is* those sacks disposed off?' When Riber replied, 'Yes, they *is*', the house and actors burst into a roar in which Tom joined as heartily as anyone. . . .

The only really important event of the Liverpool season was the return of Fanny Kemble to the stage. It was at the Theatre Royal, Manchester, that she reappeared; from thence she came to the Theatre Royal, Liverpool, where I had the honour to form her acquaintance. At that period the showman's art had not invaded the profession of a gentleman; advance agents, Press wire-pullers, and so-called acting managers were not in existence. Hence it came to pass that Mrs Kemble walked upon the Liverpool stage (where we awaited her arrival with anxiety and curiosity) alone and unattended. We had expected to see a tragedy queen. We saw instead a quiet, unassuming lady of middle age and middle height, simply attired in a black silk dress. Her pale classic features were irradiated by a pair of dark, lustrous eyes, which wore an eerie expression—imperious one moment, pleading the next—and which showed forth in vivid contrast to the glory of her abundant hair, even then slightly streaked with grey at the temples. As we simultaneously bared our heads to the last of the Kembles, she responded to the recognition in one comprehensive and gracious courtesy, then introducing herself *sans cérémonie*, to the stage manager, commenced the rehearsal.

In recalling that memorable night in Liverpool after all these years, I can see in my mind's eye the wistful, sad face, 'dumb with the depth of a divine despair', the lustre of the beauteous eyes dimmed with tears, but fixed to the last on Clifford's letter [the play was Sheridan Knowles's *The Hunchback*] as Master Walter led her despairing from the stage. I can hear the matchless melody of 'Twas Clifford's voice if ever Clifford spoke'. Best of all, I recall the *tour de force* of the last act. I have a vivid recollection of Macready's 'Good God! Ulric, yon look!' [*Werner*], of the burst of paternal emotion in *Virginius*, 'I thank thee, Jupiter, that I am still a father!', of Forrest's 'Let them come! we are prepared!' in *The Gladiator*, of Brooke's 'Oh! fool, fool, fool!', of Ristori's 'Tu!' in *Medea*, of Fechter's 'I am *not* a lackey; I am an executioner!' [*Ruy Blas*]; but not one of these illustrious actors, nay, not all of them combined, ever equalled the grace, the beauty, the tragic fire, the perfect majesty, the commingling of exquisite artifice with perfect art, which Fanny Kemble imparted to the eight commonplace monosyllables, 'Do it! Nor leave the task to me!'

John Coleman

35

Nightmare

George Henry Lewes (1817–78) is usually thought of now for his long liaison, from 1854, with 'George Eliot'. During four immediately preceding years (1850–4) he had written drama criticism for the *Leader* which he helped to found—under the pseudonym of 'Vivian'. His feeling for the theatre was hereditary, for Charles Lee Lewes, the original Young Marlow in Goldsmith's *She Stoops to Conquer*, was his grandfather. For a short period, too, he acted professionally, and he wrote a few plays.

Lewes was always independent. Today *The Duchess of Malfi*, in its black-velvet night, is an assured classic—even though a modern writer has told us alarmingly that 'in John Webster, as in the best Continental drama, reality is conceived as psychological truth in its all-embracing Existential sense'. Lewes did not like the play at all. Here is his *Leader* review of Samuel Phelps's Sadler's Wells revival in November 1850.

He refers to John Marston (*c*1575–1634), author of *The Malcontent* (1604); Richard Hengist [Henry] Horne (1803–84), author of the 'farthing epic', *Orion*, and of a tragedy, *Cosmo de Medici* (1837); Isabella Glyn, tragic actress (1823–89); Samuel Phelps (1804–78), for long the Sadler's Wells actor-manager; Helen [Helena] Faucit, later Lady Martin (1817–98), principal actress of her period; and George Bennett, actor (1800–79).

Lewes's *On Actors and the Art of Acting* appeared in 1875, but his dramatic essays from the *Leader* were not collected until William Archer and Robert W. Lowe put them in a volume (1896) with Forster's reviews from *The Examiner*.

Among the pardonable errors of my youth, I count the belief that our old English dramatists were worthy of study as men of true dramatic genius. Pardonable, I say, because I was lured into it by a reverential regard felt for Lamb, Hazlitt, and others as fine critics, and by the unmistakable beauties of the scenes and passages they quoted. My days and nights were given to Marlowe, Dekker, Webster, Marston, Kyd, Greene, Peele, and the illustrious obscure in Dodsley. Enthusiasm, however, was tamed by the irresistible mediocrity of these plays; no belief in their excellence could long stand up against the evidence of their dreariness and foolishness. I underlined fine passages; copied apophthegms and beauties into various notebooks; wrote foolish articles in magazines expressive of my admiration; but the thing could not last, and I silently gave up my former idols to the scorn of whoso pleased to vilify them. Looking backwards to the days of Lamb—especially bearing in mind his peculiar idiosyncrasies—the admiration he felt, and tried to inspire others with, is perfectly intelligible; but, as I said some months ago, the resuscitation of those dramatists has been a fatal obstruction to the progress of the drama, and has misled many a brave and generous talent. It has fostered the tendency and flattered the weakness of poets, by encouraging them to believe that mere writing suffices for a drama—that imagery will supply the place of incidents, and that tragic *intentions*, which boldly appeal to the imagination, are enough.

Nothing was needed to burst this bubble but the actual revival of a play or two upon the modern stage. Marston's *Malcontent* was rudely tried at the Olympic; and now *The Duchess of Malfi*, by John Webster, the most admired of the company excepting Marlowe, has been elaborately prepared by R. H. Horne, and produced at Sadler's Wells with all the care and picturesqueness for which that theatre is known. I have read that play four times, but although Horne has greatly lessened its absurdities, I never felt them so vividly until it was acted before my eyes. He has made it less tedious and less childish in its horrors, but the irredeemable mediocrity of its *dramatic* evolution of human passion is unmistakable. The noble lines of manly verse which charm the *reader* fail to arrest the *spectator*, who is alternating between impressions of the wearisome and ludicrous.

Consider it under what aspect you will, short of a commonplace book of 'passages', *The Duchess of Malfi* is a feeble and a foolish work. I say this fully aware of the passages which may be quoted as specimen-bricks. Other critics have declaimed against its accumulation of horrors; to my mind that is not the greatest defect. Instead of 'holding the mirror up to nature', this drama holds the mirror up to Madame Tussaud's and emulates her chamber of horrors; but the worst remains behind, and that is the motiveless and false exhibition of human nature. Take the story. The young Duchess of Malfi loves her steward, tells him so, and privately marries him. Her brothers Ferdinand and the Cardinal, caring only for the nobility of their lineage, wish to marry her to Prince Malateste; and, on hearing how she has disgraced herself, resolve to kill her. But death, simply as death, is no fit punishment for such a crime. They prepare, therefore, a waxen image (anticipating Madame Tussaud) of Antonio, her husband, which is shown to her as his corpse; they fill the palace with mad people, whose howlings are to madden her; and, having wrought upon her till they think despair can hold out no longer, they bring in the executioners and strangle her. No sooner is she dead than Ferdinand, who planned it all, turns suddenly remorseful—as villians do in the last scenes of melodramas—and in the fifth act he goes raving mad. Now, firstly, the horrors are childish, because they grow out of no proper ground. They are not the culmination of tragic motives. The insulted pride of Ferdinand might demand as reparation the life of his sister, and there is a real tragic position in the third act, where he places the poniard in her hand and bids her die. But playing these fantastic tricks to bring her to despair is mere madness. How ludicrously absurd is this Ferdinand—who has never given a hint of any love for his sister, any sorrow for her shame, any reluctance in perpetrating these cruelties—to be suddenly lachrymose and repentant as soon as she is dead! This is not the work of a *dramatist*; it is clumsy ignorance. *The Duchess of Malfi* is a nightmare, not a tragedy.

I might go through the work and point out in almost every scene evidences of a similar incapacity for high dramatic art; but to what purpose? Every year plays are published by misguided young gentlemen exhibiting this kind of incapacity, and friendly critics have no greater compliment than to declare that the 'mantle of the Elizabethan dramatists has fallen upon Mr Jones'. If Shakespeare is a great dramatist, Webster and company are not dramatists at all; and nothing exalts him more than to measure him by his contemporaries.

Despising probabilities, disregarding all conditions of art, and falsifying human nature, *The Duchess of Malfi* is, nevertheless, an attractive play to that audience. As a terrific *melodrame*, it delights the pit. It was, therefore, not a bad speculation to produce this adaptation which, let me say once for all, must have cost Horne more labour than he will gain credit for. As a poet, Horne is known to wield 'Marlowe's mighty line' like a kindred spirit. In these additions to Webster we defy the nicest critic to detect the old from the new; unless you have the two books side by side, you cannot tell whether you are reading Webster or Horne. But he would write a better play himself, and his labour would better be employed. Why waste his faculties in the hopeless task of making falsehood look like truth? *Cosmo de Medici*, impracticable though it be, is worth any amount of Webster.

The acting of this play reflects credit on the theatre. Miss Glyn was better than we have yet seen her; but this intelligent actress will never achieve the position she aspires to, unless she makes a radical change in her style, and throws aside the affectations and conventions she has acquired. Her elocution is vicious. She chaunts instead of speaking, and her chaunt is unmusical. Instead of taking the rhythm from the verse, the accent from the sense, she puts one monotonous rhythm upon the verse, and lets the accent obey the impetus of the chaunt, as if the voice mastered her, instead of her mastering the voice. Once or twice when she spoke naturally it was quite charming; and her grand burst of despair, in the fourth act, though injured by this very defect of chaunting, had so much force and fury in it that the house shook with plaudits. The comedy of the early scenes was hard, forced, and stagey. In making love to her steward she wanted tenderness, grace, and coyness. On the whole, however, one may say that, except Helen Faucit, no English actress could have played the part so well. Phelps was ill at ease in the first four acts, as if the nonsense of his part baffled him, and he could not grasp it; towards the close of the fourth act, however, he made a clutch at it, and his madness in the fifth act was terribly real. George Bennett, in Bosola, was suited to a nicety.

George Henry Lewes

MISS LAURA ADDISON AS QUEEN MARY.
IN
SCHILLER'S HISTORICAL TRAGEDY OF MARY STUART

"'O! woe
To the unhappy victim, when the tongue
That frames the law shall execute the sentence.

Act I. Sc I.

Engraved by Hollis, from a Daguerreotype by Mayall.

JOHN TALLIS & COMPANY, LONDON & NEW YORK.

36

Farewell, Macready

William Charles Macready, then fifty-seven years old, retired from the stage after his performance of Macbeth at Drury Lane on 26 February 1851. On the night of 1 March he had the ordeal of a testimonial dinner at the Hall of Commerce in Threadneedle Street. Sir Edward Bulwer Lytton, author of *The Lady of Lyons*, *Richelieu*, and *Money*, presided; Charles Dickens, the organiser, arrived in a blue dress-coat, brass-buttoned and silk-faced, a satin vest with a white satin collar, and an elaborately embroidered shirt. Hardly anyone in Macready's world was conspicuously missing, though Mr Justice Talfourd, author of *Ion*, had to be away on circuit. Lytton proposed the health of a man who had identified himself with the living drama of his period and half created it; Macready replied with both dignity and emotion; and after a variety of speeches—Dickens was witty and Thackeray wavering—John Forster rose for the toast of 'Dramatic Literature'. He waved a paper that contained, he said, a sonnet by the Poet Laureate, Alfred Tennyson (who was there that evening). 'Read it, Forster! Read it!' cried the guests; and in his stentorian voice he began: 'Farewell, Macready, since to-night we part . . .'

The great actor would live in retirement, at Sherborne and Cheltenham, through twenty-two years that brought him many griefs. At Cheltenham on the morning of 27 April 1873, he died, aged eighty; after a week his body was brought to London, and to Kensal Green where his first wife, his sister, and five of his eleven children had been buried; the names of two other children were upon the marble tablet.

A century later a small group from the Society for Theatre Research went to Kensal Green on the clear, cold morning of 27 April 1973. There in the vault before Macready's coffin, and after the laying of a laurel chaplet, Robert Eddison read Tennyson's Ode with an unforgettable grave simplicity.

Farewell, Macready, since to-night we part;
  Full-handed thunders often have confessed
  Thy power, well used to move the public breast.
We thank thee with our voice, and from the heart.
Farewell, Macready, since this night we part;
  Go, take thine honours home; rank with the best,
  Garrick and statelier Kemble, and the rest
Who made a nation purer through their Art.

Thine is it that our drama did not die,
  Nor flicker down to brainless pantomime,
  And those gilt-gauds men-children swarm to see.
Farewell, Macready; moral, grave, sublime;
Our Shakespeare's bland and universal eye
  Dwells, pleased, through twice a hundred years, on thee.

Alfred Tennyson

THOMAS'S
DRAMATIC TRAVELLING ESTABLISHMENT,

ERECTED ON THE OPEN GROUND LATELY OCCUPIED BY

FAIRLES'S TILE SHEDS,

WATERLOO VALE, SOUTH SHIELDS.

OPEN EVERY EVENING.

On WEDNESDAY, April 6th, 1842,

Will be presented a celebrated Nautical Melo-drama, replete with deep interest, entitled The

DREAM AT SEA;

Or, Penden Vau, the Haunted Cavern.

Trevanion, a wealthy Mine Owner—Mr HENRY Richard Ponderel, his Nephew.—Mr BUGLASS Launce Lynwood, a Fisherman—Mr MACFARREN Williams—Mr JONES Alley Croaker—Mr REILLY Black Ralph, a Wrecker—Mr ANDREWS Tom Tinkle, Village Muffin Man—Mr HAYES Red Norris, Trewof, Michael, (Wreckers)—Messrs DARLING, SMITH, & WILLIAMS Anne Trevanion—MAD. ADELINE MACFARREN Biddy Nuts—Mrs ANDREWS Margaret, Ralph's Wife—Mrs REILLY Henry, a Child, Master J. WATSON.

Scenery and Incidents.---THE ROCK OF THE ARMED KNIGHT.

Wreck of the Ship Neva—Plunder shared by the Wreckers—Penderell saved by Launce—Black Ralph about to despatch Penderell—Launce interferes—Deadly struggle—Launce overthrown—Ralph going to stab him—Penderell seizes a Hatchet and cuts him down—Biddy Nutts in the Dumps—the Muffin Man's Grandfather's Will—Conjugal Felicity—Love reaching an unchangeable Climax—Cupid painted without Pantaloons.

RALPH THE WRECKER'S HUT.

Launce Lynwood determined to quit the country—assisted by Ralph—exchange Clothes—Wedding Festivities—reading of Grandfather's Will—the four post Bed-stead—Tinkle's Legacy—It's a Forgery—Supper and Merrymaking—Assault and Battery—"Anne called him by his name"—She grasped his arm—He struck her—She—She fell, and

SHE IS DEAD!

Wreckers carousing—Launce returns—the Dream at Sea—the Bell of St Buryan—For whom?—Anne Trevanion—Biddy in mourning—Tinkle and his Legacy—Seized on for half a sack of Flour.

Tom ruined, Body and Breeches.

The Tax-gatherer drunk—keep Temperance in view.—" It would be some consolation to behold her once again, even in her grave"—Anne Trevanion in her Bridal Dress—the dead alive, " Earth, Air, and Sea!—She lives!"—The scene changed.

SECURE THE MURDERER!

Tinkle laying in a stock of Bread and Cheese, preparatory to his departure for London—Plenty of Money—Walk two hundred and fifty miles on three shillings—Calf's Head best hot—cutting up the Legacy—Ten Pound Note—Ten Pound Fiddlestick.

TINKLE HEIR TO TWO HUNDRED POUNDS.

Bless the old Waistcoat—no going to London now—I'll be married in it.——Trevanion pale, agitated, and almost heart-broken—Lynwood's Escape.

Penden Vau, the Haunted Cavern.

Ralph the Wrecker dying—Anne implores Ralph to tell his reason for bringing her to the Cave—he does so—" and here we must remain—no Boat will venture near the Haunted Cavern"—A ray of hope—Launce, exhausted, reaches the Cave—is pursued by Penderell and Miners—Penderell presents a pistol at the head of Launce. THE LIVING APPARITION RUSHES BETWEEN THEM. Trevanion appears at the mouth of the Cave—comes forward—Anne utters a cry, and falls into her father's Arms—the repentant Villain—Death of Black Ralph the Wrecker—The Denoument, and

REWARD OF INNOCENCE.

Comic Song by Mr. HAYS.

A Favourite Ballad by Mrs. ANDREWS.

The whole to conclude with The

EMIGRANT'S DAUGHTER;

Or, THE NEUTRAL GROUND.

Principal Characters by Messrs Macfarren, Buglass, Reilly, Hayes, Henry, Andrews, &c., and Miss Atkinson.

On THURSDAY, April 5th, 1842,

The Performances will commence with the popular and interesting Drama of

ROBERT MACAIRE

Or, The Two Murderers.

Robert Macaire, under the assumed Name of Redmond, an accomplished Thief, Mr MACFARREN Jaques Strop, under the assumed name of Bertrand, a Thief in the Rough, a timid, unpolished Artist—Mr HAYES Dumont, an Innkeeper—Mr HENRY Charles, his adopted Son—Mad. A MACFARREN Mr Germuil, a wealthy Farmer—Mr HENRY Pierre, Head Waiter at the Auberge—Mr REILLY Louis—Mr BUGLASS Sergeant Loupy—Mr GEORGE Baton, Cloupe (Gensdarmes)—Messrs HUME and SINCLAIR Marie, a poor Woman—Miss ATKINSON Clementine, daughter of Germuil—Mrs ANDREWS.

A Comic Song by Mr. HAYES.

The Entertainments will conclude with

GRUDGE, FUDGE, DUDGE, & TRUDGE!

Or, THE THREE CLERKS.

Characters by the Company.

Boxes, 1s 6d. Pit, 1s. Gallery, 6d.

Doors open at SEVEN, and to begin at Half-past. Half-price to Boxes only at Nine o'Clock. Children under Twelve Years of Age Half-price to all Parts of the Theatre. Shopkeepers will much oblige the Proprietor of this Establishment by Permitting the Bills to lie in their Windows. All Tradesmen's Bills to be sent in on SATURDAY, before Three o'Clock, for instant liquidation.

MR. MACFARREN, Stage Manager. [HEWISON, PRINTER.]

37

Fire of Genius

On Monday, 2 January 1860, the first number of a new theatre weekly, *The Players*, appeared: an issue still feeling its way, though the editor, in his fighting leader, expressed a wish 'to write impartially and consistently'. On the same page an anonymous critic, who had been on 19 December 1859 to Crosby Hall, Bishopsgate, reported 'the fire of genius' in an actor's dramatic reading of Bulwer's *The Lady of Lyons*. The actor, tall and raven-dark, was called Henry Irving, stage name of John Henry Brodribb of mingled Somerset and Cornish ancestry; he was then twenty-one years old. Though he had had a great many parts in the provinces, a few in Sunderland, the vast majority in Edinburgh, he had played only four professionally in London: all at the Princess's Theatre in the autumn of 1859 (one was Osric in *Hamlet*). True, in 1856, he had been an amateur Romeo —paying three guineas for the privilege—at the Royal Soho Theatre in Dean Street: there he used for the first time the name of Irving, not (and fortunately) as he had first intended, Baringtone.

None of the later London parts had helped very much. So it was a bold venture to take Crosby Hall for a night to read *The Lady of Lyons*: he had appeared as Claude Melnotte, the principal part, at his Edinburgh farewell 'benefit' in September. Earlier in the year, when he had hoped to give a reading of the same piece at Linlithgow, it had to be abandoned at the twelfth hour because no one arrived.

Still, at Crosby Hall, he had a good house and a genuine success: one that he repeated when he read Sheridan Knowles's *Virginius* in the same hall on 8 February. *The Players* reported later that he 'infused a degree of energy and passion into some of the passages worthy the most experienced actor'. The scene in which he stabbed Virginia was 'terribly real in its intensity and called forth the rapturous applause of its hearers'. Shortly after this he left for Dublin and a long provincial spell from which he did not return until the autumn of 1866 when he acted Doricourt in Mrs Cowley's *The Belle's Stratagem* (1780) at the St James's Theatre. That November he appeared as the villain in a new play by Dion Boucicault, *Hunted Down*. At the end 'George Eliot' said to G. H. Lewes, 'What do you think of him?' 'In twenty years,' Lewes replied, 'he will be at the head of the English stage.' 'He is there, I think, already,' she said.

The great artist's story is told definitively in *Henry Irving: The Actor and His World* (1951) by his grandson, Laurence Irving. But here now, from my volume of *The Players*, is the young man at Crosby Hall. *The Lady of Lyons; or, Love and Pride* (1838) was written by Edward Lytton Bulwer who became Bulwer Lytton. Its period is 1795; Glavis is one of the suitors rejected by the proud beauty, Pauline, who yields to the wooing of the peasant-born Claude Melnotte in the guise of the Prince of Como.

We all know the 'Dramatic Reading'. We have all—at least all who have served their apprenticeship to theatrical amusements —suffered the terrible infliction of the Dramatic Reader; but then with equal certainty we have all answered to the next gentleman's call of a 'Night with Shakespeare, with Readings, &c', and have again undergone the insufferable bore of hearing our dear old poet murdered by the aspiring genius. Thinking somewhat as we have above written the other evening, we wended our editorial way towards Crosby Hall, where our informant 'circular' assured us Mr Henry Irving was about to read Bulwer's *Lady of Lyons*. We asked ourselves who is Mr Henry Irving? and memory, rushing to some hidden cave in our mental structure, answered—Henry Irving, oh! yes, to be sure; how stupid! We at once recollected that Mr Irving was a gentleman of considerable talent, and a great favourite in the provinces. We have often seen his name honourably figuring in the columns of our provincial contemporaries. Now we were most agreeably disappointed on this present occasion; for instead of finding the usual conventional respectable-looking 'mediocrity', we were gratified by hearing the poetical 'Lady of Lyons' poetically read by a most accomplished elocutionist, who gave us not only words, but that finer indefinite something which proves, incontestably and instantaneously, that the fire of genius is present in the artist. It would be out of place now to speak of the merits of the piece selected by this gentleman; but the merits appeared as striking and the demerits as little, as on any occasion of the kind in our recollection. Claude's picture of his imaginary home was given with such poetic feeling as to elicit a loud burst of approval from his hearers, as also many other passages occurring in the play. The characters were well marked, especially Beauseant and Madame Deschappelles, whilst the little part of Glavis was very pleasingly given. Mr Irving was frequently interrupted by the applause of his numerous and delighted audience, and at the conclusion was unanimously called to receive their marks of approval.

The Players

A NEW TRAGEDY,
CALLED THE
PATRICIAN'S DAUGHTER,
WRITTEN BY
J. WESTLAND MARSTON, Esq.
Will be produced on THURSDAY.
The PROLOGUE written by
Mr. CHARLES DICKENS,
Will be Spoken by Mr. Macready.

The Earl of Lynterne, (a Statesman) Mr. PHELPS, Lord Chatterly, Mr. SELBY,
Sir Archer Taunton, Mr. M. BARNETT, Captain Pierpoint, Nephew of Lord Lynterne, Mr. HUDSON
Mordaunt, afterwards Sir Edgar Mordaunt, Mr. MACREADY,
Heartwell, Lister, } Politicians. { Mr. ELTON, Mr. G. BENNETT,
Deancourt, Colville, } Friends of Mordaunt: { Mr. W. H. BLAND, Mr. ROBERTS,
Physician, Mr. RYDER, Guests of Lord Lynterne, Mr. STANTON, Mr. HARCOURT, &c,
Mordaunt's Servant, Mr. C. J. SMITH, Notary, Mr. YARNOLD,
Lord Lynterne's Servants, Messrs. BENDER, BRADY, PAULO, &c.
Lady Mabel Lynterne, Daughter of the Earl, Miss HELEN FAUCIT,
Lady Lydia Lynterne, his Sister, Mrs. WARNER, Lady Chatterly, Miss ELLIS
Lady Taunton, Mrs. SELBY, Attendant on Lady Mabel, Mrs. WATSON.

VIVAT REGINA. W. S. Johnson, Printed Soho.

Play-bill for the Drury Lane production of *Patrician's Daughter*

38

To the Pit

This leading article appeared in the seventh number of *The Players* (13 February 1860), a weekly journal which lasted from 2 January 1860 to 20 July 1861, and was edited from the second number, for about eight months, by 'Wilfrid Wisgast, M.A.', pseudonym of Dr George Sexton. He left the chair with some dignity, observing that it was 'neither necessary nor desirable that, in the few words I have to say on this occasion, I should enter into those circumstances which have induced me to retire somewhat abruptly'. The Editor was versatile. As Wisgast, he was prepared to write entertainments and lectures, and 'to revise, edit, or correct for the press, the work of young authors'. As Sexton, he advertised his essay (price eighteenpence) on 'Hollingsworth and Modern Poetry'. It was reviewed at alarming length in the issue of 1 September 1860 by a critic who described Dr Sexton as 'a veritable Proteus in literature who is constantly appearing before the public in a new shape'; here he was rescuing from impending oblivion 'the fame of one of England's greatest poets' (the fame appears to have died). Proteus-Sexton also advertised his works on *The Human Hair and Beard*; and *Diseases of the Skin*—apparently printed together—and a defence of smoking, *The Great Tobacco Controversy*. Later he was 'open to engagements to lecture on scientific, literary, and social topics'. By then, however, a new Editor, a Mr J. B. Hopkins, had begun to enjoy himself by serialising his own abysmal tragedy, *The Yogi's Daughter* ('She draws near to Sona, pauses for a moment, then tears out his eyes') and an even more lamentable novel entitled *Public Charity*. Not surprisingly, the journal faded away.

Still, here is a leader from its Wisgast prime.

The nineteenth century has witnessed the advent of a class of preachers who, in their extreme antipathy to anything like amusement when presented on the stage, have endeavoured to furnish something to laugh at in their pulpits. The broad grin of low comedy is no longer confined to the play-house; it breaks out on Sundays in fashionable churches, amongst most pious audiences. Those lines of Wesley which a hundred years ago were considered amongst religious people to comprise nearly the whole duty of man, 'No room for mirth or trifling here', have been completely ignored—at all events, a new reading of them has been adopted. Our old friend, the clown, it appears, is no violator of the moral law if he makes his appearance in the pulpit. The dullest of all dull jokes, and the stalest of all forgotten witticisms, instead of being prohibited, are now made an essential part of sound divinity. Tragic preaching we have always been tolerably familiar with, but comic preaching is a modern phenomenon curious to observe and interesting to analyse. The Revd. C. H. Spurgeon probably stands at the head of this new school of joking divines. But his followers or imitators are legion. At Manchester, the Free Trade Hall is crowded every Sunday afternoon to hear a humorous sermon from the Revd. Arthur Mursell who seems to have so decided a comic taste that he even selects a funny text. On looking over the published discourses of this clerical disciple of Democritus, we find such texts selected as 'What ails thee?' 'Knocking at the door', 'Red, white, and blue', 'Silence in court', 'Here, there, and everywhere', 'The tricks of the trade' (his own trade, probably), 'Forbidding the banns', 'On Her Majesty's service', and many others of a kindred character. The one, however, in which we felt the greatest interest, was headed 'This way to the pit'. All these discourses are full of bits of slang, worn-out jokes, and the most wretched attempts at wit and humour, such as would hardly be tolerated on the stage of the lowest order of theatre. The Revd. gentleman, himself, did he make his debut as a clown or low comedian, would unquestionably fail for want of talent, notwithstanding his taste for 'something to laugh at'. With this, however, we have nothing to do; but what we could not help feeling some interest in, was the discourse with a theatrical heading. 'This way to the pit'—what does it mean, we said? Is Mr Mursell about to preach on the theatre and point out the superiority of the pit over the boxes and gallery, and at the same time to give instruction as to the readiest method of procuring a good seat in the former, without being squeezed to death? Or does he mean to condemn the pit, and to show that the way to get there is by spending your money at the public house, so as not to be able to afford a seat in the boxes? No, nothing of the kind. He commences:

> 'Such is the cry which the passenger down Oxford Street or the Strand will hear about seven o'clock in the evening as he passes by the Princess's or Adelphi Theatres, on Boxing Night.'

We were not aware before that the lessees of the respectable theatres named, were in the habit of adopting the course resorted to by the proprietors of penny shows at fairs, of placing men outside to shout and bawl of the performance about to commence, the price of admission, and the way to the pit. We are very old playgoers, but this is certainly something new to us. However, the Revd. gentleman is no doubt correct. He probably has had a Boxing Night experience in the pit, and is therefore entitled to speak with authority. But what more has he to say of the theatre?—oh! nothing. He flies off at once to treat of 'the ravings of the drunkard', 'the oath of passion', 'the impure jest', etc., etc., all of which are crying out, 'This way to the pit!' and to tell us that this momentous text lurks behind 'innocent and high sounding names', such as 'concert room, oyster shop, and cigar divan'. In a word, the pit of the theatre is symbolical of another pit which always stands in the foreground of these discourses, the description of which, though dealt with most minutely by our clerical comedian, we shall not attempt in our pages. There may be some resemblance between the two places for all we know to the contrary; we are not sufficiently acquainted with the latter to speak very decisively upon the subject. The pit of a theatre on Boxing Night is certainly anything but a comfortable place. It is by no means improbable that Virgil may have had his eye upon it when he penned those oft-quoted lines, describing the descent of Æneas:

> Facilis descensus Averni
> Sed revocare gradum superasque evadere ad auras,
> Hic labor sed opus est.

The labour of escaping from the crowd in a pit on Boxing Night, and the ease with which the moving mass carries you forward in entering, may have furnished the old Latin poet with the idea expressed in the above lines. At the same time we believe that Boxing Night is not the only night in the year, nor the theatre the only place, in which crowds trample each other in the mire in order to procure places. We have seen something very like it at old Covent Garden when an anti-Maynooth meeting has been held or a No Popery demonstration convened. We observed something approximating most closely to it no longer ago than last Sunday evening at the theatres opened for preaching. We have witnessed it at Exeter Hall over and over again, when gentlemen of the Revd. A. Mursell's stamp have been the principal actors. Why, therefore, is the pit of the theatre selected to illustrate the other and much deeper pit? Is it because it allows this clerical would-be humorist the opportunity of playing upon a word? If his penchant for punning be so great that he must have some word with a double meaning in his text, there is plenty of scope for him to display his powers without meddling with subjects which he clearly does not understand. Can he find nothing in his own chapel to symbolise the lower regions instead of taking the pit of the theatre? We could perhaps assist him, but that it would probably be considered profanity.

It is curious to observe the extreme dislike which these comic clergymen manifest against the theatre. They are even more inveterate against it than were the old sober-sided preachers who never tolerated a smile, and who looked upon a laugh as a heinous crime. Probably it is because the former fear rivalry. They are, no doubt, aware that if their congregations should once taste the genuine humour of a good farce or comedy, their own reputation for joking or wit would be gone for ever. Who could appreciate the wretched worn-out commonplace attempts to say something funny, seen in these discourses, but people who have no idea what real genuine wit is, nor where it is to be found?

'Wilfrid Wisgast'

THEATRE ROYAL,

Newcastle upon Tyne.

Lessee, Mr. JAMES MUNRO, No. 6, Grainger Street.

The Public is respectfully informed that in consequence of the **heavy Expense** attending the Engagement of The African Roscius, all complimentary **Orders must be suspended** (the Press excepted).

BRILLIANT RECEPTION

OF

THE AFRICAN ROSCIUS!

Whose personation of the difficult and opposite characters of OTHELLO and MUNGO created the greatest sensation, and who was received throughout with frequent bursts of Applause, by a Crowded Audience. The circumstance of a Man of Colour performing Othello on the British Stage is indeed an epoch in the history of Theatricals, and his having been called for after the performance by the unanimous voice of the Audience to receive their tribute of Applause is as highly creditable to the native talent of the sunny climes of Africa as to the universal liberality of a British Public.

ON THURSDAY EVENING, DEC. 18th, 1845,

Will be enacted Shakspeare's admired Comedy of THE

MERCHANT OF VENICE.

Duke of Venice,...... Mr COPPIN. Antonio,...... Mr T. MEAD. Bassanio,...... Mr MANLEY
Salanio,..... Mr YOUNG. Salarino,...... Mr THOMPSON Gratiano,...... Mr BUTLER FAUVARQUE. Lorenzo,..... Mr STINTON.

Shylock, - - - By the AFRICAN ROSCIUS.

Tubal, ... Mr. HUGHES. Launcelot Gobbo, ... Mr. WARE. Old Gobbo,.......... Mr SALTER Balthazar,........... Mr YOUNG
Portia,...... Mrs. W. RIGNOLD. Nerissa,...... Mrs WARE. Jessica,...... Miss SIMPSON.

To conclude with (received on Tuesday Evening with shouts of Laughter and Applause) the popular Farce of THE

VIRGINIAN MUMMY

Captain Rifle (of the Sharpshooters, serving on the Western Frontier, romantically attached to the Profession of Arms and the Ward of Doctor Galen),.................................... Mr. MANLEY.

Doctor Galen (an enthusiastic Compounder of the Elixir possessing the extraordinary quality of restoring Life, after being extinct three thousand Years, and in search of a Mummy),.................................... Mr. THOMPSON

Ginger Blue, an independent Nigger—Head Waiter—always absent when wanted, yet mindful of his Perquisites—remarkably familiar—bursting with Fun and Laughter—very industrious (by Deputy,) but receives all Gratuities in Person; a most accommodating Appetite, and love of Money induces him to become a MUMMY,.......... **By the AFRICAN ROSCIUS**

WHO WILL INTRODUCE THE FOLLOWING SONGS, &c.:—

SONG—"OPPOSUM UP A GUM TREE, OR THE NEGRO HUNT."

SONG—"The Negro's Address to his Mistress, or the Midnight Serenade."

AIR—"FANNY ELSSLER'S CACHUCHA."

Lucy (a sentimental young Lady, Ward of Doctor Galen, and attached to Captain Rifle),.................... Miss SIMPSON.

On Friday, will be performed a New Tragedy, written expressly for the African Roscius, by a Gentlemen of celebrity, in Dublin, entitled "**KARAFFA**;" Karaffa, by the AFRICAN ROSCIUS. After which a favourite Interlude. To conclude with a Drama of intense interest called "**OBI; or Three Fingered Jack**;" Obi, by the AFRICAN ROSCIUS, being the LAST NIGHT this popular and greatest Novelty in the Theatrical World can appear.

The Spectacle of "ALADDIN" is in preparation and will be shortly produced with New Scenery by Mr. FULLER, Machinery by Mr. GILL, and Dresses by Mr. ALLEN.

Newcastle upon Tyne: Printed by M. BENSON, No. 3, Foot of Dean Street.

39

Mr Waldengarver

This is the sad story of Mr Wopsle's Hamlet, as Charles Dickens tells it in the novel of *Great Expectations* (1861). Once clerk at the village church in the Kent marsh country down by the river, Wopsle had a Roman nose, a large shining bald forehead, and a deep voice; and he 'punished the "Amens" tremendously'. Years passed; he became 'the celebrated Provincial Amateur of Roscian renown' at a small metropolitan theatre. His stage name was Waldengarver. Pip, the book's hero, and his friend Herbert Pocket, attended a performance and found the Hamlet—as Herbert later expressed it with much tact—to be both 'massive and concrete'.

On our arrival in Denmark, we found the king and queen of that country elevated in two armchairs on a kitchen-table, holding a Court. The whole of the Danish nobility were in attendance, consisting of a noble boy in the wash-leather boots of a gigantic ancestor, a venerable Peer with a dirty face, who seemed to have risen from the people late in life, and the Danish chivalry with a comb in its hair and a pair of white silk legs, and presenting on the whole a feminine appearance. My gifted townsman stood gloomily apart, with folded arms, and I could have wished that his curls and forehead had been more probable.

Several curious little circumstances transpired as the action proceeded. The late king of the country not only appeared to have been troubled with a cough at the time of his decease, but to have taken it with him to the tomb and to have brought it back. The royal phantom also carried a ghostly manuscript round its truncheon, to which it had the appearance of occasionally referring, and that, too, with an air of anxiety and a tendency to lose the place of reference which were suggestive of a shade of mortality. It was this, I conceive, which led to the Shade's being advised by the gallery to 'turn over!'—a recommendation which it took extremely ill. It was likewise to be noted of this majestic spirit that where it always appeared with an air of having been out a long time and walked an immense distance, it perceptibly came from a closely-contiguous wall. This occasioned its terrors to be received derisively. The Queen of Denmark, a very buxom lady, though no doubt historically brazen, was considered by the public to have too much brass about her; her chin being attached to her diadem by a broad band of that metal (as if she had a gorgeous toothache), her waist being encircled by another, and each of her arms by another, so that she was openly mentioned as 'the kettledrum'. The noble boy in the ancestral boots was inconsistent; representing himself, as it were in one breath, as an able seaman, a strolling actor, a gravedigger, a clergyman, and a person of the utmost importance at a Court fencing-match, on the authority of whose practised eye and nice discrimination the finest strokes were judged. This gradually led to a want of toleration for him, and even—on his being detected in holy orders, and declining to perform the funeral service—to the general indignation taking the form of nuts. Lastly, Ophelia was a prey to such slow musical madness, that when, in course of time, she had taken off her white muslin scarf, folded it up, and buried it, a sulky man who had been long cooling his impatient nose against an iron bar in the front row of the gallery, growled, 'Now the baby's put to bed, let's have supper!' Which, to say the least of it, was out of keeping.

Upon my unfortunate townsman all these incidents accumulated with playful effect. Whenever that undecided Prince had to ask a question or state a doubt, the public helped him out with it. As for example; on the question whether 'twas nobler in the mind to suffer, some roared yes, and some no, and some inclining to both opinions said 'toss up for it', and quite a Debating Society arose. When he asked what should such fellows as he do crawling between earth and heaven, he was encouraged with loud cries of 'Hear, hear!' When he appeared with his stocking disordered (its disorder expressed, according to usage, by one very neat fold in the top, which I suppose to be always got up with a flat iron), a conversation took place in the gallery respecting the paleness of his leg, and whether it was occasioned by the turn the ghost had given him. On his taking the recorders —very like a little black flute that had just been played in the orchestra and handed out at the door—he was called upon unanimously for Rule Britannia. When he recommended the player not to saw the air thus, the sulky man said, 'And don't *you* do it, neither; you're a deal worse than *him*!' And I grieve to add that peals of laughter greeted Mr Wopsle on every one of these occasions.

But his greatest trials were in the churchyard: which had the appearance of a primeval forest, with a kind of small ecclesiastical wash-house on one side, and a turnpike gate on the other. Mr Wopsle, in a comprehensive black cloak, being descried entering at the turnpike, the gravedigger was admonished in a friendly way, 'Look out! here's the undertaker a-coming to see how you're getting on with your work.' I believe it is well known in a constitutional country that Mr Wopsle could not possibly have returned the skull, after moralising over it, without dusting his fingers on a white napkin taken from his breast; but even that innocent and indispensable action did not pass without the comment 'Wai-ter!' The arrival of the body for interment (in an empty black box with the lid tumbling open), was the signal for a general joy which was much enhanced by the discovery, among the bearers, of an individual obnoxious to identification. The joy attended Mr Wopsle through his struggle with Laertes on the brink of the orchestra and the grave, and slackened no more until he had tumbled the king off the kitchen-table, and had died by inches from the ankles upward.

We had made some pale attempts in the beginning to applaud Mr Wopsle; but they were too hopeless to be persisted in. Therefore we had sat, feeling keenly for him, but laughing, nevertheless, from ear to ear. I laughed in spite of myself all the time, the whole thing was so droll; and yet I had a latent impression that there was something decidedly fine in Mr Wopsle's elocution—not for old association's sake, I am afraid, but because it was very slow, very dreary, very uphill and downhill, and very unlike any way in which any man in any natural circumstances of life or death ever expressed himself about anything. When the tragedy was over, and he had been called for and hooted, I said to Herbert, 'Let us go at once or perhaps we shall meet him.'

We made all the haste we could downstairs, but we were not quick enough either . . .

Charles Dickens

40

Peculiar Drama

I have cherished this review of a 'peculiar drama' in which a villain is continually shooting somebody', the Angel of Death has a strenuous evening, and an anonymous critic (*The Players*, 8 June 1861) is in breathless trouble with his pronouns.

At this period the journal, with a new proprietor, had left Shoe Lane for Pounceby's Steam Printing Works in Leman Street, Whitechapel. Not so far off, in Shoreditch, the Standard Theatre, holding more than 3,000 people within its horseshoe, needed drama larger than life-size, a need its directors had not failed to gratify. At this time Alice Marriott (always 'Miss Marriott', though married to a theatre manager, Robert Edgar) was newly in command: a vigorous player with a capacious memory and given to performing Romeo and Juliet 'with equal ease and effect'. She was also a notable female Hamlet. 'The intonation of her rich musical voice and significant expression of countenance,' said the *Glasgow Bulletin*, 'can only be the result of profound study and correct appreciation.'

Invariably a ready tragedienne in the provinces and in London—she acted at Drury Lane, the Surrey, the Standard, and Sadler's Wells which she ran for a few years—it has been suggested that Pinero had her in mind when he created Mrs Telfer (Miss Violet Sylvester) in *Trelawny of the 'Wells'*. But she was a far more accomplished actress than Mrs Telfer would have been. Her son, Richard Horatio Edgar (1848–94)—the Horatio derived from *Hamlet*—appeared with her for a time; in 1875 he was the father, by an actress, Marie (Polly) Richards, of an illegitimate child, christened Richard Horatio Edgar, with the surname Wallace added as a blind. The paternal grandmother, Alice Marriott, who died on Christmas Day, 1900, aged 76, knew nothing of the boy who would become one day the novelist and dramatist, Edgar Wallace. He would have made a better job of the plot of *The Midnight Angel; or, Twelve o'Clock and the Spirit of Death.*

J. T. Douglass, the adapter, was the son of John Douglass, who had directed the Standard and who would again; Douglass Jr later succeeded his father in the new theatre (the first was destroyed by fire in October 1866).

The new drama entitled *The Midnight Angel; or, Twelve o'Clock and the Spirit of Death*, was produced at the Standard Theatre on Monday. The drama (which is an adaptation from the French) is by Mr J. T. Douglass, jun., and in six tableaux. It is styled a 'Peculiar drama', and we think it fully deserves the name. Of the piece we will only say that it was placed upon the stage with very great care, and with all due regard to scenery, which was indeed all that could be desired, and one scene especially (a grove of weeping willows) was met, as the curtain rose, with a perfect burst of applause from the immensely crowded house. The piece was powerfully cast, embracing the names of those established favourites, Miss Marriott, Henry Sinclair, Frederick Villiers, Mr O'Sullivan, and Mr John Neville.

The chief attraction in the drama is Miss Marriott, who undertakes the arduous task of representing five different characters. We first see her appearing to Gaston de Bressane, a young physician (Henry Sinclair) as the Midnight Angel of Death, and so motionless did she stand, as he gazes upon her in wonder, and so beautiful did she look, that the audience could not restrain themselves, but burst into a tremendous round of applause, and some seconds elapsed before he could be heard addressing her. We next see her as a Clerk, amazing all around her by relating what was going on in the adjoining sick chamber of the Count de Prix (Mr John Neville), and here it is that the angel of death claims her victim as the clock strikes twelve, in the person of Pagio, a centenarian (Mr T. B. Bennett). The third character she represents is Love at a masquerade ball, where she captivates Raymond, son of Count de Prix (Mr O'Sullivan) with all the loveliness this charming *artiste* really possesses. Next we see her as a Woodcutter at a duel, which takes place between Baron Struelino (Mr F. Villiers) and Gaston de Bressane, where she rapidly changes into the Angel of Death, and claims the second victim, which change is rapturously appreciated by the audience. The fifth character she impersonates is the Spirit of Death, hovering over her prey the bride of Gaston de Bressane (Miss Mandlebert), and here the drama ends.

The plot of this peculiar drama is this. A young physician is introduced into the play very poor, owing, as he says, to the presence of a quack doctor, who has appropriated the works and other productions of his brain to his use, and has got the credit of being *the* doctor to the extinction of all support to the one he has thus robbed. At this portion of the play he is tempted by a desperate villain, Baron Struelino, to become his doctor. This villain was continually shooting somebody, half-killing his servants and all others who came in his way, and he thus found himself in need of a doctor to attend to their wounds, the offer of which situation he makes to Gaston de Bressane, who scorns it, of course, and commands the Baron to leave the house. The Quack (Mr R. Norman) also makes him a dishonourable offer, and is passionately refused; and after some assistance from his friend Raymond, they adjourn to 'La Taverne', where the young physician first beholds the Angel of Death and enters into a compact with her, namely that wherever at a death-bed he was attending, he saw her there and her hand raised, he was to cease all assistance, and let her claim her victim. He leaves his mother in her power as hostage, for the fulfilment of the compact, and swoons.

The Baron Struelino whose father (as he believes) has been murdered by the Count de Prix, at a masquerade ball, appears at the sick chamber of that nobleman in the dress of Satan—the same dress his father was assassinated in—and it is at this point of the play he expects to hear the dying man make a confession, or rather to force one from him. The Angel of Death here appears as a clerk, defies the young physician to administer to the aid of a dying man by uplifting her hand; all is here cleared up respecting the death of the Baron's father, by the young physician who is in possession of the facts, proving that death was caused from natural causes which had taken place before the pistol the Count de Prix confessed to have fired, had taken effect. Twelve o'clock here strikes, the Angel of Death's hand descends, and is uplifted to the head of the Centenarian who falls dead at the last stroke.

The Baron is in love with the daughter of the Count de Prix, as is also the young physician, and at length the rivalry ends in a duel, first with her brother Raymond whom the Baron wounds, and next with her lover, Gaston de Bressane. The duel takes place amid the falling snow, and the Angel of Death in the guise of a woodcutter, hovers o'er her second victim: he is mortally wounded by Gaston de Bressane, and deserted by all but the Angel of Death, who hovers around him as the snow is quickly covering him in his death struggle. He dies, and Gaston is about to marry his bride when the Angel of Death appears in the chapel and strikes the bride, who sinks into the arms of her betrothed. He begs to be left alone, and the Angel of Death, unseen by anyone but him, stands with her hand uplifted. A very affecting scene here ensues between the Angel of Death and the young bridegroom, who at first beseeches her to take his mother, all but to spare his love, but at last offers to resign her, imploring the angel to resign the hostage his mother. The angel stands all this while motionless; at length she slowly drops her hand, and, as the hour of twelve chimes, the Spirit of Death announces that their compact is broken, his science has triumphed over death, and that his mother is free. The marriage party are all joined in happiness, and here ensues a grand apotheosis: the Angel of Death, in company with other angels, is seen to ascend.

Here ended this extraordinary drama, a parallel for the effects and scenic displays of which we have not seen placed upon the Standard stage for years. The parts throughout were well sustained, and the applause at some of the fine points of Miss Marriott's acting was indeed deafening, and that lady was called no less than four times before the curtain to receive the approbation of an appreciative audience. This charming actress seems to be gaining in favour every time she appears, and she has now been starring at this theatre upwards of a twelvemonth . . .

The performance ended with the successful drama of *Ireland as It Was*, introducing those now established favourites, Mr O'Sullivan and Miss Mendelhurst. The house was crowded to the very ceiling.

The Players

MADAME CELESTE AS MIAMI.
IN
MR. BUCKSTONE'S DRAMA OF THE GREEN BUSHES.
"Oh I could not bear to think you ever loved another."
Act 2. Sc. 1.

Engraved by Hollis from a Daguerreotype by Mayall
For Tallis's Drawing Room Table Book of Theatrical Portraits, Memoirs, and Anecdotes.

JOHN TALLIS & COMPANY, LONDON & NEW YORK.

41

Rachel

This, printed in 1867, is the third in the trinity of sonnets that Matthew Arnold (1822–88) wrote in memory of the great French tragic actress, Rachel (Elisabeth-Rachel Félix, 1821–58). Born of a poor French-Jewish family—her parents were pedlars—her art was as extraordinary as her life, with its many liaisons, was fevered. She died of consumption at her villa in the South of France.

Of all people, Charlotte Brontë (1816–55) left a famous memory in the twenty-third chapter of *Villette* (1853). There, in the theatre at Villette (Brussels), the heroine, Lucy Snowe, sees a tragic actress who is not named:

> . . . I found upon her something neither of woman nor of man; in each of her eyes sat a devil. These evil forces bore her through the tragedy, kept up her feeble strength—for she is but a frail creature; and as the action rose and the stir deepened, how wildly they shook her with the passions of the pit! They wrote *Hell* on her straight haughty brow. They tuned her voice to the note of torment. They writhed her regal face to a demoniac mask. Hate and murder and madness incarnate she stood. It was a marvellous sight, a mighty revelation . . .

That, allegedly, was Rachel in 1842. Charlotte Brontë saw her in London during 1851 (Corneille's Camille) and wrote, at various times: 'A wonderful sight . . . she made me shudder to the marrow of my bones,' and 'It is scarcely human nature that she shows you; it is something wilder and worse; the feelings and fury of a fiend.'

One of my favourite index entries, under 'Rachel, Mlle, French actress', in an edition of Mrs Gaskell's *Life of Charlotte Brontë*, directs one to the phrase, '[he] had begun his service to her in the same tender and faithful spirit as that in which Jacob served for Rachel'.

Sprung from the blood of Israel's scatter'd race,
At a mean inn in German Aarau born,
To forms from antique Greece and Rome uptorn,
Trick'd out with a Parisian speech and face,

Departing life renew'd, old classic grace;
Then soothing with thy Christian strain forlorn,
A-Kempis! her departing soul outworn,
While by her bedside Hebrew rites have place—

Ah, not the radiant spirit of Greece alone
She had—one power which made her breast its home!
In her, like us, there clash'd, contending powers,

Germany, France, Christ, Moses, Athens, Rome.
The strife, the mixture in her soul, are ours;
Her genius and her glory are her own.

Matthew Arnold

42

Man and Prince

The actor was Henry Irving (1838–1905); the place, the Lyceum Theatre, London, on the night of 31 October 1874; the critic, Clement William Scott (1841–1904). Irving, not yet in management himself—this would begin in 1878—was moving into the full splendour that, for thirty years, accompanied his name at the summit of the English stage.

Clement Scott, who wrote for so long in the *Daily Telegraph*, and from 1880–9 also edited *The Theatre*, is remembered too often as an opponent of Ibsen. But, in spite of his occasional blindness, his vanity and his floridity—very much of the period—he knew the theatre from all sides and he could be a most valuable, as well as copious, impressionist critic. See his *From 'The Bells' to 'King Arthur'* (1896) from which this extract is taken.

Henry Compton (Charles Mackenzie, 1805–77) was notable for his Shakespearian clowns; he was the grandfather of Compton Mackenzie and Fay Compton, and father-in-law of R. C. Carton, the dramatist.

All present longed to see Hamlet. Bernardo and Marcellus, the Ghost, the platform, the grim preliminaries, the prologue or introduction to the wonderful story, were, as usual, tolerated —nothing more. Away go the platform, the green lights, the softly-stepping spirit, the musical-voiced Horatio. The scene changes to a dazzling interior, broken in its artistic lines, and rich with architectural beauty; the harps sound, the procession is commenced, the jewels, and crowns, and sceptres, dazzle, and at the end of the train comes Hamlet. Mark him well, though from this instant the eyes will never be removed from his absorbing figure . . . How is he dressed, and how does he look? No imitation of the portrait of Sir Thomas Lawrence, no funereal velvet, no elaborate trappings, no Order of the Danish Elephant, no flaxen wig after the model of M. Fechter, no bugles, no stilted conventionality. We see before us a man and a prince, in thick robed silk and a jacket, or paletot, edged with fur; a tall, imposing figure, so well dressed that nothing distracts the eye from the wonderful face; a costume rich and simple, and relieved alone by a heavy chain of gold; but, above and beyond all, a troubled, wearied face displaying the first effects of moral poison.

The black disordered hair is carelessly tossed about the forehead, but the fixed and rapt attention of the whole house is directed to the eyes of Hamlet: the eyes which denote the trouble—which tell of the distracted mind. Here are 'the windy suspiration of forced breath', 'the fruitful river in the eye', the 'dejected 'haviour of the visage'. So subtle is the actor's art, so intense is his application, and so daring his disregard of conventionality, that the first act ends with comparative disappointment. Those who have seen other Hamlets are aghast. Mr Irving is missing his point, he is neglecting his opportunities. Betterton's face turned as white as his neckcloth when he saw the Ghost. Garrick thrilled the house when he followed the spirit. Some cannot hear Mr Irving, others find him indistinct. Many declare roundly he cannot read Shakespeare. There are others who generously observe that Hamlets are not judged by the first act; but over all, disputants or enthusiasts, has already been thrown an indescribable spell. None can explain it; but all are now spellbound. The Hamlet is 'thinking aloud', as Hazlitt wished. He is as much of the gentleman and scholar as possible, and 'as little of the actor'.

We in the audience see the mind of Hamlet. We care little what he does, how he walks, when he draws his sword. We can almost realise the workings of his brain. His soliloquies are not spoken at the footlights down to the audience. Hamlet is looking into a glass, into 'his mind's eye, Horatio'. His eyes are fixed apparently on nothing, though ever eloquent. He gazes on vacancy and communes with his conscience. Those only who have closely watched Hamlet through the first act could adequately express the impression made. But it has affected the whole audience—the Kemble lovers, the Kean admirers, and the Fechter rhapsodists. They do not know how it is, but they are spellbound with the incomparable expression of moral poison.

The second act ends with nearly the same result. There is not an actor living who on attempting Hamlet has not made his points in the speech, 'Oh! what a rogue and peasant slave am I!' But Mr Irving's intention is not to make points, but to give a consistent reading of a Hamlet who 'thinks aloud'. For one instant he falls 'a-cursing like a very drab, a scullion'; but only to relapse into a deeper despair, into more profound thought. He is not acting, he is not splitting the ears of the groundlings; he is an artist concealing his art; he is talking to himself; he is thinking aloud. Hamlet is suffering from moral poison, and the spell woven about the audience is more mysterious and incomprehensible in the second act than the first.

In the third act the artist triumphs. No more doubt, no more hesitation, no more discussion. If Hamlet is to be played like a scholar and a gentleman, and not like an actor, this is the Hamlet. The scene with Ophelia turns the scale, and the success is from this instant complete. But we must insist that it was not the triumph of an actor alone; it was the realisation of all that the artist has been foreshadowing. Mr Irving made no sudden and striking effect, as did Mr Kean. 'Whatever nice faults might be found on this score,' says Hazlitt, 'they are amply redeemed by the manner of his coming back after he has gone to the extremity of the stage, from a pang of parting tenderness to press his lips to Ophelia's hand. It had an electrical effect on the house.' Mr Irving did not make his success by any theatrical *coup*, but by the expression of the pent-up agony of a harassed and disappointed man. According to Mr Irving, the very sight of Ophelia is the keynote of the outburst of his moral disturbance. He loves this woman; 'forty thousand brothers' could not express his overwhelming passion, and think what might have happened if he had been allowed to love her, if his ambition had been realised. The more he looks at Ophelia, the more he curses the irony of fate. He is surrounded, overwhelmed, and crushed by trouble, annoyance, and spies.

They are watching him behind the arras. Ophelia is set on to assist their plot. They are driving him mad, though he is only feigning madness. What a position for a harassed creature to endure! They are all against him. Hamlet alone in the world is born to 'set it right'. He is in the height and delirium of moral anguish. The distraction of the unhinged mind, swinging and banging about like a door; the infinite love and tenderness of the man who longs to be soft and gentle to the woman he adores: the horror and hatred of being trapped, and watched, and spied upon were all expressed with consummate art. Every voice cheered, and the points Mr Irving had lost as an actor were amply atoned for by his earnestness as an artist. Fortified with this genuine and heart-stirring applause, he rose to the occasion. He had been understood at last. To have broken down here would have been disheartening; but he had triumphed.

The speech to the players was Mr Irving's second success. He did not sit down and lecture. There was no affectation or princely priggishness in the scene at all. He did not give his ideas of art as a prince to an actor, but as an artist to an artist. Mr Irving, to put it colloquially, buttonholed the First Player. He spoke to him confidentially, as one man to another. He stood up and took the actor into his confidence, with a half deferential smile, as much as to say, 'I do not attempt to dictate to an artist, but still these are my views on art.' But with all this there was a princely air, a kindly courtesy, and an exquisite expression of refinement, which astonished the house as much from its daring as its truth. Mr Irving was gaining ground with marvellous rapidity. His exquisite expression of friendship for Horatio was no less beautiful than his stifled passion for Ophelia. For the one he was the pure and constant friend, for the other the baffled lover.

Determined not to be conquered by his predecessors, he made a signal success in the play scene. He acted it with an impulsive energy beyond all praise. Point after point was made in a whirlwind of excitement. He lured, he tempted, he trapped the King, he drove out his wicked uncle conscience-stricken and baffled, and with a hysterical yell of triumph he sank down, 'the expectancy and rose of the fair state', in the very throne which ought to have been his, and which his rival had just vacated. It is difficult to describe the excitement occasioned by the acting in this scene. When the King had been frighted, the stage was cleared instantaneously. No one in the house knew how the people got off. All eyes were fixed on Hamlet and the King; all were forgetting the real play and the mock play, following up every move of the antagonists, and from constant watching they were almost as exhausted as Hamlet was when he sank a conqueror into the neglected throne.

It was all over now. Hamlet had won. He would take the ghost's word for a thousand pounds. The clouds cleared from his brow. He was no longer in doubt or despair. He was the victor after this mental struggle. The effects of the moral poison had passed away, and he attacked Rosencrantz and Guildenstern in the Recorder scene with a sarcasm and withering scorn which were among the results of a reaction after pent-up agony. But this tremendous act was even now not yet over. There was the closet scene still to come—a scene which still further illustrates the daring defiance of theatrical tradition exhibited by Mr Irving. If the Hamlet was to be a mental study it should be one to the last. The actor who could conquer prejudices so far was bound to continue, and when the audience looked at the arras for the pictures, or round the necks of the actor and actress for the counterfeit presentment of two brothers, they found nothing.

Mr Irving intended to conjure up the features of the dead King by a mental struggle, not by any practical or painted assistance. Speaking of David Garrick, Mr Percy Fitzgerald says, 'It was a pity he did not break through the stale old tradition of Hamlet's pulling out the two miniatures instead of the finer notion suggested by Davies of having them on the tapestry *—or the better idea still of seeing them with the mind's eye only.*' It is this idea which Mr Irving adopts, and with so striking a success that the audience could scarcely believe that they had been for so many years misled. It is unquestionably the correct view to take, and it can be done with the best possible effect. An act which was such an intellectual strain as this for both actor and audience could not fail to be felt. It was exhausting, overpowering . . .

The strain upon the nervous system of Mr Irving upon so important an occasion, the growing lateness of the hour, and the wealth of beauty in the play, prevented the success which will yet be obtained by Ophelia's mad scene, by Mr Compton's acting of the Clown, or Gravedigger, and by Hamlet's churchyard passion. But let it not for a moment be supposed that *Hamlet* ended in an anticlimax. A fencing scene which would have rejoiced the heart of M. Angelo . . . to say nothing of the murder of the King by Hamlet, which, as regards impulse, determination, and effect, has never been equalled, put the final touches to this overwhelming work . . . a performance which will make its mark in the dramatic history of our time. The position of Mr Irving, occasionally wavering and pleasantly hesitating in the balance, has now been firmly established. The Hamlet of Henry Irving is a noble contribution to dramatic art.

Clement Scott

43

Portia

Oscar Wilde (1856–1900), as a young man, wrote this sonnet to Ellen Terry, then in her first Lyceum Theatre glory; she had joined Henry Irving at the end of 1878. Wilde had celebrated her Henrietta Maria in *Charles I*; here now was Portia which she first played, to Irving's Shylock, at the Lyceum on 1 November 1879. The poet was among the 350 guests at a Lyceum reception in the following February on the night of the hundredth performance. His theatrical sense was not always true. Thus a sonnet to Irving included the unlucky phrase, hardly applicable to the actor's strange, subtle voice, 'Thou trumpet set for Shakespeare's lips to blow.'

Ellen Terry, born at Coventry in 1847, died at Smallhythe, Kent, in 1928.

I marvel not Bassanio was so bold
To peril all he had upon the lead,
Or that proud Aragon bent low his head,
Or that Morocco's fiery heart grew cold;
For in that gorgeous dress of beaten gold
Which is more gorgeous than the golden sun,
No woman Veronese looked upon
Was half so fair as thou whom I behold.
Yet fairer when with wisdom as your shield
The sober-suited lawyer's gown you donned,
And would not let the laws of Venice yield
Antonio's heart to that accursed Jew—
O Portia! take my heart! it is thy due:
I think I will not quarrel with the Bond.

Oscar Wilde

44

Strictly Personal

Edward Dutton Cook (1830–83) was a practised Victorian drama critic—at first for the *Pall Mall Gazette*, later for *The World*—and a prolific and informed miscellaneous writer. We quote now from his posthumously published volume of essays, *On the Stage*. Among the people mentioned are Charles Mathews, Sn (1776–1835), actor and entertainer; Charles Macklin (*c*1700–97), celebrated Shylock; James Quin (1693–1766), declamatory tragedian; Richard ('Gentleman') Jones, comedian (1778–1851); William Bodham Donne (1801–82), fifth Examiner of Stage Plays; William Augustus ('Handsome') Conway (1789–1828), who committed suicide by drowning; and Charles Albert Fechter (1824–79), Lewes's 'lymphatic, delicate' Hamlet, with his 'long flaxen curls, quivering nostrils, fine eyes, and sympathetic voice'.

Acting is so personal and physical a matter that mannerism is inevitable to it. The player is involved in the character he sustains, and invests it with his own peculiarities of aspect and conduct. Now and then an actor may succeed for a time in discarding, as it were, his own individuality, in so changing himself as to escape identification. It was said of the elder Mathews that he possessed the 'art of extracting his personal nature from his assumptions', insomuch that 'he was always least happy when he had nothing to assume', and that 'in a plain straightforward part, where he had only to speak in his own personal character, he was scarcely above mediocrity'. Mimetic power of this kind is, of course, very rare, nor is it likely that it could be effected in relation to the loftier efforts of the drama.

Assuredly the performances of our greatest actors have been marked by a confirmed mannerism. It could hardly be said of them that they extracted their personal nature from their assumptions. We read of Betterton that his voice was low and grumbling, though he could tune it by an 'artful climax' so as to enforce attention even from the fops and orange-girls; that his 'fat short arms were rarely lifted higher than his stomach; his left hand frequently lodged in his breast, whilst with his right he prepared his speech'. Quin's action, we are told, was either forced or languid, his movement ponderous or sluggish; he was prone to long pauses, and to an artificial or cadenced delivery. According to Macklin's spiteful criticism, Garrick's 'art in acting consisted in incessantly pawing and hauling about the characters with whom he was concerned in the scene; and when he did not paw or haul the characters about, he stalked between them and the audience . . . squeezed his hat, hung forward and stood almost upon one foot, with no part of the other to the ground but the toe of it; his whole action when he made love in tragedy or in comedy, when he was familiar with his friend, when he was in anger, sorrow, rage, consisted in squeezing his hat, thumping his breast, strutting up and down the stage, and pawing the characters that he acted with.'

Mrs Crawford described the histrionic methods of the

Kembles as 'all paw and pause'. Edmund Kean's acting was abundantly mannered, for all its brilliancy and genius. His alternation of long pauses and rapid utterances bordered on the verge of extravagance; his familiarity of speech and abruptness of gesture were often ludicrous in effect. Of a special instance, Hazlitt notes that 'the motion was performed and the words uttered in the smallest possible time in which a puppet could be made to mimic or gabble the part'. It was Coleridge, I think, who said of Edmund Kean's acting that it was like reading Shakespeare by flashes of lightning; an equivocal compliment after all, for a more uncomfortable mode of studying a poet could not be conceived. Of Macready's mannerisms it is scarcely necessary to speak. He was, as all who recollect him will readily acknowledge, curiously angular of attitude and stilted of gait; as Mr Donne, the late Examiner of Plays, has written, he was 'unquestionably a man of genius, and as unquestionably, in our judgment, he inoculated his profession with a style of elocution which sets poetry, music, and nature alike at defiance'.

There is danger, of course, of the physical conditions under which an actor may labour being classed among habits or vices of manner. To some, perhaps, the squint of Talma or the lameness of Foote seemed liable to critical approach as mannerisms. John Kemble might possibly have mended his system of pronunciation could he have been convinced of its erroneousness; but his hollow tones and 'foggy throat' were certainly beyond his control. Hazlitt remarks upon the set of ingenious persons, who, having discovered that Kean was of small size and inharmonious voice, of no very great dignity or elegance of manner, went regularly to the theatre 'to confirm themselves in this piece of sagacity'. Yet Hazlitt was himself chargeable with similarly defective criticism when he complained of Jones, the popular light comedian, that he was always 'the same Mr Jones, who shows his teeth, and rolls his eyes, and looks like a jackdaw just caught in a snare'; and when he descanted so frequently upon the tall stature of Conway. Probably Mr Jones could not help rolling his eyes or showing his teeth, or, from the point of view of Hazlitt, looking like a snared jackdaw; if Kean could not add a cubit to his stature, neither could Conway decrease his height. It may be noted, indeed, that Conway, feeling himself personally injured by the observations of the critic, called upon him for an explanation, and obtained a disavowal in the following terms: 'Some expressions in my view of the English stage relating to Mr Conway having been construed to imply personal disrespect to that gentleman and to hold him up to ridicule, not as an actor, but as a man, I utterly disclaim any such intention or meaning in the work alluded to; the whole of what there is said being strictly intended to apply to his appearance in certain characters on the stage and to his qualifications or defects as a candidate for theatrical disapprobation. *W. Hazlitt.* May 24, 1818.'

How far a performance is injured by peculiarities of manner, each spectator must decide for himself. . . . The public may have always something to forgive the players; but forgiveness has rarely been denied to them. In less than a quarter of an hour Mr Fechter's English audiences accommodated themselves to his French accent; Mr Betterton's Hamlet, probably in a very few minutes, constrained the spectators to forgetfulness concerning the actor's age and clumsiness of form and manifold infirmities. And as much may be said, without doubt, of later representations of Hamlet and of other characters.

Dutton Cook

45

No Excuse

When the Shelley Society was founded in 1886, it decided to stage *The Cenci* (1819), tragedy of incest, parricide, and retribution. This was founded upon the horrors of 1599, during the Pontificate of Clement VIII, which ended in the destruction of one of the noblest families of Rome. Because the Lord Chamberlain withheld a licence, the production had to be technically in private. Eventually, the organisers secured the Grand at Islington, and there on 7 May, the 74th birthday of Robert Browning (who was present), the tragedy was performed. The audience included such figures as George Meredith, James Russell Lowell, Bernard Shaw (then only 29), and Henry Arthur Jones. Alma Murray (1854–1945) played Beatrice who, with her stepmother, is driven to murder, and Hermann Vezin (1829–1910) the Count, violent, cruel, and incestuously passionate. In the theatre, clearly an exciting occasion; but newspaper critics must have a little dashed the spirits of the Society. The notice that follows is from *The Theatre* (then edited by Clement Scott) of 1 June 1886; it was written by the journalist and author, Austin Brereton (1862–1922).

Sybil Thorndike played Beatrice superbly at the New Theatre, London, in Lewis Casson's production (1922; brief Empire Theatre revival in 1926). Robert Farquharson was originally the Count, and Hubert Carter took up the part at the Empire: in the second cast, as Orsino's Servant, was Laurence Olivier. In 1959, at the Old Vic, Barbara Jefford, among our best classical players, acted Beatrice to the Count of Hugh Griffith. One might have said of the newest Beatrice, as of Dame Sybil's, in a borrowing from Shelley: 'One of the rare persons in whom energy and gentleness dwell without destroying each other.'

This was the first and probably the last performance of the most repulsive play that has been produced this century. For even if the enthusiastic members of the Shelley Society purposed again acting *The Cenci*, it is more than likely that a repetition of the tragedy in anything like so public a manner as that accorded to it at Islington would be forbidden by the licenser of plays, inasmuch as the payment of a guinea to the Shelley Society constitutes membership, and, consequently, the privilege of witnessing its stage representations. The guinea a year also entitles the subscriber to bring a friend to each performance. This attempt to evade the law is somewhat similar to that practised in the old days of unlicensed theatres, when a charge was made for admission to a concert, the theatrical entertainment being 'given *gratis* by persons for their diversion'. Such an excuse would avail but little now, and the Shelley Society, we may rest assured, would hardly venture upon a second presentation of a tragedy which has no excuse for its existence.

'To excite pity and terror' is doubtless a laudable ambition on the part of a poet, but it is not the all in all of a tragedy. Tragedy should ennoble; it should, as Messrs Alfred and Buxton Forman rightly urge, purify the passions. But no elevation of the mind, no purification, can arise from the contemplation of that which is mere horror and abomination, unrelieved by sympathy. It is difficult to see where good can come from working on the vile criminal passion of a man who is little short of a monster—a man in outward semblance only—and the consequence of his loathsome degradation. There would have been some slight excuse for this sad exhibition had Shelley's play contained any grand language, any lofty thought, or any special theatrical effectiveness. But in none of these respects is it noteworthy. Its 'word-painting' has no particular excellence, and, regarded as a stage-play, it is positively ineffective. The construction throughout is weak, displaying a very inexperienced hand indeed; the real climax to the piece, the death of the Count Cenci, strongly reminds one of the murder scene in *Macbeth*; but even after this imitation of Shakespeare the greater parts of two acts are occupied by the heroine, whom everyone knows to be guilty of her father's murder, proclaiming her innocence of it; and Beatrice also strongly asserts at one time that she has been foully outraged, while on another occasion she declares herself to be as spotless as the driven snow.

These are blemishes that ought to be patent to those least inexperienced in the matter of plays; and yet *The Cenci* is acted, despite the repulsive nature of its story, its weakness of language, and its absolute unfitness, in other respects, for representation on the stage. And all to do honour to Shelley. Honour, forsooth! The only result of this silly experiment of the Shelley Society has been to bring dishonour down on the devoted head of their departed hero, whose name must henceforward be recorded in theatrical annals in conjunction with the least reputable of its records. To those who respect the stage and sympathise with its more laudable efforts, it must be a matter of sincere congratulation that this injudicious step received but scant support from those directly connected with the theatre.

Austin Brereton

MR. CRESWICK AS HOTSPUR.

HOT: Ha! you shall see now, in very sincerity of fear and cold heart, will he to the king and lay open all our proceedings.

KING HENRY IV. *Part 1, Act 2, Sc. 3.*

46

London Assurance

This piece on the 1890 revival of *London Assurance*, at the Criterion, appeared in a volume of *Playhouse Impressions* (1892) by Arthur Bingham Walkley, who then wrote principally for *The Speaker*, *The National Observer*, and *The Star*. From 1900 to 1926 he was drama critic of *The Times*, an elegant, classically minded writer, always more at home with the quality of the plays than with their players. A Civil Servant (various Post Office appointments), a lover of France, and in his spare time an apple-grower, he appears in the Introduction and Epilogue of Shaw's *Fanny's First Play* as the critic Trotter: 'Wears diplomatic dress, with sword and three-cornered hat.'

I met *London Assurance* first in the mid-1920s, acted by a provincial repertory company and treated as a near-classic. Yet by the time of its Royal Shakespeare Company revival, in a drastic but successful adaptation during 1970, the comedy had been practically forgotten. It was regarded indeed as a discovery. Ronald Eyre controlled his changes of structure and language so well that I imagine this will be the definitive future text.

Dion Boucicault (1820–90) was born in Dublin, probably son of the encyclopaedist Dr Dionysius Lardner, by his mistress Anne Boursiquot, sister of George Darley, the poet-dramatist. By 1838 Dion was acting, as Lee Moreton, in an English provincial stock company at Cheltenham; he had already written one play when Madame Vestris (with exciting new scenery to help) presented *London Assurance* at Covent Garden during the spring season of 1841; Louisa Nisbett, with whom Boucicault was infatuated, played Lady Gay Spanker. He was then twenty (not nineteen as Walkley says):

the play triumphed, and Boucicault, who would be known through life as an expert technician in the theatres of New York and London—he put together about 200 plays—would find that it remained his best-known work, with the three Irish dramas of *The Colleen Bawn* (1860), *Arrah-na-Pogue* (1864), and *The Shaughraun* (1874). His life was complicated and amorous. So, amusingly, is the comedy of *London Assurance*, braced by a variety of love affairs.

It had had nine London revivals since the 1841 production (Charles Mathews as Dazzle, William Farren as Sir Harcourt, Mrs Nisbett as Lady Gay) when the RSC took it up in the Eyre version. In their time Lady Gay and Sir Harcourt had become show-pieces. Walkley, reviewing the comedy in November 1890, does not mention the principal players, Charles Wyndham and Mrs Bernard Beere. This was the last London revival, for a run, before the RSC's, but it had an all-star performance in aid of King George's Pension Fund for Actors and Actresses, at the St James's in 1913, and it held its place for a time with repertory companies.

At the Aldwych in June 1970 I felt that this most mercurial of artificial comedies could have been re-named Gay Spanker. It was lucky in its cast, especially in Donald Sinden's massive, pouting Narcissus, Sir Harcourt Courtly, vainest of elderly bucks, who looked like the Prince Regent crossed with Max Beerbohm's Lord George Hell; Elizabeth Spriggs's horsey Lady Gay, with the exhilaration of a cross-country canter; Judi Dench as the articulate heroine, cunningly refreshed by actress and director; Michael Williams as one of the more involved heroes, and Barrie Ingham as the ubiquitous Dazzle with all of Alfred Jingle's resource.

Good; but Walkley here is writing in 1890. *The Love Chase* (1837), which he mentions, was by Sheridan Knowles (1784–1862), author of Macready's favourite *Virginius*. Charles Wyndham (1837–1919) was knighted in 1902.

In a letter to Monckton Milnes, who had found his patience overtaxed by some of the nicknames too freely bestowed upon him by his friends, Sydney Smith writes: 'The names of "Cool of the Evening", "London Assurance", and "In-i-go Jones", are, I give you my word, not mine.' This was in 1842, and the choice of at least one of the nicknames attests the vogue of a comedy which had been produced at Covent Garden in the previous year—*London Assurance*—by a youngster of nineteen who afterwards called himself Dion Boucicault. In the ensuing half-century the popularity of the piece has slowly dwindled, but never quite to vanishing point. Its vitality, persistent if feeble, has puzzled observers who do not allow for the peculiar conditions of the stage. It is not a classic, say these. It is not literature. It is not life.

The truth is that *London Assurance*, though it has no pretensions to being an organic whole or to holding the mirror up to nature, belongs to a class of plays which the players themselves, despite the indifference of playgoers, will not willingly let die. It is what is known as an actors' play—in this connection the word might perhaps be more correctly written display—a medium, that is, for the exercise of virtuosity—an affair of *bravura* passages, wherein the technical execution is everything and the subject-matter nothing, or next to nothing. Such plays may be taken as the actors' refutation of Euclid, for their aim is to show that a 'point' has magnitude, and that a 'part' is sometimes greater than the whole. Assuredly it is so with *London Assurance*, in regard to which play the wise man may ask the question, How will Lady Gay Spanker deliver the 'Steeplechase speech?' or how will the 'business' between Cool and Meddle be managed? but will at once perceive that to pursue his inquiries into the naturalness of this or that personage, into the credibility of the play as a whole, would be sheer waste of time.

That is the conventional critical standpoint on the subject—and, having adopted it, I feel instantly tempted to shift my ground. Is the play so very unreal as a picture of a time, are its characters so very artificial after all? Might not diligent search reveal some of M. Zola's 'human documents' even in this 'actors' play'? Suppose, *par impossibile*, that all record and memory of the year 1841 were obliterated except this comedy of *London Assurance*, and let us examine how far it will enable us to 'reconstitute an epoch'. To begin with, it is evident from the very first scene that in the year of grace—or of the want of it—1841, the social institution known as Tom-and-Jerryism was still flourishing. Charles Courtly comes home with the milk in a state of riotous intoxication, and empties his pockets of the knockers which he has wrenched from his neighbours' doors. He is empty-headed, he is vicious, he is, if not a Yahoo, a good deal of a Mohock. Yet the author evidently puts him forward as what would now be called a 'sympathetic' personage. For he has everything his own way, is reproved by nobody, and is rewarded in the end with the hand of the pretty girl of the piece.

Here, then, we get our first 'document'. We have 'constated' the existence of Tom-and-Jerryism so late as 1841. Picking our way through the dialogue, we find much valuable evidence as to the social habits of the time. Burgundy might then be drunk in the morning. 'Come into my room,' says Courtly to Dazzle at the breakfast hour, 'and I'll astonish you with some Burgundy.' And in the evening it might be followed by brandy-punch. 'It was all that cursed brandy-punch on the top of Burgundy,' groans Dolly Spanker. Madeira, too, was still in fashion. Dazzle: 'Max, that Madeira is worth its weight in gold; I hope you have more of it.' Max: 'A pipe, I think,' etc. Smoking-rooms had not yet been established; when the gentlemen wish to practise the vice of cigar smoking, they retire to the billiard-room. For it is still a voice in 1841. 'No cigar smoking,' says Sir Harcourt; 'Faints at the sight of one,' adds Cool—both speaking of a grown man. After dinner, when the ladies have departed, the gentlemen are expected to sing songs. Stage direction: ('Spanker *is heard to sing* "A Southerly Wind and a Cloudy Sky"—*after verse, chorus*'). Antimacassars justified their existence in 1841. Max Harkaway refers to Sir Harcourt's 'oily perfumed locks'. From Charles's description of the delights of London to the rustic Grace, we find that the fashionable entertainment was not the opera, but the ballet. The fopperies of Sir Harcourt show that in 1841 we are still in the Age of the Dandies, further evidence of which is forthcoming in Grace's allusion to 'our literary dandyisms and dandy literature'. In other words, scratch this play and you find both D'Orsay and Bulwer. The entry of Mr Solomon Isaacs in the last act shows that people were still arrested for debt. And they still travelled from London to Gloucestershire in post-chaises (hence a sharp distinction between the Town Mice and the Country Mice of the play, which gives another 'note' of 1841). Duelling (but here our 'document' perhaps becomes untrustworthy) did not yet involve a trip across the Channel. Sir Harcourt and Spanker manage their little affair in the billiard-room. Minor points are: that 'buttonholing' was not yet a mere figure of speech ('He would actually,' says Lawyer Meddle, 'have taken the Reverend Mr Spout by the button'); and that architectural taste was still barbaric ('the fine Elizabethan mansion' of Scene Two has 'large french windows at the back').

So much for *London Assurance* as a 'document'. And that is not all. Even the language of the play, untrue as it must have been to the actual life, yet reflected a side of the literary taste of the time. Certainly no living young lady of 1841 ever rhapsodised as Grace Harkaway does:

> I love to watch the first tear that glistens in the opening eye of morning, the silent song that flowers breathe, the thrilling choir of the woodland minstrels, to which the modest brook trickles applause; these, swelling out the sweetest chord of sweet creation's matins, seem to pour some soft and merry tale into the daylight's ear, as if the waking world had dreamed a happy thing, and now smiled o'er the telling of it.

But read the English of the 'Keepsake' and the 'Beauty's Annuals'. (And, inasmuch as Grace's uncle describes the glories of 'the chase in full cry' in precisely the same dithyrambic strain, take note that, long before Ibsen wrote *Ghosts*, 'the drama of heredity', the stage had glimpses of the drama of consanguinity.) Even Lady Gay Spanker's amazing 'impression of the hunt'—

> Time then appears as young as love, and plumes as swift a wing. Then I love the world, myself, and every living thing —a jocund soul cries out for very glee, as it could wish that creation had but one mouth that I might kiss it—

has its historic justification. For Lady Gay was first played by Mrs Nisbett, and had not Mrs Nisbett previously achieved fame for her delivery of Constance's glowing description of the raptures of the hunting-field in Sheridan Knowles's *The Love Chase*? He, then, who laughs at Dion Boucicault is laughing, all unaware, at Sheridan Knowles.

My excuse for dwelling on the documentary aspect of the play is that Mr Charles Wyndham, in the present revival at the Criterion, has frankly presented *London Assurance* as a document. For the first time in the history of its revivals, we have the players habited, with punctilious correctness, in the high-collared, wasp-waisted, tight-legged garments of 1841, so that the student of costume may find in every curly wig, stock, *jabot*, military cloak, white beaver hat, turnover shirt-cuff, and satin waistcoat, a documentary ecstasy.

A. B. Walkley

47

Pooter at the Tank

The Diary of a Nobody, substantially enlarged from its *Punch* original, appeared in 1892. According to its authors, the Grossmith brothers, George (1847–1912), entertainer and Gilbert-and-Sullivan comedian, and [Walter] Weedon (1852–1919), actor, dramatist, and artist, the 'Nobody', Charles Pooter, and his dear wife Carrie, lived about 1890–1 at The Laurels, Brickfield Terrace, Holloway: a solid little house with a stucco-pillared portico like a four-poster bedstead.

Pooter, a highly respectable, gently pompous City clerk, is plagued by minor disasters. Silly though he is, he is progressively lovable; and the Grossmiths' idea of his journal (originally with Weedon's drawings) has become a minor classic. 'Exaggerated burlesques of the era are dead,' said J. C. Squire; 'this transcript from life appears destined to a perennial popularity among the discerning.' In creating a Nobody the Grossmiths raised a Somebody. For all we know, there may be a fold of time in which Charles Pooter, with his soft brown beard, and his many friends are still toasting themselves in a bottle of the sparkling Algéra that Mrs James of Sutton sent as a present.

Here is the unlucky visit to the theatre. That play at the Tank, *The Brown Bushes*, sounds like J. B. Buckstone's famous Adelphi drama, *The Green Bushes; or, A Hundred Years Ago* (1845). Curiously, a revised version of this was done at the Grand, Islington, in 1903.

April 19 Cummings called, bringing with him his friend Merton, who is in the wine trade. Gowing also called. Mr Merton made himself at home at once . . . He said he should treat me as a friend, and put me down for a dozen of his 'Lockanbar' whisky, and as I was an old friend of Gowing, I should have it for 36s, which was considerably under what he paid for it. He booked his own order, and further said that at any time I wanted any passes for the theatre, I was to let him know, as his name stood good for any theatre in London.

April 20 Carrie reminded me that as her old school friend, Annie Fullers (now Mrs James), and her husband had come up from Sutton for a few days, it would look kind to take them to the theatre, and would I drop a line to Mr Merton, asking him for passes for four, either for the Italian Opera, Haymarket, Savoy, or Lyceum. I wrote Merton to that effect.

April 21 Got a reply from Merton, saying he was very busy, and just at present couldn't manage passes for the Italian Opera, Haymarket, Savoy, or Lyceum, but the best thing going on in London was the *Brown Bushes*, at the Tank Theatre, Islington, and enclosed seats for four; also bill for whisky.

April 23 Mr and Mrs James (Miss Fullers that was) came to meat tea, and we left directly after for the Tank Theatre. We got a 'bus that took us to King's Cross, and then changed into one that took us to the Angel, Mr James each time insisting on paying for all, saying that I had paid for the tickets and that was quite enough.

We arrived at theatre where, curiously enough, all our 'bus-load except an old woman with a basket seemed to be going in. I walked ahead and presented the tickets. The man looked at them, and called out 'Mr Willowly! do you know anything about these?' holding up my tickets. The gentleman called to, came up and examined my tickets, and said: 'Who gave you these?' I said rather indignantly: 'Mr Merton, of course.' He said: 'Merton? Who's he?' I answered rather sharply: 'You ought to know, his name's good at any theatre in London.' He replied: 'Oh! is it? Well, it ain't no good here. These tickets which are *not* dated, were issued under Mr Swinstead's management, which has since changed hands.' While I was having some very unpleasant words with the man, James, who had gone upstairs with the ladies, called out: 'Come on!' I went up after them, and a very civil attendant said: 'This way, please, box H.' I said to James: 'Why, how on earth did you manage it?' and to my horror he replied: 'Why, paid for it, of course.'

This was humiliating enough, and I could scarcely follow the play, but I was doomed to further humiliation. I was leaning out of the box when my tie—a little black bow which fastened on to the stud by means of a new patent—fell into the pit below. A clumsy man not noticing it had his foot on it for ever so long before he discovered it. He then picked it up and eventually flung it under the next seat in disgust. What with the box incident and the tie, I felt quite miserable. Mr James, of Sutton, was very good. He said: 'Don't worry—no one will notice it with your beard. That is the only advantage of growing one that I can see.' There was no occasion for that remark, for Carrie is very proud of my beard.

To hide the absence of the tie I had to keep my chin down the rest of the evening, which caused a pain at the back of my neck.

April 24 Could scarcely sleep a wink through thinking of having brought up Mr and Mrs James from the country to go to the theatre last night, and his having paid for a private box because our order was not honoured; and such a poor play too. I wrote a very satirical letter to Merton, the wine merchant, who gave us the pass, and said, 'Considering we had to *pay* for our seats, we did our *best* to appreciate the performance.' I thought this line rather cutting, and I asked Carrie how many p's there were in appreciate, and she said, 'One.' After I sent off the letter I looked at the dictionary and found there were two. Awfully vexed at this.

Decided not to worry myself any more about the James's; for, as Carrie wisely said: 'We'll make it all right with them by asking them up from Sutton one evening next week, to play at Bézique.'

George and Weedon Grossmith

MR. G. V. BROOKE AS PHILIP OF FRANCE.

The Pope, my Lords! Four letters, things not names!
The Pope! Did earth receive him from the stars;
Or sprang he from the ocean? Did the sun
Wake earlier on his birthday?
Let him ban the fields
The grass will grow in spite of him.

Act 3. Sc. 3.

48

Understudy

Early in 1960 Margaret Halstan (1874–1967), then eighty-five, would sit at tea in a little café opposite the Theatre Royal, Drury Lane, remembering more than six decades on the stage. In her presence, as Wendy Monk—who was with her, discussing her career—now recalls, the plastic table-top seemed to become white damask and the wall-tiles embossed paper. The veteran actress, who had understudied Dorothea Baird as Trilby in the mid-nineties, was then appearing, as she did for more than 2,000 performances, in her last part, the Queen of Transylvania, with ball-dress and tiara, in *My Fair Lady*: a single line but a grand stage presence. 'When Miss Halstan walks across the stage, the footlights glitter,' said Moss Hart, the director, after the first night.

It had been an extraordinary life: acting with Tree, Wyndham, Alexander, Ellen Terry, Benson, leading players between the wars and after World War II: Shakespeare heroines, drawing-room comedy, Galsworthy and Shaw, musical comedy, farce. Her real name was Maud Hertz. Born on Christmas Day 1874, the beautiful daughter of wealthy parents, she became tri-lingual. She developed an early passion for the stage; several famous theatre people visited them in Hampstead and later in St John's Wood. Bernard Shaw was there one afternoon and wrote later to Maud's mother: 'Is this rumour true that your daughter is going on the stage? How absurd! She would have to turn your house upside down before she could possibly succeed. I suggest that you wrap up this exotic young creature very carefully in cotton-wool and place her under a glass case in the centre of your drawing-room mantelpiece . . .' In the years ahead Maud Hertz, as Margaret Halstan, would be acting for Shaw.

During her long life she grew into an endeared figure of the stage. Though at her death her autobiography was unfinished, Wendy Monk had collected several of the memories that would pour out, night by night, across that café tea-table. Among the names in the following extract: Max Hecht was a backer of plays who would be connected with Tree and the rebuilding of Her (His) Majesty's; his grand-daughter is the actress Maxine Audley. Dorothea Baird (1875–1933) became the wife of H. B. Irving, Sir Henry's elder son. *Trilby* would not have been produced if Herbert Tree had taken the opinion of his half-brother, Max Beerbohm, who saw the Paul Potter dramatisation (of George du Maurier's novel) in Philadelphia. But Herbert went himself in New York on the last night of his American visit and the result would be stage history; nothing could have suited him better than the fantastic figure of Svengali. Lionel ('Lal') Brough (1836–1909), McAlister in *Trilby*, belonged to a distinguished stage family.

I had made up my mind to go on the stage, and my parents accepted the decision. They understood how I felt, for both of them had wanted to do the same but had been prevented by their own parents. Though the rules of society were slightly less rigid than when they were young, the stage was still thought to be a dangerous and unconventional calling for a girl well brought up. Actors and actresses, charming to meet on rare ephemeral occasions, lived more mysteriously than they do now. Were they not a trifle disreputable? The general idea was that daughters should stay at home and wait for a suitable offer of marriage. Boredom at the prospect of such a future sent Florence Nightingale into nursing. And certainly the prospect did not excite me.

One night Mr and Mrs Hecht gave a party. After dinner Paderewski played for the guests, who included Beerbohm Tree; the Forbes-Robertsons; Cyril Maude and his wife, Winifred Emery; Sir Ernest Cassel; and Mrs Patrick Campbell. I leant over the grand piano and watched Paderewski's luxuriant hair bobbing about as he played. (Tree's half-brother, Max Beerbohm, once drew a short-sighted dowager at a flower show, awarding Paderewski's head first prize in the chrysanthemum class.) Presently I was asked to recite, and I did a scene from *As You Like It*, which I can still speak from memory, and which begins:

> *Rosalind:* Pray you, what is't o'clock?
> *Orlando:* You should ask me what time o'day. There's no clock in the forest.

When it was over, Tree came up to me and said: 'I don't care for this sort of recitation, but if ever you think of going on the stage, I promise you I'll give you your first chance.'

Soon the chance came. I read in the theatrically-minded Sunday newspaper, *The Referee*, that Tree wanted a young actress to understudy Dorothea Baird in *Trilby*, which had opened to much enthusiasm at the Haymarket. A temporary understudy had been engaged, but Tree did not think she was the 'du Maurier type', and this was essential. My mind went back to a day when old Mr Stamp, the Hampstead chemist, had mistaken me for one of George du Maurier's daughters. True, the artist used them as models for his *Punch* drawings; but did this make me a du Maurier type? I looked into the mirror, and the reflection reassured me. With my father's help I wrote to Tree, reminding him of his promise, saying that my parents had consented to my stage career, and could I have a shot at the Trilby understudy? I remember my heart thudding as I ran to the pillar-box on the corner. This was in the late autumn of 1895. Tree's reply came by return of post: an appointment for me to see him at the Haymarket at the end of the week. On the day I was shown to his first-floor office; he stared at me for some time with his pale eyes, and then handed me a copy of the script. 'You certainly look right,' he said; then, taking half-a-sovereign from his pocket, he added while spinning the coin, 'But it's heads or tails if you'll be able to play it.' He told me that he would leave two tickets for me at the box office so that I could see the play that evening—I had already been to the first night with my parents—and I was to come back on the following Tuesday, word-perfect.

The play, adapted from du Maurier's novel by Paul M. Potter, an American dramatist, had already triumphed in the States—so much so that a new town in Florida had been christened Trilby. At the end of his first American tour Tree saw it with his wife, left their box after the second act, completed the purchase on the spot, and sailed next day with the script in his pocket. William Terriss, who had bought the English rights for £75, agreed for £100 to surrender them. The problem was the casting of Trilby O'Ferrall, the Franco–Irish model hypnotised by the ruthless musician Svengali into becoming a great singer, but only under his influence. After some weeks George du Maurier's neighbour at luncheon—he was the host's son, Nigel Playfair, still not a professional actor—suggested a girl he had admired as Rosalind at Stratford-upon-Avon. Tree went to see her in Ben Greet's company in the provinces and eventually engaged her. In London, after a long tour, she was a great success. It was this girl, Dorothea Baird, whom I now sought to understudy.

After going to the theatre with my mother we sat up half the night studying the script. Between us we were able to recall the moves and 'business', for my mother had an almost photographic memory for things she had seen on the stage; she could describe settings and costumes in detail and quote some of the lines of plays she had seen when a child. Learning the part was no problem to me; I could 'fix' my lines after reading the script three or four times—a trick many actors share. When I went on the Tuesday to the Haymarket stage door in Suffolk Street, I was taken to Dorothea Baird's dressing-room and told to put on her first-act clothes, the 'Trilby uniform', a French infantry soldier's grey overcoat and a vivandiere's striped petticoat. That was all. I was also given a pair of list slippers several sizes too large; but I had to appear on the stage bare-footed, something that in itself created a sensation in the Nineties.

Until I walked on the stage I had no idea at all whether it would be an audition or a rehearsal. Probably, I thought, I would be playing with other understudies. It was a little frightening, then, to find that for my benefit the scene was to be performed with the original cast, except for Tree himself who was going to watch from the dress circle. My Svengali would be S. A. Cookson, his understudy for several years. Though I was nervous I was also happy and excited; it never occurred to me that it was asking a good deal of an unknown girl to appear, without rehearsal, in that company of talented, experienced players.

On my cue I stood outside the studio door, gave the English milkman's yodel, 'Milk below-o,' with which Trilby announces herself, and then burst into the room with that rather alarming line, '*Salut, mes enfants,* the top of the morning to you, boys! . . . Zutalots-tarra-pat-a pouffe—Houp-la!' After this I had to swing round in a circle on my toes and sink cross-legged on the floor down stage centre. A superb entrance, but tricky.

Soon after this I had to smoke a cigarette, something I was not accustomed to off-stage. Lionel Brough, who played the Laird, lit it for me. In my nervousness I blew out the match; Brough quickly lit another, and that went out, too.

I heard him murmur under his breath, 'Steady, girl, steady!' At the third match the cigarette was lighted, and all went calmly to the end of the scene when the curtain fell and rose again at once. 'I don't want to see any more!' Tree called from the circle. Terrified, I turned to Lionel Brough, standing beside me. 'Oh God!' I said, 'I've lost it!' 'You damn little fool,' he said cheerfully, 'you've got it!' And I had. Everyone congratulated me; Tree came round and seemed delighted. He took me, still in Trilby's costume, into his office, and handed me a contract: 'Understudy, and to play as cast. Salary: two guineas a week.' (The young Gerald du Maurier, proud to be playing the small part of Dodor, received £4 a week.)

Trilby ran on through the autumn and winter. I had chosen the stage name of Margaret Halstan: we loved to go to Cornwall for holidays, and I took my new surname from Halsetown, near St Ives, where—as it happened—Henry Irving had spent his boyhood. It did not appear on a programme until January 1896 when Tree took *Hamlet* (he was always glad of a chance to play the part) to the New Theatre, Cambridge, for a flying matinee, and I acted the Player Queen, shivering on a raw winter day in boy's tights and short tunic; as I stood in the wings, 'Lal' Brough, the First Gravedigger, insisted on putting his fur-lined overcoat around my shoulders . . .

While I was understudying at the Haymarket I met Mrs Patrick Campbell for the first time; it was at a dinner party Max Hecht gave for the company of *For the Crown*, a version of a play by François Coppee, set in Bulgaria during the fifteenth century. Johnston Forbes-Robertson, then in management with Frederick Harrison at the Lyceum, played a prince of the family that coveted the crown; Winifred Emery (Mrs Cyril Maude) and Mrs Pat, as a fatally alluring gipsy girl, were the leading ladies. Besides the company, the Trees were at the party, with Fred Terry and Julia Neilson, Sir Ernest Cassel, the financier and friend of the Prince of Wales, and Sir Felix Semon, the throat specialist, and his wife. Mrs Pat failed to arrive and we went in to dinner where the table had as its central decoration flowers arranged in the shape of a crown. An hour late, to the minute, an unmistakable voice was heard in the hall. Quite unabashed, Mrs Pat made an entrance. 'I know I'm late,' she cried, 'but I had two *beautiful* new dresses, and I couldn't make up my mind which suited me better. But here I am now.' No one knew quite what to say. Forbes-Robertson hastily jumped up and led her to a seat by Sir Ernest Cassel and she began purring to him. When she felt the charm had worked, she pulled a hair from his beard, dipped it into champagne, and held it up with the cry, 'This will bring me luck.' If she had been on the stage she could hardly have caused a bigger sensation. Then, after a startled silence, we all began to talk at once . . .

After the London run we went out on tour, and at length, in Glasgow, I had my first chance to go on as the artist's model who posed in the nude, who had 'the handsomest feet in all Paris', and who fell in love with Little Billee, one of *les trois Angliches* who shared a studio in the Latin Quarter. To produce the right impression of 'angel's feet', as Little Billee calls them, the toe-nails had to be made up; and I still cherish the memory of Mrs Tree and Kate Rorke kneeling before me and painting them pink. When news came through that Dolly Baird could not play, these experienced actresses—as excited as if they were going on themselves for the first time—insisted on helping me to get ready.

I remember especially the final scene at that Glasgow matinee. A large, framed portrait of the dead Svengali is delivered to the studio and placed in its wrapping on an easel in the corner. Trilby is drawn towards it; she tears off the paper, sees Svengali, begins to sing as if still in his power, and dies. Always Tree would stand behind the empty frame, masked by drapery, to add to the theatrical effect. Though I knew it would happen, I had a genuine shock when I saw him there, standing eerily in the green stage lighting, and I screamed so realistically that Tree congratulated me afterwards. How I enjoyed myself that afternoon!

Margaret Halstan

MR. BUCKSTONE AND MRS. FITZWILLIAM,
AS
TOM DIBBLES AND THE ORPHAN NAN
IN MR. BUCKSTONE'S CELEBRATED COMIC DRAMA OF
GOOD FOR NOTHING

TOM. "Now I'm not going to put myself in a passion

49

Temple

When Bernard Shaw (1856–1950)—'Nothing exasperates me more than to be Georged,' he said once—wrote this in 1906, he was in his fiftieth year and at the heart of the theatre of ideas. The passage appears in *The Author's Apology* first prefixed to the American edition of *Dramatic Opinions and Essays*, edited by James Huneker. Shaw was drama critic of *The Saturday Review* between January 1895 and May 1898.

Only the ablest critics believe that the theatre is really important: in my time none of them would claim for it, as I claimed for it, that it is as important as the Church was in the Middle Ages and much more important than the Church was in London in the years under review . . .

When I wrote, I was well aware of what an unofficial census of Sunday worshippers presently proved: that churchgoing in London has been largely replaced by playgoing. This would be a very good thing if the theatre took itself seriously as a factory of thought, a prompter of conscience, an elucidator of social conduct, an armoury against despair and dullness, and a Temple of the Ascent of Man. I took it seriously in that way, and preached about it . . .

Bernard Shaw

50

Druriodrama

Although Weedon Grossmith's Drury Lane appearance was not in one of the more successful plays—it was Cecil Raleigh's 'new and original melo-farce', *The Flood Tide* (1903)—he had an excellent chance of seeing, at first hand, the kind of sensational effect that an 'autumn drama' needed. Most disasters, from earthquakes to explosions and train smashes, could be simulated on the vast stage of Drury Lane; and they were. Cecil Raleigh (1856–1914), whose real name was Rowlands, was involved with more than thirty dramas, including a dozen for the Lane. Arthur Collins (1863–1932), manager of the theatre, was a relishing master of spectacle. The extract is from Grossmith's autobiography, *From Studio to Stage* (1913).

Collins took me into the Saloon to talk business. By the way, the Saloon is big enough to hold another theatre for comedy and farce. We paced up and down the palatial room while he was propounding his scheme, which was an offer for me to play the chief comedy part in the forthcoming autumn drama, a very sensational play by Cecil Raleigh, called *The Flood Tide*.

Now I confess that I had always yearned to play in a Drury Lane drama. It would be something new to me, accompanied with plenty of excitement, getting far away from loafing through a four-act comedy in dress clothes all the time, or rushing and tearing in the same costume, through doors, under tables, or out of windows, or into beds in a three-act farce. So I put my cards on the table and confessed that I should love to play in a Drury Lane drama. Arthur Collins then assumed a very grave expression, saying that nothing would please him better also, but that it was a matter of terms. I had never seen that expression on his face before.

I named the salary that I had hitherto received, and told him that I would take the same from him. For a moment, and *only* for a moment, his expression showed surprise. I observed a slight elevation of his eyebrows. I am positive he was prepared for me to mention a much higher sum, for his answer was not quite consistent with his previous gravity. He assumed perplexity and muttered, 'By Jove, yes!' and then bit his lip. This was rather bad acting, and with a slight shake of the head he said, 'That's a lot of money,' and he had to consider his duty to his directors, and perhaps he 'ought to place it before them first', etc., then quite suddenly he said, 'Well, come into the office.'

I knew of course the directors had left the matter entirely to him. Collins produced a printed agreement and in an open-hearted, generous manner, said: 'Perhaps you had better sign at once, otherwise Cecil Raleigh will approach—er' (he was thinking who Cecil Raleigh *would* approach). 'As a matter of fact,' continued Collins, 'he *has* approached I daresay you know *who*, and *he* is simply dying to play the part, and, by the way, I promised to send him a telegram.' Though none of these remarks impressed me, I signed the agreement with the greatest pleasure in the world and without any conditions.

On asking to be allowed to read the play, as is usual when a manager is arranging with an alleged 'star', I was told that it was 'quite impossible', and indeed the last act was not written, and the author generally completed that irksome task at Folkestone during the week-ends, while the other acts were being rehearsed. This proceeding I thought not unusual as I had always heard that Sheridan wrote the last act of *Pizarro* on the first night of the production at Drury Lane while the play was proceeding.

There was one very important matter that was not mentioned before I signed the agreement, and that was whether I should have to appear in the great sensational scene in *The Flood Tide*. This 'plum' is always kept in reserve—so I heard afterwards. In this sensational scene you may have to be run over by a train, thrown from a precipice—sometimes wired, not always. If a comedian has to play the part, he will probably not be wired, as his fall is sure to be amusing, or [else he will] be blown up to the giddy heights of the borders and, with a carefully fixed wire, drawn up in a couple of seconds . . .

These little events come as a happy surprise to the actor or actress who plays in a Drury Lane drama for the first time. Nothing could have been more pleasant than the rehearsals which commenced at the convenient time of two o'clock and continued till six, with tea served to all members of the company at four o'clock. This is a much more sensible plan than the usual time selected by managers, beginning at eleven and continuing till three with no interval for lunch . . . One cannot work without food, and it is exceedingly selfish of a manager, because *his* habit is to make a big breakfast at ten and lunch at three-thirty, to expect everyone else to fall in with his eccentricities, whereas if an adjournment is made for half an hour, everyone returns fit for their work again.

An adjournment for an hour and a half is fatal, as I have discovered, where Charles Hawtrey has been holding the managerial reins; he is a good-natured, irresponsible chap, who refuses to take anything too seriously, and who will lunch during the interval, at the Carlton, in the leisurely style of an English squire quite oblivious of the fleeting time. Even this is far preferable to the selfish, dogmatic, narrow-minded tyrant who cares not whether you are hungry as long as he or she is not.

The two-to-six plan of Arthur Collins is an admirable one. You are not dragged out of your bed early in the morning, and you have all that part of the day to attend to your private business and study your part and learn the words, always a very difficult accomplishment with me. I wander for hours round the outskirts of London, ride in four-wheel cabs (taxis are no good), and frequently take a non-stop train to, say, Peterborough. If you are quite alone in the carriage and buy nothing to read, you have nothing to distract you. I went to East Ham one day and had to change at Stepney and wait half an hour for a train, at which I was delighted, for a more unattractive station it had never been my good fortune to wait at. The result was I learned nearly half an act. I never learn from the typewritten part but always copy it into a little book.

The rehearsals at Drury Lane were wonderfully conducted. It requires a considerable knowledge of management and a Napoleonic power to control between three or four hundred people, and I found Collins the personification of coolness and self-control. Only on one occasion he seemed for a minute to lose control of his temper when addressing the mechanics down below the stage who were working the huge lifts, or, to be more correct, had omitted to do so. His language even then was not objectionable because it was not understandable; otherwise Lady Tree, then Mrs Beerbohm Tree, who was playing the adventuress, would not have said in a very innocent voice to Miss Margaret Halstan (the good girl of the play), 'What does he mean, dear?'

I had to make my entrance in a dog-cart, the near wheel catching the wing as I drove on. I had then to leap from the cart, accompanied by loud and exhilarating music composed by James Glover, which terminated with a big chord as I embraced Polly, my sweetheart, played by Miss Claire Romaine. I had plenty of excitement right through; in the racing scene when it was discovered that I had 'scratched' my horse (the favourite), I was welshed and carried off on their shoulders by a huge crowd of supers, some of them hailing from Covent Garden Market. But whatever trouble and excitement I had gone through, and I must say the welshing was conducted on very realistic principles, it was nothing compared to what was in store for me at the end of the third act. The parts were handed out to Norman McKinnel and C. W. Somerset, who played the two villains, for the big sensational scene, Scene IV, Act III, 'The Boathouse at Blackmere Lake.' I heard McKinnel growling to Somerset, 'Oh! We're in for it!' I cheerily remarked, 'I'm sorry for you chaps, but, thank goodness, I am not on in the "sensation" scene.' 'Oh yes, you *are*,' said Somerset with a fiendish grin. I thought he was joking till the stage manager handed me my part, and I read the following description of what I was expected to do: Wellington Clip (that was the part I played) has to witness a terrible encounter between the two men on the small island of the great Blackmere Lake:

> Clip is terrified and rushes into the boathouse, and climbs the stairs to the top of a two-storied house. Finding he is pursued, he scrambles on to the roof where he hangs clutching on to the sloping gable, as he is being pursued by the villains who are intent on murdering him. A terrific roar is heard. The great dam has burst, and a huge volume of water floods the stage. The boathouse is swept away, and as it is falling and breaking to pieces, Clip leaps on to a big branch of a tree which is rapidly passing in the swirl of the flood.

After reading this description, I walked round to the Law Accident Insurance Society in the Strand, and took out an accident insurance policy for a large sum. I was half inclined to take this step after rehearsing the welshing scene at the races, but the curious incidents that were to occur at Blackmere Lake quite decided me. Scene III, Act III, was what is termed a front scene. It was very dark, and a couple of dozen men dressed as workmen, with lanterns in their hands and pickaxes, were discussing the seriousness of the continuance of wet weather.

It was difficult to hear all they said, for dozens of men were knocking and hammering behind, getting ready the big sensational scene. After this, Lady Tree was heard bribing Norman McKinnel, an Italian scoundrel, to murder the lunatic millionaire, played by Charles Somerset, to slow music.

When they had departed the workmen re-entered. Some had struck work, fearing a great accident, and the chief of the gang, who shouted—and he had to shout loudly—to give the 'music cue', informed his mates at the top of his voice: 'Things can't go on much longer, lads. The masonry is giving already. We have had three nights of continuous rain, and with another night of this cursed deluge, the great dam which-has-taken-seven-years-to-build-will *be in Blackmere* Lake by—the—*morning*!!'

The stage suddenly blackened out. We are all in total darkness, black gauzes are lowered. There are shouts from the stage manager: 'Strike! Lower your borders!' Stage hands rush in every direction, carrying something or pushing something. 'Mind your backs!' they shout. 'You jump aside!' The safest place is close to the curtain, down by the footlights . . . 'Get on your blues! Down with the borders! Take care! Who's working the lifts? Then why the devil don't you do it? Come on! Look out! Get your cloth down above there. Now then, boys!'

'Number three is too low! Do you hear?—*Too low*. Get your props. D——n it, mind the batten! Why the tum, tum, fum rum, don't you do what you're told?' etc. The front row of the stalls frequently complain of the loudness of the band, particularly the brass, and wonder why it is not remedied, but James Glover, the conductor, knows why.

'Look out for your calls!' Then a boy with an electric torch leads you through rocks, rivers, spars of iron, cautions you against an open trap, and leads you to your place. The band is still crashing and booming; an electric sign to the orchestra, and the music changes to the tremolo and mysterious. The gauzes rise slowly, opening on the big sensational scene. The gallery is noisy with shouts of 'Down in front! Order, please! Take off your 'at!', 'Lay down!'

I shall never forget that first night when the flood commenced.

Tons of rice and spangles poured from the side to indicate the bursting of the dam. Children floated by, clinging to barrels and floating trees, screaming and yelling, especially as some of them got frightened and, tipping sideways, fell down the trap, to be caught by the men underneath. Then the boathouse with myself hanging outside from the roof, began to wobble, and the whole structure toppled over. A huge floating tree, with a well-concealed mattress, passed by, and Somerset and myself jumped on to it and were supposed to be saved as the curtain descended slowly.

One night the tree passed too quickly for us to jump on, and we were both drowned.

I must say it was great fun.

Weedon Grossmith

Standard Theatre,

Licensed by the Lord Chamberlain, 6 Vic. cap 9.] Shoreditch, Facing the Eastern Counties Railway. [Lessee.—Mr. John Douglass Weymouth Terrace, Hackney Road.

Under the Direction of - - - - - - Mr. JOHN DOUGLASS.

For the Benefit of Mrs. R. HONNER.

On TUESDAY, MARCH 5th, 1850.

The Performances will commence with, for the First and only Time at this Theatre, a Drama, in Three Acts, by J. B. BUCKSTONE, Esq., (represented by the express permission of that Gentleman and B. WEBSTER, Esq.) entitled

ISABELLE!

ACT 1.—THE GIRL.—PERIOD 1794.

Eugene Le Marc .... (a young Soldier) .... Mr. BASIL POTTER
Scipio ...... (his Comrade) ...... Mr. LYON
Andrew .... (a Peasant of the Tyrolise) .... Mr. H. LEWIS
Michael .. (Father to Isabelle) .. Mr. JOHN GATES Phillipe .. Mr. LOOME George .. Mr. BIRD
Isabelle ...... (a Tyrolean Peasant Girl) ...... Mrs. R. HONNER
Sophia .... (her companion) .... Miss ELIZA TERRY
Savoyards, Soldiers, Guests, &c.

ACT 2.—THE WIFE.—PERIOD 1802.

General Le Marc .... (in the Service of the Republic) .... Mr. BASIL POTTER
Scipio ...... (his former companion—a broken-down Roué) ...... Mr. LYON
Coquin and Epirionne ..... (Two Gamblers) ...... Messrs. G. HERBERT & C. ROBY
Apollo Bazazet .... Mr. R. HONNER
Andrew .... Mr. H. LEWIS
Madame Le Marc .... Mrs. R. HONNER
Sophia .... Miss ELIZA TERRY
Susie .... (an Attendant on Madame Le Marc) .... Mrs. J. W. DOUGHTY

ACT 3.—THE MOTHER.—PERIOD 1815.

Monsieur Le Marc .... Mr. BASIL POTTER
Scipio ...... (now a Mountain Brigand) .... Mr. LYON
Coquin and Epirionne ...... (Two Ruffians) . ... Messrs. G. HERBERT & C. ROBY
Andrew .... Mr. H. LEWIS
Apollo Bazazet .. .. Mr. R. HONNER
Phillipe .... Mr. LOOME Vincent .... (a young Soldier) .... Miss BROOK
Madame Isabelle .... Mrs. R. HONNER
Madame Sophia .... Miss ELIZA TERRY

In the course of the Evening

MR. FRAZER WILL SING A GRAND SCENA.

The Drama of "Isabelle," to be succeeded by the Farce of

THE SPOILED CHILD!

Little Pickle .... Miss SARAH THORNE
(Whose performance of which Character has lately elicited such universal admiration.)
Old Pickle .... Mr. JOHN GATES John .... Mr. LOOME Thomas .... Mr JONES
James .... Mr. BIRD Tag .... Mr. J. W. DOUGHTY
Miss Pickle .... Mrs. J. GATES Maria .... Mrs. J. W. DOUGHTY
Margery .... Miss PEARSON Susan .... Miss H. TERRY

TO BE SUCCEEDED BY

A BALLET DIVERTISSEMENT

IN THE COURSE OF WHICH, THE

INIMITABLE FLEXMORE

WILL DANCE A PAS BUFFO,

Pas de Cossaque - by Mr. W. H. HARVEY

And a Pas de Nationes, by Miss HARRIETT SAVILLE.

A PAS DE DEUX - - BY MR. H. SAUNDERS AND MADEMOISELLE PAULINE.

"Buy a Broom," ....by Miss CARTER.

The whole to conclude with J. B. BUCKSTONE, Esq.'s, Popular Drama (for the First and only time here,) called

Abelard and Heloise!

Mons. Falbert .... (reputed Uncle of Heloise) .... Mr. E. B. GASTON
Laurenadie ...... (a Bravo) ...... Mr. LYON
Augustin .... (his Brother—a Clerk) .... Mrs. R. ATKINSON
Barnabic .... (an Innkeeper) .... Mr. JOHN GATES
Maxamillian and Sampson .... (two Embryo Philosophers) .... Mr. R. HONNER & Mr. H. LEWIS
Daniel Gautlier .... (Betrothed to Heloise) .... Mr. BASIL POTTER
Abelard - (a Student) - Mr. E. F. SAVILLE (his original Character)
Bernard ...... (Abbe of Clairvaux) ...... Mr. C. ROBY Students, Monks, Soldiers, &c.
Heloise .... Mrs. R. HONNER
Jocette .... Miss ELIZA TERRY
Beatrice .... Mrs. J. GATES Nuns, Dancing Girls, Peasants, Scholars, &c.

Stage Manager - - - - - - - Mr. R. HONNER.

BOXES........1s.—Half-Price, 6d. at half-past 8. PIT........6d.—No Half-Price. GALLERY....... 3d.
Box Keeper.......... ...Mr. J. T. HUMPHREYS. Officer....... ....Mr. J. RAWSON.
RETURN CHECKS NOT TRANSFERABLE. TOWNCEBY's Steam Press, 7, Cannon Street, East.

51

In the Mind

James Evershed Agate (1877–1947), a Lancastrian, a Francophil, and an acute judge of acting, was drama critic of the *Sunday Times* from 1923 to his death. He had written earlier for the then *Manchester Guardian* and *The Saturday Review*. His articles, zestful, learned, and idiosyncratic, were influential, if capricious at times, and he made another reputation as the diarist of the nine *Ego* volumes (this extract is taken from the first, 1935), as well as for much vigorous miscellaneous writing. He collected his drama and film criticisms assiduously; those on the theatre are an important record of the London stage between the wars.

In the following passage he returns to his earlier playgoing: (Sir) Frank Benson (1858–1939), Shakespearian actor-manager; Irene Vanbrugh (1872–1949) in *His House In Order* (1906) by (Sir) Arthur Pinero (1855–1934); Lewis Waller (1860–1915) as Henry V; (Dame) Madge Kendal (1848–1935) as Mrs Hyacinth in *A Tight Corner* (1906) by Herbert Swears (in 'Run like the swift hare' he borrowed one of the actress's everyday phrases); Hilda Trevelyan (1880–1959) in *What Every Woman Knows* (1908) by J. M. Barrie (1860–1937); Edward Terry (1844–1912) in Pinero's *Sweet Lavender* (1888); *The Bells* (1871) by Leopold Lewis, from the French; *The Lyons Mail* (1877) by Charles Reade, from the French; J. M. Barrie's *Alice Sit-by-the-Fire* (1905); (Sir) Johnston Forbes-Robertson (1853–1937) in *The Light That Failed* (1903) by 'George Fleming' from Kipling's novel; Lawrence Anderson (1893–1939); *Berkeley Square* by John L. Balderston and J. C. Squire (1936); Leslie Howard (1893–1943).

Of stage utterances that I remember

It would be easy to make a list which would do credit to one's literary sense. But the point is to tell the truth, even if the lines which come to me unbidden are not necessarily great lines, though some may be. In no particular order, then, I remember:

Benson in *Coriolanus* saying 'There is a world elsewhere.' I was fourteen and it was at the Theatre Royal, Manchester. I burst into tears and laid my head down on the wooden partition separating pit from stalls.

Irene Vanbrugh in *His House in Order* saying: 'I go to no park tomorrow.' Later I took my landlord, George Potter, to see a performance of this play in Buxton. When the provincial actress got to this line George brought his enormous fist down on to the brass rail separating the orchestra from the stalls and shouted: 'And I'd go to no bloody park, noather, Miss!'

Lewis Waller's 'Once more unto the breach, dear friends, once more', pitched in the key of a silver trumpet. Your modern Henry intones 'Once moah unto the breach, deah friends, once moah' in the manner of a curate urging his flock to a silver collection.

Mrs Kendal sitting on the lid of an oak chest containing her lover, drumming her heels and bidding her husband 'R-r-run like the swift hare.'

Louis Calvert in *Antony and Cleopatra* saying to the attendant announcing news from Rome: 'Grates me: the sum.' . . .

Janet Achurch in *A Doll's House* saying to Doctor Rank: 'Let me pass, please.' Janet used to drop her voice a full third on the word 'pass'. The last fool I saw play Nora not only did this bit skittishly but contrived to get herself seated on the wrong side of the doctor, so that she did not have to pass him at all!

Hilda Trevelyan in *What Every Woman Knows* bringing the curtain down on the cry: 'My constituents!'

Edward Terry in *Sweet Lavender* saying: 'Have you seen my dress-suit, Clemmy, my boy? The coat and waistcoat are in fair preservation, but the rest of it has been attending funerals for years.' With enormous emphasis on 'funerals' (high note) and 'years' (low note). Unlike any other comedian I have ever seen, Terry declined to let his laughs have their full value; when the audience was three-quarters way through a laugh Terry would decide that that was enough, and the great voice would again come booming through . . .

Of stage-pictures that recur

Irving in *The Bells* brushing the snow from his boots. Irving's look when Dante sees Ugolino starving in his tower. Irving's gusto when in *The Lyons Mail* Dubosc, with a face like a dirty hatchet, goes through the pockets of the dead postilion. The same mask, now sunset-gilded, which Lesurques turns on his accusers.

Ellen Terry, at the Gaiety Theatre, Manchester, playing *Alice Sit-by-the-Fire* on the night after Irving died. Just before the end Alice has to say: 'It's summer done, autumn begun. Farewell, summer. Alice Sit-by-the-Fire henceforth. The moon is full tonight, Robert, but it isn't looking for me any more. Taxis farewell—advance four-wheelers. I had a beautiful husband once, black as the raven was his hair—' Here Ellen broke down utterly. The curtain fell in silence, and we all left the theatre quietly, feeling that we had intruded on a private sorrow.

Benson's entry in *King Lear* with the body of Cordelia in his arms. Benson's gnarled walk across the stage as Hamlet. Benson as Caliban hanging head downwards from a palm-tree.

Forbes-Robertson in *The Light That Failed* making me cry so much that the whole scene was blotted out. (Jean Forbes-Robertson with Lawrence Anderson did the same thing in *Berkeley Square*, and again in the revival with Leslie Howard.) . . . I always wanted Forbes-Robertson to play Antony in *Antony and Cleopatra*, if only to give form and moving to 'that noble countenance, Wherein the worship of the whole world lies.'

James Agate

ROYAL

PRINCESS'S THEATRE.

OXFORD STREET

UNDER THE MANAGEMENT OF Mr. CHARLES KEAN, No. 3, TORRINGTON SQUARE

This Evening, SATURDAY, Nov. 11th, 1854,

The Performances will commence with (25th Time) a New Comedietta, in One Act, by A. C. TROUGHTON, Esq., entitled,

LIVING TOO FAST:

Or, A TWELVE MONTHS' HONEY-MOON.

Mr. Charles Prudent — Mr. WALTER LACY
The Hon. Captain Craven Plausible — Mr. G. EVERETT
Mr. Cotton — Mr. J. CHESTER
William — (Prudent's Servant) — Mr. CORMACK
Mrs. Prudent — — — — Miss MURRAY
Mary — (Julia's Maid) — Miss J. LOVELL.

After which, (47th Time) a Comic Drama, in Two Acts, by Mr. J. M. MORTON, entitled

FROM

VILLAGE TO COURT

The Baron Von Grosenbach, — Mr. HARLEY
Captain Ernest Manheim. — — Mr. J. F. CATHCART
Lieutenant Schwabb, Mr. F. COOKE
Maximilian Krootz, - - - Mr. DAVID FISHER
Bertha. Countess of Lindenberg. — Miss MURRAY
Rose Walstein, — — — — Miss HEATH

After which, will be performed (6th Time),

A NEW MELO-DRAMATIC SPECTACLE,

In Three Acts and Eight Scenes, including an Epilogue, (Adapted from the French), entitled

SCHAMYL

THE WARRIOR-PROPHET.

The Scenery Painted under the Direction of Mr. GRIEVE.
The Dances and Action by Mr. OSCAR BYRN. The Dresses by Mrs. and Miss HOGGINS
The Machinery by Mr. G. HODSDON The Appointments, &c., by Mr. E. W. BRADWELL
The Overture, Entre-Actes, and a portion of the Incidental Music by Mr. ISAACSON.

Prince David Vassiloff, (Governor of Georgia) Mr. JAMES VINING
Captain Alexis Vassiloff, (his Nephew) Mr. DAVID FISHER
Schamyl. — (Son of the Prophet Khasi-Moullah) — Mr. RYDER
Halim, (his Half-Brother) Mr. J. F. CATHCART
Dr. Daniel, (an English Physician, travelling in Georgia) Mr. WALTER LACY
Masbook, (a Circassian Chief, in League with Russia, "Father to Halim") Mr. GRAHAM
Yedig. — } Circassian Chiefs { Mr. RAYMOND
Arvad, — Mr. G. EVERETT
Zarolta, — Mr. TERRY
Other Circassian Chieftains, Mr. J. COLLETT, Mr. CORMACK
Messrs. DALY, STOAKES, COLLIS, BUSH, &c.
Emin, and Zarif. (Jugglers) Mr. F. COOKE and Mr. ROLLESTON
Lieutenant Paramanoff, — Mr. PIKE
Sowabbachkin, — (a Cossack) — Mr. H. MELLON
Ghesil, (a Boy) Miss KATE TERRY

Zenda — (Mother of Schamyl and Halim) — Mrs. PHILLIPS
Fedora Vassiloff. (Daughter to the Prince) Miss HEATH
Lodine, (Fedora's Attendant) Miss DALY.
Russian Officers & Soldiers, Georgians, in the Pay of Russia, Mongolians, Circassians, Murids, Adighans, Circassian Priests, Women, &c., &c.

Scene—In Georgia & Circassia

PERIOD, — 1834.

ACT 1

HALL IN THE PALACE OF THE RUSSIAN GOVERNOR AT TEFLIS (F. Lloyds)

THE SUMMIT OF MOUNT DARBELA,

Commanding a View of the

VALLEY OF THE CAUCASUS Night. (W. Gordon)

ACT 2

A PLAIN BEFORE THE FORTRESS OF ACHULGO

IN DAGHESTAN. (W. Gordon)

INCIDENTAL BALLET

AND

TABLEAUX VIVANS!

By Mesdlles. C. Parkes, Adams, C. Adams, Cushale, Cutmore, Clifford, Dring, Hendrick, Lovell, J. Lovell, Maile, Stapley, Startin, Watson, Healey, Brazier, Hastings, Hughes, Grey, Wood, Gilbert, Weston, &c. Messrs. Paulo, Brown, Kent, Wilson, Roberts, Elliston, &c.

INTERIOR of the FORTRESS!

THE DYKE of KOISON

WITH DISTANT LAKE AND FORT. Moonlight (W. Gordon).

Cutting of the Dyke & Inundation of the Fortress

ACT 3

The SANCTUARY of ACHULGO,

AND TOMB OF THE PROPHET KHASI-MOULLAH. (F. Lloyds)

The Citadel & City of Teflis. (F. Lloyds)

THE EPILOGUE!

TWENTY YEARS ARE SUPPOSED TO HAVE ELAPSED.

PERIOD. — 1854.

Scene—A BAY on THE COAST of CIRCASSIA!

Introducing Schamyl's Reception of the Representatives of the (W. Gordon)

ENGLISH, FRENCH, AND TURKISH NAVY,

Concluding with a NATIONAL CIRCASSIAN DANCE, by the Ladies of the Corps de Ballet.

MONDAY—The Courier of Lyons, and Schamyl, the Warrior-Prophet!
TUESDAY—Faust and Marguerite, and Schamyl, the Warrior-Prophet!

THE COURIER OF LYONS—on Monday & Thursday Next.
FAUST AND MARGUERITE—on Tuesday and Friday Next,
THE CORSICAN BROTHERS—on Wednesday Next.

SCHAMYL,

THE WARRIOR-PROPHET!

EVERY EVENING.

DRESS CIRCLE, 5s. BOXES, 4s. PIT, 2s. GALLERY, 1s.
Second Price—DRESS CIRCLE, 2s. 6d. BOXES, 2s. PIT, 1s. GAL. 6d.
Orchestra Stalls, 6s. Private Boxes, £2 12s. 6d. £2 2s. £1 11s. 6d.
Box-Office Open from 11 till 5, o'Clock. Doors Open at Half-past 6. The Performances to Commence at 7.
Half-Price will commence as near Nine o'Clock as is consistent with the Non-Interruption of the Performance.
☞ The Saloons under the Direction of M. EPITEAUX, of the Opera Colonnade.

Gallery Door in Castle Street. Children in Arms will not be admitted

Private Boxes and Stalls may be obtained at the Libraries, and of Mr. MASSINGHAM, at the Box-Office of the Theatre, Oxford Street. Any Person wishing to secure Places, can do so by paying One Shilling for every Party not exceeding Six, which Places will be retained until 9 o'Clock in the Boxes, and in the Stalls, the Whole Evening.

Applications respecting the Bills to be made to Mr. TREADAWAY, at the Stage Door

VIVANT REGINA ET PRINCEPS.] [John K. Chapman and Company, 5, Shoe Lane, and Peterborough Ct. Fleet Street

52

These Fine People

In the record of the Irish dramatic renaissance, John Millington Synge (1871–1909), a grave, dark-haired man with eyes 'at once smoky and kindling' (John Masefield speaks), was to the prose play what W. B. Yeats was to the poets' stage. When Yeats insisted on the need for 'beautiful and appropriate language', he did not realise that the finest fulfilment of his wish would not be the language of the Celtic-myth verse plays, but what has been called popularly the Synge-song: the prose rhythms of the short tragedy of *Riders to the Sea*; the peasant sketch, *In the Shadow of the Glen*; the bitter-sweet comedy, *The Well of the Saints*; and, unexampled, *The Playboy of the Western World* (1907), based upon a tale Synge had heard in Aran. He was more of a natural technician than Yeats; he, too, had the same belief in a simplicity that, in fact, was profoundly complex.

During the birth-pangs of *The Playboy* at the Abbey Theatre, Dublin, its 'fine bit of talk' infuriated myopic patriots and began a pandemonium which was to beat again over the head of a dramatist of a later day, Sean O'Casey. On the first night in January 1907, Irishmen responded with hisses; on the second with an angry hullabaloo. It was simply that some of these Dubliners held that Synge had defamed his country by his uncompromising treatment of the Irish peasant character. 'We shall have to establish a Society for the Preservation of Irish Humour,' he murmured as he listened to the uproar. That is an old story now. It has been said sagely that *The Playboy* is as much and as little of an insult to Ireland as *Don Quixote* is to Spain.

Christy Mahon comes to the country shebeen (inn) near a village on the wild coast of Mayo, boasting that he has killed his father 'in a windy corner of high distant hills': all Synge's verbal genius is in the phrase. The awed locals treat Christy as a hero ('making a mighty man of me this day by the power of a lie').

Here is a scene from *The Playboy*, with Synge's preface.

In writing *The Playboy of the Western World*, as in my other plays, I have used one or two words only that I have not heard among the country people of Ireland, or spoken in my own nursery before I could read the newspapers. A certain number of the phrases I employ I have heard also from herds and fishermen along the coast from Kerry to Mayo or from beggar-women and ballad-singers nearer Dublin; and I am glad to acknowledge how much I owe to the folk-imagination of these fine people. Any one who had lived in real intimacy with the Irish peasantry will know that the wildest sayings and ideas in this play are tame indeed, compared with the fancies one may hear in any little hillside cabin in Geesala, or Carraroe, or Dingle Bay. All art is a collaboration; and there is little doubt that in the happy age of literature, striking and beautiful phrases were as ready to the story-teller's or the playwright's hand, as the rich cloaks and dresses of his time. It is probable that when the Elizabethan dramatist took his ink-horn and sat down to his work, he used many phrases that he had just heard, as he sat at dinner, from his mother or his children.

In Ireland those of us who know the people have the same privilege. When I was writing *The Shadow of the Glen* some years ago, I got more aid than any learning could have given me from a chink in the floor of the old Wicklow house where I was staying, that let me hear what was being said by the servant girls in the kitchen. This matter, I think, is of importance, for in countries where the imagination of the people, and the language they use, is rich and living, it is possible for a writer to be rich and copious in his words, and at the same time to give the reality, which is the root of all poetry, in a comprehensive and natural form. In the modern literature of towns, however, richness is found only in sonnets, or in prose poems, or in one or two elaborate books that are far away from the profound and common interests of life. One has, on one side, Mallarmé and Huysmans producing this literature; and on the other, Ibsen and Zola dealing with the reality of life in joyless and pallid works. On the stage one must have reality, and one must have oy; and that is why the intellectual modern drama has failed, and people have grown sick of the false joy of the musical comedy, that has been given them in place of the rich joy found only in what is superb and wild in reality. In a good play every speech should be as fully flavoured as a nut or an apple, and such speeches cannot be written by anyone who works among people who have shut their lips on poetry. In Ireland, for a few years more, we have a popular imagination that is fiery, and magnificent, and tender; so that those of us who wish to write start with a chance that is not given to writers in places where the springtime of the local life has been forgotten, and the harvest is a memory only, and the straw has been turned into bricks.

[*From the first act of the play. Pegeen Mike, the publican's daughter, with Christy Mahon, the playboy.*]

Pegeen You should have had great people in your family, I'm thinking, with the little small feet you have, and you with a kind of quality name, the like of what you'd find on the great powers and potentates of France and Spain.

Christy (*with pride.*) We were great, surely, with wide and windy acres of rich Munster land.

Pegeen Wasn't I telling you, and you a fine, handsome young fellow with a noble brow?

Christy (*with a flush of delighted surprise.*) Is it me?

Pegeen Aye. Did you never hear that from the young girls where you come from in the west or south?

Christy (*with venom.*) I did not, then. Oh, they're bloody liars in the naked parish where I grew a man.

Pegeen If they are itself, you've heard it these days, I'm thinking, and you walking the world telling out your story to young girls or old.

Christy I've told my story no place till this night, Pegeen Mike, and it's foolish I was here, maybe, to be talking free; but you're decent people, I'm thinking, and yourself a kindly woman, the way I wasn't fearing you at all.

Pegeen (*filling a sack with straw.*) You've said the like of that, maybe, in every cot and cabin where you've met a young girl on your way.

Christy (*going over to her, gradually raising his voice.*) I've said it nowhere till this night, I'm telling you; for I've seen none the like of you the eleven long days I am walking the world, looking over a low ditch or a high ditch on my north and south, into stony, scattered fields, or scribes of bog, where you'd see young, limber girls and fine, prancing women, making laughter with the men.

Pegeen If you weren't destroyed travelling, you'd have as much talk and streeleen, I'm thinking, as Owen Roe O'Sullivan or the poets of the Dingle Bay; and I've heard all times it's the poets are your like—fine, fiery fellows with great rages when their temper's roused.

Christy (*drawing a little nearer to her.*) You've a power of rings, God bless you, and would there be any offence if I was asking are you single now?

Pegeen What would I want wedding so young?

Christy (*with relief.*) We're alike so.

Pegeen (*she puts sack on settle and beats it up.*) I never killed my father. I'd be afeard to do that, except I was the like of yourself with blind rages tearing me within, for I'm thinking you should have had great tussling when the end was come.

Christy (*expanding with delight at the first confidential talk he has ever had with a woman.*) We had not then. It was a hard woman was come over the hill; and if he was always a crusty kind, when he'd a hard woman setting him on, not the divil himself or his four fathers could put up with him at all.

Pegeen (*with curiosity.*) And isn't it a great wonder that one wasn't fearing you?

Christy (*very confidentially.*) Up to the day I killed my father, there wasn't a person in Ireland knew the kind I was, and I there drinking, waiting, eating, sleeping, a quiet, simple, poor fellow with no man giving me heed.

Pegeen (*getting quilt out of cupboard and putting it on the sack.*) It was the girls were giving you hard, maybe, and I'm thinking it's most conceit you'd have to be gaming with their like.

Christy (*shaking his head, with simplicity.*) Not the girls itself, and I won't tell you a lie. There wasn't anyone heeding me in that place, saving only the dumb beasts of the field.

(*He sits down at fire.*)

Pegeen (*with disappointment.*) And I thinking you should have been living the life of a king of Norway or the eastern world. (*She comes and sits beside him after placing bread and mug of milk on the table.*)

Christy (*laughing piteously.*) The like of a king, is it?

And I after toiling, moiling, digging, dodging from the dawn till dusk; with never a sight of joy or sport saving only when I'd be abroad in the dark night poaching rabbits on hills, for I was a divil to poach, God forgive me (*very naively*), and I near got six months for going with a sung fork and stabbing a fish.

Pegeen And it's that you'd call sport, is it, to be abroad in the darkness with yourself alone?

Christy I did, God help me, and there I'd be as happy as the sunshine of St Martin's Day, watching the light passing the north or the patches of fog, till I'd hear a rabbit starting to screech and I'd go running in the furze. Then, when I'd my full share, I'd come walking down where'd you see the ducks and geese stretched sleeping on the highway of the road, and before I'd pass the dunghill, I'd hear himself snoring out a loud, lonesome snore he'd be making all times, the while he was sleeping; and he a man'd be raging all times, the while he was waking, like a gaudy officer you'd hear cursing and damning and swearing oaths.

Pegeen Providence and Mercy, spare us all!

Christy It's that you'd say surely if you seen him and he after drinking for weeks, rising up in the red dawn, or before it maybe, and going out into the yard as naked as an ash-tree in the moon of May, and shying clods against the visage of the stars till he'd put the fear of death into the banbhs and the screeching sows.

Pegeen I'd be well-nigh afeard of that lad myself, I'm thinking. And there was no one in it but the two of you alone?

Christy The divil a one, though he'd sons and daughters walking all great states and territories of the world, and not a one of them, to this day, but would say their seven curses on him, and they rousing up to let a cough or sneeze, maybe, in the deadness of the night.

Pegeen (*nodding her head.*) Well, you should have been a queer lot. I've never cursed my father the like of that, though I'm twenty and more years of age.

Christy Then you'd have cursed mine, I'm telling you, and he a man never gave peace to any, saving when he'd got two months or three, or be locked up in the asylums for battering peelers or assaulting men (*with depression*), the way it was a bitter life he led me till I did up a Tuesday and halve his skull.

Pegeen (*putting her hand on his shoulder.*) Well, you'll have peace in this place, Christy Mahon, and none to trouble you, and it's near time a fine lad like you should have your good share of the earth.

Christy It's time surely, and I a seemly fellow with great strength in me and bravery of . . . (*Someone knocks.*) (*Clinging to Pegeen.*) Oh, glory! it's late for knocking, and this last while I'm in terror of the peelers, and the walking dead.

(*Knocking again . . .*)

J. M. Synge

NEW ROYAL LYCEUM THEATRE

Licensed Pursuant to Act of Parliament.

Proprietor & Manager, — MR. E. D. DAVIS.

The Erection being completed, the NEW ROYAL LYCEUM THEATRE

WILL BE OPENED

FOR THE RECEPTION OF THE PUBLIC

ON MONDAY EVENING NEXT, SEPT. 29th. 1856.

Mr. DAVIS wishes that his kind Friends and Patrons should themselves judge of the efforts made for their accommodation rather than be guided by any comments from him, he will therefore only express his hopes that it will be apparent to all how anxiously he has laboured to redeem the promise made as to the time of opening.

Architect - - - - MR. THOS. MOORE.
Assistant Architect and Superintendent of Works, - - MR. JOS. POTTS.
The Decorative Department from the Pencil of MR. JAS. LINDSAY.
Executed under his direction by Messrs. SAUNDERS & JOHNSON.
The Masonry by MESSRS. THOMPSON AND TERRY.
The Joiner Work by MR. J. TAYLOR.
The Gas and other Fittings by Mr. DANNATT and Mr. CLASPER.
The Upholstery by Messrs. ALCOCK, BRYDON, HERRING, &c.
The Painting Work by Mr. ARNISON.

MONDAY EVENING, Sept. 29, 1856

The Season will commence with Sir E. L. BULWER LYTTON's beautiful Play

RICHELIEU

Louis the Thirteenth........Mr. COURTENAY Gaston (Duke of Orleans)........Mr. IRVING
The Sieur de Beringhen (a Courtier)........Mr. ALFRED DAVIS
Baradas (Favourite of the King)..Mr. ORVELL The Chevalier de Mauprat..Mr. J. C. COWPER
Richelieu, (First Time in Sunderland)........Mr. DAVIS
Father Joseph Mr. FOOTE Huguet (a Spy) Mr. BRUNT Francois (a Page) Miss AGNES MARKHAM
Pages to Richelieu........Misses POULSON and MONTAGUE
Pages to the King........Misses MILNER, LEIGH, CARTER
Count de Clermont........Mr. GIBSON Captain of Guard........Mr. WAITE
Gaoler........Mr. BRODERICK Governor........Mr. S. JOHNSON
First Secretary Mr. MASTERS Second Do. Mr. EDOUIN Third Do. Mr. MORELLI
Julia de Mortemar (Richelieu's Ward)........Mrs. ALFRED DAVIS
Marion de Lorme........Miss DE CLIFFORD

To Conclude with the highly successful New Piece of Oriental Sentimentality, or Sentimental Orientality, extracted from Dreams of the Arabian Nights, by the indefatigable Visionary, HOO-ZURE-ATAR, and which to be appreciated must be seen, as the most extravagantly laudatory eccomiums must fall immeasurably short of the gigantic merit of

THE ENCHANTED LAKE!

OR THE FISHERMAN AND THE GENIE.

Achmet (Autocrat of Bagdad, of imperial splendour and imperious disposition) Mr. S. JOHNSON
Mooney Pacha (his much-abused Vizier) Mr. FOOTE Abdallah (the Black Enchanter) Mr. MASTERS
Hassan (a Fisherman, who finds out that honesty is the best policy) Mr. ALFRED DAVIS
Monkey (who though at first, "a beast," ultimately proves himself "a gentleman") Mr. EDOUIN
Genius of the Bottle........(who has no connection with the Bottle Imp)........Mr. COURTENAY
Selim........Cook of the Palace)........Mr. GIBSON
Azor and Azim........(Two Young Princes)........Mrs. COURTENAY and Miss CARTER
Cooks........Messrs. BRUNT, IRVING, WAITE, BRODERICK, OWEN
Fatima and Zelica (interesting young Ladies, Daughters of Achmet) Misses OWEN and DE CLIFFORD
Queen of the Peri........Miss MILNER
Peris Misses LEIGH, POULSONS, C. BROCK, B. BROCK and F. BROCK, &c.

In the Course of the Burlesque the following SONGS, &c., &c.:—

SONG—"The Lop-necked Jar,"........Mr ALFRED DAVIS.
SONG—"'Tis a Place of Beauty rare,"........Mr ALFRED DAVIS.
CHORUS—"Come away my pretty little Peri,"........PERIS.
SONG—"Wanted a Genius,"........Miss MARKHAM.
SONG—"The Lake of the Mountain's surprisingly deep,"........Miss MARKHAM.
DUET—"The Keel Row,"—Miss MARKHAM and Mr ALFRED DAVIS.
CHORUS—"Here you see a wretched Set,"........COOKS.
SONG—"Pray Daddy, pray put bye your Sword,"........M. OWEN.
SONG and CHORUS—"The Sultan comes down,"........COOKS.
CHORUS—"Get along Black Man,"........THE FISHERS.
CHORUS—"Trip, trip,"........CHARACTERS.
DUET & CHORUS—"Spread out our Tents, my Boys,"........CHARACTERS.
SONG—"On the Lake's Green Banks,"........Miss MARKHAM.
SONG—"On yonder Rocks reclining,"........Miss MARKHAM.
SONG—"Rise from the Waves,"........Miss MARKHAM.
FINALE—"Great as the Crown of all our Wishes,"
Miss MARKHAM and CHORUS.

IN THE COURSE OF THE BURLESQUE,

DANCING BY THE VIENNOISE SISTERS.

THE ARGUMENT.

Do you know the argument of this play? | They do but jest!—POISON in jest!!!
From Shakspeare. [A long way—P. D.

1.—How the Peri puzzled their Peri-craniums about a subject, and what an effort of Genius it required to find one.
2.—How Hassan got into a mess with the Genie, and how he ingeniously got out of it.
3.—How Hassan and his Master fished in the Enchanted Lake, and what were the net proceeds of the nett proceeding.
4.—How the Sultan bought the fish, and how the Cook was embroiled by frying them, together with other matters only related in this history.
5.—How the Sultan and Court watched in the kitchen, and how the fish showed themselves no common soles.
6.—How the Sultan and Court went a wild-goose chase in the wilderness, and the Mirage they saw there.
7.—How the two Princes were roused from their mesmeric trance, and how the Black Enchanter took up his abode in rather narrow quarters than he liked.
8.—How Omar disenchanted the Lake, and what a splendid finale it made.

TUESDAY EVENING, Sept. 30, 1856

The Performances will commence with Sir E. L. Bulwer's celebrated Play of the

LADY OF LYONS!

Claude Melnotte........Mr. COWPER
Mons. Deschapelles........Mr. MASTERS Beauseant........Mr. ORVELL
Colonel (afterwards Gen. Damas)........Mr. ALFRED DAVIS
Glavis........Mr. S. JOHNSON Gaspard........Mr. COURTENAY
Landlord........Mr. FOOTE Servant........Mr. THOMSON
1st Officer........Mr. BRUNT 2nd Officer......Mr. IRVING 3rd Officer......Mr. F. OWEN
Pauline (the Lady of Lyons)........Miss ADELAIDE BOWERING
Widow Melnotte........Miss AGNES MARKHAM
Marion........Miss LEIGH Janet........Miss MILNER
Madame Deschapelles........Mrs. DAVIS

To conclude with the celebrated Burletta written expressly for Mr. DAVIS, entitled

THE ENCHANTED LAKE!

CHARACTERS AS BEFORE.

WEDNESDAY EVENING, OCT. 1.

The Performances will commence with Sir E. L. BULWER'S beautiful Play of

RICHELIEU!

CHARACTERS AS BEFORE.

To conclude with the New and Laughable Farce, called

THAT BLESSED BABY!

Mr. Frank Finnicke........Mr. COURTENAY John Thomas........Mr. S. JOHNSON
First Policeman........Mr. GIBSON Second do........Mr. OWEN
Mrs. Lever........Miss DE CLIFFORD Mary Jane........Miss AGNES MARKHAM

☞ A Numerous and Efficient Orchestra will be provided.

THE PRICES OF ADMISSION WILL BE TO

Private Boxes and Orchestra Stalls....3s. 6d. | Pit........1s. Second Price,........6d.
Second Price,........2s. 6d. | Gallery,........6d.
Centre Boxes,........2s. Second Price,......1s. | Second Price,........3d.

Second Prices to commence as near Nine o'clock as the termination of an Act will allow.

REFRESHMENTS OF FIRST QUALITY will be provided at the most Reasonable Charges.
RETIRING ROOMS and other Accommodations will be found attached to the various parts of the Theatre.

☞ On THURSDAY will be Performed Shakspeare's beautiful Play, THE MERCHANT OF VENICE.
SHYLOCK - - - - - MR. T. MEAD.

Performances to commence at 7 o'clock precisely, and to terminate as nearly as possible at a quarter before 11.

STAGE MANAGER · MR. ALFRED DAVIS

Play-bill for *Richelieu* at the Royal Lyceum Theatre, Sunderland, with Henry Irving as Gaston, Duke of Orleans

53

Saint Joan

When Shaw chose to write about Saint Joan, he took a theme—suggested to him by Mrs Shaw—that to a romantic would have meant heroics, fanfares, the pageantry of conquest, court, and Coronation, and a tremendous melodramatic to-do round the stake at Rouen. The first audiences found, not unexpectedly, that there was nothing conventional. Joan, devoid of the more obvious theatrical blazonry, was a country girl with a country accent ('Where be Dauphin?'). True, there were moments and speeches unlooked-for, the changing of the wind on the silver Loire, the voices in the Cathedral bells; but instead of the Coronation, Shaw went straight to the ambulatory at Rheims, when all the pomps had passed, and instead of the stake in Rouen market-place supplied that extraordinary epilogue on a restless midnight of summer lightning in the year 1456. Here the ages kissed and commingled in the bedchamber of Charles VII; and Joan, the Venerable and Blessed, had the play's last word, 'O God that madest this beautiful earth, when will it be ready to receive Thy saints? How long, O Lord, how long?'

The New York Theatre Guild staged the play first, at the Garrick, New York, on 28 December 1923; it ran for 214 performances with Winifred Lenihan as Joan. In London Mary Moore and Sybil Thorndike presented it at the New Theatre on 26 March 1924; a run of 244 performances. There have been several revivals. Dame Sybil is always regarded as the definitive Joan, pillar of faith and fire; others who have acted the part in London include Ludmilla Pitoëff, Mary Newcombe, Constance Cummings (Streatham Hill, 1939, soon after the outbreak of war), Ann Casson (King's, Hammersmith),

Celia Johnson, Siobhan McKenna, Barbara Jefford, Joan Plowright, and Angela Pleasence. Dorothy Holmes-Gore played the part in the first touring company. Wendy Hiller and Elisabeth Bergner each appeared as Joan during the Malvern Festivals in the 1930s. The list of revivals is long (a collector's prize would have been Jean Forbes-Robertson at the Theatre Royal, Brighton, in 1936). Katharine Cornell was an American Joan.

The principal players in the New Theatre cast of 1924 were: Joan, Sybil Thorndike; the Dauphin, Ernest Thesiger; Dunois, Robert Horton (his Page was Jack Hawkins); Richard de Beauchamp, Earl of Warwick, E. Lyall Swete; Chaplain de Stogumber, Lewis Casson; the Inquisitor, O. B. Clarence; Brother Martin, Lawrence Anderson. The play should always be referred to as *Saint Joan* (not in the shortened form, 'St').

Here is James Agate's review from *The Contemporary Theatre 1924*.

The thing to do with a new work by Mr Shaw—and, indeed, with any new work—is to find out its particular quality of interest, enlightenment, ecstasy, and provocation, to discover the exact kind and degree of emotion which that particular work, and not some other, contains. The point is to get at an author's meaning, and not to attempt to discover corroboration of your own conceptions. What like is Mr Shaw's 'Joan'? For the moment nobody else's matters. You are not to find yourself aggrieved because her memorialist has not seen fit to bathe his subject in the sentimental mysticism of M. Anatole France, or to make her the central figure of some romantic melodrama, all gilt armour and mellifluence, unfurling her replies to her judges in words silken as the banner of France. Incidentally, if ever you saw Sarah's Maid, half angel and half bird—who, to the charge of being a witch, retorted, 'Si je l'étais, je ser-r-r-ais déjâ loin!' with a gentleness and ineffability unknown to celestial choir or cooing dove—incidentally, if you remembered this most pathetic impersonation, the thing to do was to forget it and put it out of your consciousness altogether.

You are not, I suggest, to 'worrit' because in the play Joan is not really the principal personage, nor yet because the play does not pan out quite as you would have it. Let me admit that it is a trifle disconcerting to see Joan plunged at the rising of the curtain into so very much the middle of things, ordering a noble lord about as though she were one of Mr Arnold Bennett's 'managing' young women. It would have been pleasant and romantic to find Joan tending sheep in her native fields of Domremy, hearing her 'voices', and rejecting some loutish suit. It is, to the conservative playgoer, distressing to have no glimpse of the coronation in Rheims cathedral—what a 'set' they would have made of it in the old Lyceum days!—and to be fobbed off with the less important cloisters, and what for a time looks like mere desultory chatter. But I must not waste space in describing what the play is not, but rather try to make plain what it is.

Saint Joan seems to me—and I stand open to any amount of correction—to be a history of privilege. It is in seven scenes. The first merely sets the play going in so far as it establishes the immaculacy and immunity of the Maid, and provides her with armour, horses, men, and means of access to the Dauphin. The second scene shows her conquest of the Court. Let me say here, since I may not have space later on, that the Dauphin was beautifully played by Mr Thesiger, who showed beneath his astonishing grotesquerie the pity and pathos of all weakness. It is during this scene that Mr Shaw strikes one of his very few false notes. Joan is challenged: 'You tell us that Saint Catharine and Saint Margaret talk to you every day?' 'They do!' comes the retort. 'Through your imagination?' they suggest to her, and she replies, 'That is the way God talks to us.' Now Joan never said that and never believed it. If I am wrong, and if she would have admitted this, then we must deem her to have been five hundred years in advance of her time. Similarly, an Archbishop who defines a miracle as 'an event which creates faith', in contradistinction to a supernatural happening which has to be believed whether you like it or not—such a cleric has read rather more Herbert Spencer than is good for, or probable in, a fifteenth-century divine. The third scene shows a miracle—the change of wind—happening before Joan prays for it, which seems to indicate that Mr Shaw would have belief follow in the wake of reason. But I would not be dogmatic here. Throughout the play the author is at his old trick of what in music I think they call 'overtones'. Simpler, perhaps, to say that he runs two hares at once, and that the value which accrues when old speeches are informed with present-day meaning must obviously be at some cost of authenticity.

The real play begins with the fourth scene, in which the Bishop of Beauvais, the Earl of Warwick, and Chaplain de Stogumber assemble round a table and 'get down to it'. The English peer wants Joan burned, not so much because her continued prestige is a danger to English arms, but because, by going direct to the Dauphin and not through the intermediacy of the Court, she has struck at the very existence, and reason for being, of the peerage. The Bishop wants Joan burned because she pretends to the ear of God by ways other than through his Ministers. This scene is enormously long; we lose sight of Joan;

and there is danger, as the trio review the whole field of religion and politics from 1429 to the present day, and we sit and hope in vain that each fresh turn in the argument will be the last—there is danger, I repeat, of both physical and intellectual cramp. Will Mr Shaw never learn to distinguish between length and significance? Cut this scene in two and you double its meaning; quarter it and you quadruple its effect. One was so weary of the flood of talk that the ensuing colloquy in the Cathedral hardly got the attention it deserved. There was great pathos in the repeated warnings of Archbishop, General, and King that not one prayer, man, or louis would be expended on Joan's salvation, should she fall into enemy hands. Joan had her second opportunity here, and her passage comparing the loneliness of the human soul with the loneliness of God was immensely fine.

After the much-needed interval came the Trial scene in the Hall at Rouen. In an author's note on the programme, Mr Shaw states that Joan's confessions, recantation, relapse, and execution, which actually occupied several days, on the stage occupy forty minutes. This is inaccurate. The scene lasts forty minutes, but for the first half of it Joan is still in her cell, and the time is taken up with an exhaustive and exhausting disquisition on heresy. It may be true that all evil begins in good, but the lecture, or so much of it, held up the action and ultimately became a weariness. However good the cackle—and it *was* good—one was conscious of a growing impatience for the 'osses. The trial and all that followed was masterly. When Warwick entered, called for attendants, and received no answer, the silence betokening that all that little world had gone to the burning, you realised that the theatre was being put to its proper purpose. And this was reinforced when Stogumber rushed in with the horror of the accomplished martyrdom written on his face, its terror quaking in his voice, his whole soul shaking with the sudden realisation of cruelty. There was another sermon here—one-tenth the length of the others and ten times more effective.

The play then draws rapidly to what ought to be its close. Warwick ascertains from the executioner that not a nail, not a hair, not a vestige which might become a relic remains. The legend of Joan is destroyed. But the priest who held the Cross before her dying eyes avows that it has just begun. 'I wonder!' says the English murderer as the curtain falls. This should have been the end. There is a faintly jovial, quasi-satirical, and wholly unnecessary epilogue, conceived in a vain of lesser exaltation. Mr Shaw excuses this on the ground that without it the play could be 'only a sensational tale of a girl who was burnt'. Do not believe it; Mr Shaw does himself injustice here. There is not an ounce of sensation anywhere in the piece, and the epilogue is implicit in all that has gone before. It is the greatest compliment to this play to say that at its tragic climax every eye was dry, so overwhelmingly had its philosophic import mastered sentiment. None in the audience would have saved Joan, even if he could.

The production was beyond any praise of mine. The scenery, designed by Mr Charles Ricketts, was neither frankly representational nor uncompromisingly expressionistic, but a happy blend of the two. The dresses made a kind of music in the air, and at the end Joan was allowed to stand for a moment in all that ecstasy of tinsel and blue in which French image-makers enshrine her memory. As Joan Miss Thorndike had three admirable moments: when she said 'They do!', when she listened in the Ambulatory to the pronouncement of desertion to come, and when she listened to the reading of her recantation. May I beseech Mr Shaw to allow her to drop the dialect? Whatever the quality of Lorraine peasant-speech, it cannot have been Lancashire, and there was too much the smack of Oldham about such sentences as 'Ah call that muck!' and 'Th'art not King yet, lad; th'art nobbut t'Dauphin!' Apart from these eccentricities, which were not of the actress's seeking, Joan was excellent—boyish, brusque, inspired, exalted, mannerless, tactless, and obviously, once she had served her turn, a nuisance to everybody. The part is one which no actress who is leading lady only and not artist would look at. But Miss Thorndike is a noble artist, and did nobly.

It is in keeping with the spirit of the play that the character which remains most with me is not Joan. Since Thursday I find myself thinking continually of Mr Lyall Swete's Warwick, who was the materialistic fox of the Middle Ages come to life, and of Mr O B Clarence's Inquisitor, about whose silver serenity there was real awe, and whose long speech was a very notable performance. Mr Casson, in his outburst on cruelty, gave one more proof of those talents as to which he is altogether too modest; and there should be good words for Messrs Robert Horton, Eugene Leahy, Lawrence Anderson (very sincere and moving as Joan's comforter), Victor Lewisohn, Milton Rosmer, Bruce Winston, Raymond Massey, and Shayle Gardner.

James Agate

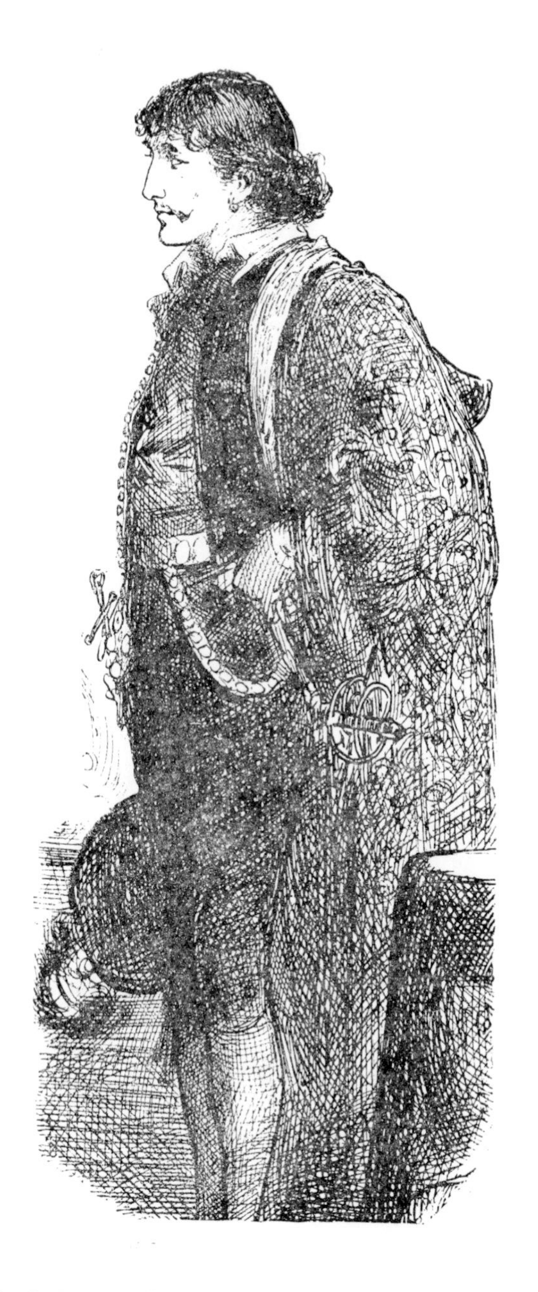

Sketch of Henry Irving as Iago at the Lyceum Theatre, London

54

Sydney Morgan

Sydney Morgan, the Irish actor (1885–1931) could have had no richer tribute when he died than this essay by Ivor Brown (a Scot) which appeared first in the *Week-End Review*. Ivor Brown, who wrote on the theatre for the then *Manchester Guardian* (1919–35) and for *The Observer* (1928–54), was the sagest and most respected drama critic of his time. He had, too, six splendid years as Editor of *The Observer* (1942–8) when he gave his personality to every page of the paper. He has a passion for words, their derivations and their shades of meaning; and he detests all forms of jargon. He has written an enduring sequence of 'Word-books' besides very much else: for example, the best modern biography of *Shakespeare* (1949); a satire, *Master Sanguine* (1934); and his autobiography, *The Way of My World* (1954).

Plays named here are three by Sean O'Casey (1880–1964), *The Shadow of a Gunman* (1923), *Juno and the Paycock* (1924), *The Plough and the Stars* (1926); *Birthright* by T. C. Murray (1910); *The Silver Box* by John Galsworthy (1906); *The New Gossoon* by George Shiels (1930). Personages are Arthur Sinclair (1883–1951), Fred O'Donovan (1889–1952), and Barry Fitzgerald (1888–1961), actors; and the brothers Fay, Frank (1870–1931) and William George (1872–1949), actors and producers.

There was inadequate tribute to Sydney Morgan, Irish actor, who died in London at the age of forty-six.

He was not a top-liner of the troupe, to use, perhaps unfairly, the idiom of that starring system against which the Irish Players did once put up a fight. I suppose that you must be a top-liner to lay a strong posthumous grasp on the graveyard columns of the Press, whose mortuary editors must accept conventional values of space for fame. In matter of rank Morgan was second player, while Arthur Sinclair and, later, Barry Fitzgerald were first clowns. But if ever the rank was but the guinea stamp this was the case. Morgan was a first-rater. I never saw him spoil a part or impede the play for the privy delight of an unchartered flourish or uncovenanted 'laugh'. Sinclair, an obvious genius, is always capable of bubbling over with that which is not in his part. I watched him so clowning in *The Shadow of a Gunman* as to destroy the end of the play. Morgan never obtruded. He may have had his personal resentments. It is the way of all artists, particularly of those who are always Horatio and never Hamlet, to murmur bitterly beneath the scorpions of the world's inequity. But whatever Morgan may have felt, he always appeared the good ally on the stage. In the big O'Casey plays he was Joxer to Sinclair's Paycock and the Young Covey to Sinclair's Fluther Good, grand performances both in parts that were largely 'feeds', adding to the already substantial deposits of 'fat' upon his colleague's platter.

Morgan is not often an Irish name, and one did not think of the square head on the shambling frame as essentially Irish or even Celtic. O'Donovan, with the tall skull and the long, flickering nose, was to me the typical Gael of the party, as far as physiology went. Nor had Morgan the full trick of the lilting cadence and of the sentences that run up hill to their lyrical climax or their comic point, singing as they run. He had a deeper, huskier register than was common in the company, but the flow of his speech was copious, vehement, and varied. It was a liquid, gurgling voice with a head on it. 'Give us a glass o'malt for God's sake' continually did cry The Covey, that thirsty hammer of the 'Boorzwawzee'. Sydney Morgan's voice, as he spoke of this bitter need, welled up like a pint of Guinness through a beer-engine, rich, dark, and syrupy beneath its crust of froth.

Morgan had twenty-three years of it. I remember him first as Bat Morrissey in *Birthright*. It was more than twenty years ago, and it was my first view of the Irish Players. There were things to be discovered in those days. The Manchester Gaiety Company were carrying *The Silver Box* in their luggage. The theatre was shedding its frippery and playgoing had become as homelike as a wet Sunday, with the family fractious. It was a glorious change for serious young people, whose appetite for drab delights had been cockered up by the Shavian slamming of the romantic theatre. Then came the Irishmen, so alien, so curious, so overwhelming in attack, now riding majestically into seas of tragedy, now turning ploughboys' banter to a madrigal. There is a fight of two brothers at the end of *Birthright*, and the combatants flew at each other as though blood were their argument in every particle of brain and body. Of course, one had heard all about conflict on the stage and seen much perfunctory brawling. But here, suddenly, was the reality of rancour. I can see it still, the very ecstasy of hate.

What was so strange about the Irish players was the speed of the accomplishment. There is one school of stage-mastery which talks ever of patience; one reads of Stanislavsky's infinite broodings on a play, his incessant rehearsals; the Moscow Art Theatre won by waiting, year after year. One is told, too, how Irving had played 429 parts before he really began. But the Irishmen, mostly starting as amateurs who turned drama into an evening's job, went slap into the fullness of achievement. When I first saw Sydney Morgan he had been an actor but a short time. He acted raw farmers and corner-boys to perfection; he himself was never raw. Much was due to the Brothers Fay, who founded that school of speech and of strong, clear, presentation. Sincerity alone never made an actor. The Irishmen had to learn the tricks; but they seemed to learn, by some happy magic, the chief trick of all, which is to leave out all the wrong tricks.

Great stress was laid at first on the group spirit; that sort of idealism is always showing its courageous head in the advanced, rebellious theatre. It usually withdraws its head under the bludgeoning of events. A little mundane success and out pop the stars. Leadership, supremacy, egotism, pride, or vanity—call the emergent impulse what you will—are inevitable in the theatre, whose glamour is a natural magnet to the exhibitionist. We needs must love the highest when we see it; isolation is the reward of merit; the great droll cannot top the bill without the power to climb; but we should acknowledge the men who stand on the rung below, year after year, filling the corner, composing the star-centred picture of the stage. If the Paycock and Fluther were the planets of the O'Casey plays, Joxer and The Covey were not satellites only; they were mighty in themselves, and I shall remember for ever the angular slouch, the dragging walk, and the whole apparatus of a lean yet sensual squalor which moved in the broken boots of the actor who played these parts. So surely did Sydney Morgan work himself into the essence of these crapulous corner-boys that you felt that not the boots only, but the entire creature was held together by bits of string and by such welding and cohesive power as a glass of malt can exercise upon a thing of rags and patches. Sinclair's rascal-parts were the full-blown bladders of a taproom knavery; Morgan's were the wry starvelings of the game. They dripped no fatness and larded no gutter. They were less largely droll than Sinclair's, but more actual, more terrible in their harsh and absolute rejection of the humbug which is so theatrically picturesque as to be endearing and refreshing.

His last part in London was, I think, in *The New Gossoon* by Mr George Shiels. The play did not last. But Sydney Morgan, now second to Barry Fitzgerald, came as near as might be to outplaying his leader; he rarely had the showy parts, and in this case his rôle was the quiet matter of a patient suitor, too slow for action and too shy for speech. It was done with a rare beauty; the acting had a canine, fawning, tail-wagging quietude as the faithful peasant spanieled his lady at heels and showed the strained eye of the dumb friend's adoration. Fitzgerald is a magnificent comedian, and he was carrying on the humours of roguery in the good old way. But Morgan, second player, was first in the discerning eye.

Let us now praise second players. The stage, with its bright personal triumphs, is often unkind to them. They are not the 'darrlins', as Joxer would have said. But they are the pillars of the stage more often than common judgment will allow, and it is the pleasure as well as the duty of criticism to redress the balance of celebrity so absurdly tilted by the machinery of 'featuring'. The paycock side of the game is not for second players. The plough is their symbol, while the stars shine for others. Morgan, plodding the furrows of 150 parts, touched nothing which he did not fertilise. He is remembered.

Ivor Brown

Since the completion of *Theatre Bedside Book*, Ivor Brown (1891–1974) has died at Hampstead. We can say of him, as he said of Sydney Morgan: 'He is remembered.' I.B. was a noble figure of his day. Time will establish his pre-eminence in English drama criticism; all else apart, he was a man who gave to words 'a new meaning and magic'.

Herbert Beerbohm Tree as Svengali in *Trilby*

55

Lord of Misrule

This century no other writer of English farce, that most difficult medium, has matched Ben Travers (b1886), our triumphant Lord of Misrule. We think of him first for what became known as the 'Aldwych farces' of 1925–33, listed now—and beginning with *A Cuckoo in the Nest*—in a passage from his autobiography, *Vale of Laughter* (1957). But before the Aldwych he had had a packed life. He reached the theatre relatively late, and the forty and more years after the Aldwych brought another range of farces—one of the best, *Banana Ridge*, in 1938. As far on as 1968 he showed in *Corker's End* (Yvonne Arnaud, Guildford) that his technique remained certain and his sense of fun inimitable. Always his characters are recognisable human types, firmly and endearingly established before they take off into the upper air.

The plays, with their flow of lyric, crumble-top nonsense, have that quality so alarming to the Shakespearian Duke. 'Why, what an intricate impeach is this? . . . I think you all are mated or stark mad.' One of my favourites from the Tribe of Ben is *Thark* (1927). After the butler at the haunted house has confided that his name is not Jones but Death (thunder and lightning here), he brings the last post, tells the visiting manservant that he will follow with the sheets, and asks the guests when they would like their call. As I wrote once, imagine the sepulchral dining-room of Thark, the storm outside, Ralph Lynn (of the Aldwych) quivering like a monocled mayfly, his partner (Tom Walls) like an apprehensive walrus, Jones-Death with a double-demon scowl, the complexities of the plot behind them, and the haunted bedroom waiting upstairs: this way to the tomb.

But back now to the beginning; a partnership created.

. . . During the next nine years I wrote nine of the eleven farces produced at the Aldwych. I supplied six in a row; then, in the autumn of 1930, Tom Walls had a dispute with Golding Bright which led to a temporary breach, though dispute is hardly a possible description of any fracas in which Golding Bright was one of the parties concerned. I returned to provide two more and then, after another lapse of a few months, the final farce to round off the series. My complete Aldwych tally during this whole period reads:

Name of Play	Produced	Number of Performances
A Cuckoo in the Nest	22 July 1925	376
Rookery Nook	30 June 1926	409
Thark	4 July 1927	401
Plunder	26 June 1928	344
A Cup of Kindness	7 May 1929	291
A Night Like This	18 February 1930	268
Turkey Time	26 May 1931	263
Dirty Work	7 March 1932	195
A Bit of a Test	30 January 1933	142

Tom Walls did not appear in the last two. If truth be told he did not appear at a good many performances of the others.

Rehearsals of the *Cuckoo*, which began five days after I had first met Tom Walls, gave me my first experience of some of his singular methods as actor-producer. For the first two of the three-weeks rehearsal he sat and directed the rest of the company, including his understudy. At the beginning of the third week he resigned himself, with a groan of effort, to participation in the acting. But during the past fortnight he had, of course, been much too busy to study his lines; and when the play started out on its one week's probation at some provincial theatre his performance was liable to hiatus. This didn't embarrass him at all. He would cross to the prompt corner and rally the dithering stage-manager with a rasping and resounding aside—'Come on, Bobbie—let's have it, can't you?' He had no compunction or shame about this. He took a contemptuous view of audiences at the best of times. But it is only fair to say that on first nights in London he was not only word-perfect but gave what was probably his best performance of the entire run of a play. 'In every play there's only one show that really matters,' he used to say; a candid admission of his cynical outlook on the whole concern. But he never hesitated to be candid about himself when he chose to be; just as he was always ready to see the funny side of his own mistakes and discomfitures.

Another of his peculiar practices was to ignore the third act completely until the last week of rehearsals. In the case of the *Cuckoo* this resulted in the most distressing ordeal for me. By the end of the second week the first and second acts had been cut, re-invented, transcribed, gagged and generally tinkered into fairly promising shape. On the Saturday—or was it the Sunday?—morning the company read through the original third act. What they read or the way they read it or both made it sound like a prolonged incantation to Gloom. I sat squirming in self-conscious anguish. The material had been in keeping with the original first two acts, but now the first two acts had been translated into Aldwych and the poor little original third seemed about as applicable as a death-knell. Tom Walls handed me a script of it. 'Go back to your room,' he said, 'and rewrite the whole bloody thing. Don't strain yourself. Thursday morning will do, so long as you get it right.'

My wife was down at Burnham with the three children who all had whooping-cough. So had I. I was lodging in a bed-sitting-room somewhere in London, and it was quite bad enough to have to spend the next fifty-four hours hard at work, and without a thought of sleep; let alone having to jump up from my chair every few minutes to pace the room, beating my chest and fighting for breath. But Tom Walls got his re-written—and in fact completely re-devised—third act by the middle of the week, and a very successful one it proved to be.

Ralph Lynn was an exception to all the others in being given a free hand in the way he acted his part. Tom Walls might occasionally criticise this but he refrained from interfering. Ralph delighted me at the very outset when we were talking together about the farce and he told me he had agreed to play in it after reading only the first act, having rejected scores of other scripts submitted to him for his opinion. His reason was that the character in the *Cuckoo* didn't try to be funny and was actuated by honest and serious motives. This won my heart at once. Here was somebody who really appreciated my theory about farce. I remember thinking at the time how mistaken I had been in suspecting that monocle.

And it is true that Ralph Lynn has always been funniest in characters impelled by the most earnest and striving motives; and it goes without saying that these characters must be the victims of embroilment or menace. I have never seen or heard of any actor with so instinctive and unerring a gift for timing; and in writing of him I have always exploited another distinctive and inimitable feature of his, the throw-away line; or perhaps what, in his case, would more aptly be called the give-away line. He makes a deliberate, unfunny, definite and convincing declaration; then, unable to contain his self-satisfaction, he ruins its whole effect by some ill-considered afterthought.

He has always relied to a great degree on instinct and impromptu, taking the form of a sudden whim during any one performance, momentary and almost unintentional. Often in the course of our long years together I have looked into his dressing-room after a show and said, 'That was a lovely piece of business tonight in the second act. Don't forget to keep it in.' And he has asked blankly, 'Why, what did I do?' The bit of business or the extraneous remark may not always have been so lovely, but he has only to be told that it was out of character for him to spurn it with remorse and shame. When before I became acclimatised to the Aldwych, I sat at rehearsals of the *Cuckoo*, racked with suspense and whooping-cough, I listened to Ralph's interpolations with aversion. Some, admittedly, were good; but I felt uneasy about taking the nominal responsibility for a line like this: when having written a false name in the inn visitors' book, his entry is inspected by the puritanical landlady:

> 'You don't write very clear.'
> 'No, I've just had some very thick soup.'

I gently protested but Ralph said he'd like to try it, and it always got a big laugh. And after all it's exactly the sort of thing Ralph himself would have said in the circumstances.

A Cuckoo in the Nest was topical in a way. It was a comment, in very jaunty form, on the contemporary state of the divorce laws. It had always been taken for granted that any unmarried couple who spent a night together in an hotel must, incontestably, be guilty of adultery; as in most cases no doubt they were. But at this time divorce judges were beginning to get rather restive and inclined to hanker after some pretty solid evidence. I thought it might be a good idea to show a couple fortuitously separated from their respective spouses and compelled by circumstances to spend a completely blameless night together not only in the same inn but in the same bedroom. And a good idea it was, though little did I foresee—in my pitiable moments of diffidence before my first meeting with Tom Walls—that the essential absurdity of the situation could not possibly be better brought out than by having Ralph Lynn and Yvonne Arnaud as the joint occupants of my bedroom.

The credit for getting them there must go entirely to Tom Walls. He had an extraordinary gift for sensing the potentialities. I think he must have persuaded, or perhaps even bluffed, Yvonne Arnaud into accepting her part in the *Cuckoo* on the strength of her successful association with Ralph in *Tons of Money*; for it wasn't worthy of her. But the fact that she was little better than a picturesque foil for Ralph never seemed to occur to anybody, and if any tribute were needed to Yvonne Arnaud's abilities this in itself would seem to suffice. But tribute should also be paid to Tom Walls's perception of how immensely valuable her very presence and personality would be to the scene.

All she had to do was to sit up in bed, looking very attractive in the midst of her primitive and forbidding surroundings, and complacently to read a book, while Ralph wandered about, irresolute and woebegone, with a blanket and a pillow. Nobody but Yvonne Arnaud could have conveyed so perfectly the sheer impossibility of there being anything morally wrong in the situation and at the same time her mischievous amusement at their joint dilemma. And yet almost every line she was given to speak was a feed line:

> 'My husband hasn't got a nasty mind. Has your wife got a nasty mind?'—'No, but she's got a nasty mother.'
>
> 'To any decent-minded person there's nothing wrong in your sleeping on the floor of my bedroom, is there?'—'No. But where's the decent-minded person?'

The Lord Chamberlain's Office expressed great concern about this bedroom scene when the script was presented for consideration. So much so that, for the only time in my experience, a special (and very inconvenient) rehearsal was called for inspection by a representative of the Censorship Department. The genial major detailed to pass final judgment did so without hesitation and almost apologetically; which was in itself a further unspoken, and perhaps unconscious, compliment to the art of Yvonne Arnaud.

The first night in London took place during a violent thunderstorm which must have upset the calculations of any Roman augurs who happened to be about; for the farce was a definite success. Tom Walls did not discard his red nose; but his glorious study of a Major of Yeomanry in decay quite justified this. He was the sort of old fellow who would have been bound to have had a red nose in real life. Mary Brough had been in *Tons of Money*, but it was her landlady in the *Cuckoo* that constituted her an indispensable member of the Aldwych team from this time onwards. She was in all nine of my Aldwych farces and had one remarkable trait. She always retained and observed the traditional but by this time archaic attitude of deference to the author when on duty. All through the nine years, once we were in the theatre she would address me as 'Sir'. I never told her not to; I knew that would be asking her to forsake her principles. It must have been Mary Brough, or someone very like her, who inspired the original use of the term 'trouper'.

She lived—the object I am sure of enormous local esteem—at Clapham. Every night during the run of the *Cuckoo* she used to be hoisted into the sidecar of a motor bicycle and conveyed to her home by a young member of the company who was no less a person than Roger Livesey. He played Alfred, the inn barman and general factotum—another example of Tom Walls's genius for casting. I always remember Roger Livesey in one particular moment typifying the obstinate density of my home-grown Somerset chawbacon at cross-purposes with the hero's clamorous mother-in-law:

> 'Where is the landlady?'
> 'Gone to get some milk.'
> 'Where from?'
> 'From the cow.'
> 'Yes, but where is the cow?'
> 'Being milked.'
> 'Yes, but where is the cow being milked?'
> 'Wull, you knows whurr to milk a cow, don't 'ee?'

There were two others in that cast who, with Ralph Lynn and Mary Brough, appeared in all nine of the farces. One was Ralph's elder brother, Sydney Lynn, who acted under the name of Gordon James. The other was, at that time, a conscientious and punctilious little support-player named Robertson Hare.

People of middle age and upwards still sometimes talk about the Aldwych of those nine years as a landmark in theatrical history. My own memory dwells perhaps less on the plays themselves than on my association with Tom and Ralph and, beyond everything else, the participation in their laughter. Tom might be despotic and, at times, arrogant and quick to assert his position as the boss of the place, but he would no more let this interfere with his laughter than he would let it interfere with his methodical, and apparently quite innocuous, patronage of the bottle. As for Ralph, he has always had a nimbleness of wit as individual as his methods on-stage. He not only sees the ridiculous side of things; he searches for it. His first instinctive thought is to spot something funny in anything he sees or hears or reads. Usually his sallies are as unpremeditated as his stage gags; but sometimes he will remain silent and pensive for a moment or two, looking as if he were trying to work out a sum in his head and then suddenly produce some odd quip. He originated, in the course of everyday conversation with me, one very familiar joke—the one about the Elephant Old Bailey, with the disreputable-looking elephant accused giving evidence on his own behalf and, asked what he had been up to on the night of the crime, protesting, 'I can't remember.' I was always fond, too, of Ralph's bookmaker caught in a shipwreck on board a liner, running up and down the deck and shouting, 'Women and children third.' . . .

Ralph has always been tremendously painstaking about his work. He was never satisfied so long as there was a single line in any of his scenes which wasn't right. All through the run of a farce he would worry and experiment until he got the thing to his liking. In those moments there were none of the waggeries and wisecracks of his leisure hours; we were concentrating on the solemn problem of creating laughter. No one ever appreciated so well as Ralph how intensely serious is the job of being funny.

Ben Travers

56

National Theatre

Robert Speaight (b 1904) is a major classical actor; one of his favourite parts is Lear, and he created Becket in T. S. Eliot's *Murder in the Cathedral.* He is also among the most eminent biographers of his day, joining a stylist's art to a researcher's craft: his subjects have included William Poel, Hilaire Belloc, Teilhard de Chardin. Moreover, his *Shakespeare on the Stage* (1973) is definitive.

For years I have treasured his novel, *The Angel in the Mist* (1936), which offers this prophetic picture of the opening of the English National Theatre. The narrator is Captain Christopher Marlow, RN, who is back in London in the early summer of 1965 after an absence of twenty years in Kenya. He goes to the private view of the National Theatre, newly built beside the Thames, and later to the première of *Macbeth,* with Ambrose Baring, veteran drama critic of a prominent Sunday newspaper.

As we drove away in a taxi, I asked him about the National Theatre . . . By the time he had finished we had reached the site of the old Charing Cross bridge. A fine structure had taken its place, and on the farther bank where the wharves had been, stood the English National Theatre. It was a massive, concrete structure, planned on simple lines, sufficiently traditional yet fully consonant with the modern material in which it was wrought. There was a square central Tower from which floated St George's flag.

'Home Rule for Scotland has at last rid us of the Union Jack,' remarked Baring acidly. 'Our country is once more represented by a Christian and intelligible emblem.'

The clock above the principal entrance announced that it was a quarter to three, and the people were arriving in large numbers. They were a well dressed, seasonable crowd, such as you would see at any important function during the summer. I was reminded of private view day at the Royal Academy, and I wondered if they were here with the same motives.

We passed up a few steps into a lofty vestibule . . . The place seemed to me well proportioned in its modern way. There was a fountain at the farther end, presided over by a statue of David Garrick.

'Of course,' said Baring, 'they would choose Garrick rather than Kean!'

'Why?' I asked.

'Garrick was buried with the Kings in Westminster Abbey, and Kean died of drink. They were both very great actors, but Kean was the greater of the two. Kean would have broken his contract with a National Theatre in six months, and Garrick would have been its constant star. He would have been the permanent president of an infinitely mutable Committee, for he could walk with statesmen and poets without losing the theatrical touch. He had a foot in two worlds, and was certainly a snob. Besides, the facade of his marriage was fairly happy; Mrs Garrick had always seen to that. I suppose they were right to put his statue in the foyer.'

A wide stone staircase led out of the vestibule at either end, and people were ascending the one and coming down the other Congestion was relieved in this way. We went up to our right and at the top we found ourselves at the end of a circular gallery, which apparently included the whole of the auditorium. On one side of this were tall balconied windows looking on the river; on the other were oil paintings or pastel drawings of playwrights and actors famous in the English Theatre. It was a promenade and a picture gallery in one.

'They've copied this from the Burg in Vienna,' said Baring, taking a glance around him. 'It's not bad, not bad . . . Let's have a look at the pictures.'

Most of these had been given by museums and private donors, and the Garrick Club, in particular, had presented a part of its valuable collection. No name which criticism had made famous was unrepresented on the walls. Kean as Richard, Macready as Macbeth, Garrick as Lear (in a powdered wig), Phelps as Wolsey, Kemble as Coriolanus and Hamlet, Irving as Shylock, Tree as Falstaff with Ellen Terry and Madge Kendal beside him, Mrs Stirling as Juliet's nurse, all these, many of them well-known pictures, had their place in the Gallery and provoked Baring to a flood of historical anecdote. They sharpened his vitality and gave pith to his phrases. I remember that he couldn't stop laughing at John Philip Kemble nursing Yorick's skull.

'What do you imagine Kemble's acting was like?' I asked him.

'The Parthenon in trunk and hose,' he replied, and went on to speak of Mrs Siddons, whom he declared to have been the greatest classical actress of all time.

'She must have had everything that John Philip lacked,' he said. 'Her formalism was lit with fire. Her acting was subject to a rule of rhythm, intonation, and physical poise, which she would have no more dreamed of transgressing than the great Racine would have dreamed of stepping outside his Alexandrine metre. She stands before actresses of all time as the mistress and the slave of discipline. On second thoughts I think she must have transcended the normal and rather confusing categories of classical and romantic. Her genius was epic . . .'

We were making the complete circle of the gallery, and had passed the big central window which gave on to a terraced balcony. I thought how pleasant it would be to sit out there on summer evenings through the intervals. The mellow historical portraits were behind us now, and the remaining pictures were of people lately dead or recently retired. Many players that I had seen myself lived for me again in the more vivid portraiture of our time.

[*On the following night Marlow and Baring went to the National Theatre's opening performance*, Macbeth.]

A steady stream of people filed up the great staircase . . . The interior was splendid in its rich, subdued colouring and its remarkably bold design. There were only two tiers, which followed the crescent of the walls, and from which there would everywhere be a good view of the stage. The gradual slope of the ceiling was interrupted where lights were hid, whose effect was to soften the colour and enhance the dignity of the whole. There was a wide apron-stage with steps covering the orchestra. The curtain of crimson damask fell in long, straight folds from the curved arch of the proscenium and reinforced the lighter red of the carpet and the rich upholstery of the seats.

'It's very good,' said Baring, as we took our places in the fifth row of the stalls. 'It's really very good indeed. You see, it's a modern theatre with just enough concessions to an old reactionary like myself. All this red immediately warms the heart of the playgoer; you could even bring a child here. If we live long enough we may see Shakespeare matinees on Sunday afternoons, which will absolve anyone of the necessity for going to church. It will be a field-day for the understudies, and I sincerely hope a concentration camp for *The Merchant of Venice*, *The Merry Wives of Windsor*, and *The Taming of the Shrew*. But I do think they've erected a national institution where it's reasonably possible to enjoy oneself. And that's a great deal. I could even have borne a building like a church; what I was afraid of was a building like a bank. As it is, the Cupids are no longer a lantern to our eyes, and we are deprived of the adorable rococo which in my youth distinguished the real from the repertory theatre; but we have got a place which is elegant as well as imposing and where neither Racine nor Chekhov will be out of place.'

Ticket-holders were requested to be in their seats by eight-fifteen and the theatre was nearly full. The tang of expectancy was in the air. Two or three latecomers slipped into our row and occupied the seats beyond us. The doors were gently closed by liveried attendants. The lights were dimmed. Gradually the conversation died down, and when there was perfect quiet the band struck up the opening chords of the National Anthem. On a unanimous impulse and almost with a single movement the audience rose and stood erect. Then as the curtain trembled and began to rise slowly on the fourth bar we all took up the words in equal chorus to greet the King and the company on the stage.

He was a familiar figure to the majority of that audience, but it was many years since I had seen him and he fulfilled the emotion of my return. He stood behind a carved oak table with a microphone before him and a sheet of paper in one hand. He was in evening dress without decorations. On his right was the Archbishop of Canterbury in a purple cassock and cape and on his left was the Chairman of the Governing Board. Other high officials, unknown to me, stood grouped on either side.

The Archbishop read a few prayers, and when he had done he deferred to the King with a slight inclination of his head. The King then began to read in a clear and measured voice from the paper in front of him:

'Your Grace, my Lords, ladies, and gentlemen. We are gathered together in this place to do honour to a great art . . .'

The speech concluded on a note too solemn for applause. We remained standing as the curtain closed and only sat down when the orchestra began the overture to *Macbeth*. This, with the rest of the incidental music, had been composed by Arnold Bax. I remembered hearing his *Tintagel Suite* many years before, and I caught many haunting reminiscences of that earlier approach to an heroic theme. The Tintagel melodies had been a perfect evocation of their subject; they breathed the pure essence of chivalry. It was interesting, therefore, to see the extent of the musician's advance along the same lines. Perhaps I can best explain it by saying that where we had before heard the wash of the sea against the rocks, we now caught the howling of the gale. The rhythm flowed less evenly; it conveyed the surge of violent emotion. And the overture, like the beginning of the play, was ominous with impending doom . . .

I do recall the picturesque appearance of Macbeth on his first entrance. He was an actor new to me and was, if anything, a trifle young for the part, but I liked his resonant voice and proud bearing. He stood immediately apart from his surroundings, directly confronting his alternative, a victim or a conqueror of fate. When the weird sisters accosted him, he reared like a racehorse at their words. His acting showed from the start the workings of ambition on a morbid imagination and a superstitious soul. He seemed to fulfil Baring's definition of Macbeth. 'Macbeth,' he had once said to me, 'is among the aristocrats of failure. He is too credulous to be really religious, and he is too intelligent to be really simple; he is too good to be really wicked, and he is too weak to be really good; he has the sense to let his imagination run away with him but he is without the strength to prevent it from running in the wrong direction. He is tragic because he is unsuccessful.'

The full measure of the actor's realisation of the part along these lines was only later to declare itself—and I viewed the whole evening from so subjective an angle that I don't think I was able to appreciate his interpretation at its proper worth until I could see it in a retrospect illuminated by Baring's comment. I couldn't, however, fail to grasp the excellence of the stage-setting, nor to remark how closely the music between the first and second acts matched the expectancy of my mood.

The full tide of the orchestra subsided and only the violins announced the rise of the curtain on Macbeth's castle. They stated a new theme with a slow, deliberate emphasis which removed the play from the sphere of the preternatural on to a level where its action would be determined by the human will. Although its event was precipitated by the marriage of a woman's resolution and a witch's prophecy, there was in this march of the strings no hint of the mystery with which the overture had been freely coloured. It was in tune with a mind made up.

The curtain rose on a bare stage. There was no furniture of any kind. Two semicircular flights of stairs led from either side to a gallery that ran along the back and gave on to a wide arch, uncurtained and open to the night. At the foot of each staircase the head of a mythical beast adorned the banister where it curved to a finish with the wider sweep of the steps, and the gallery was protected by a balustrade. Below it were a pair of high doors embossed with barbaric ornament. These were closed. The colouring throughout was steel grey deepening to sapphire blue where the night sky was thrown on the cyclorama. There was no illumination but the moonlight streaming through the arch.

The firm melody of the strings accompanied the rise of the curtain and introduced the scene. Then, slowly, they ceased. There was a pause dense with the contained excitement of the audience. My heart knocked inside me, and my thought anticipated the ovation with which we should receive her. It seemed as if the whole assembly were making of this silence a vessel for her splendid speech. And then, to surprise us with its daring and purposely to frustrate our applause, there floated from some near corridor of the castle that for which we had been waiting. I had never heard her speak on the stage but in comparing her voice to a violin, I imagined that the years had deepened and enriched it. I told myself the harmony was fuller, the utterance more majestic and more sure. It came more clearly with every syllable, prefiguring her entrance and thrilling me with its just alliance of music and meaning. And it bore the gift of which it remains for me the inspired messenger—the Word:

'*They met me in the day of success and report says they have more in them than mortal knowledge.*'

Robert Speaight

ALDWYCH THEATRE

Proprietor - - - - - - - - - A. E. Abrahams
Licensees and Managers - - TOM WALLS & LESLIE HENSON

General Manager - - { For Tom Walls and Leslie Henson, Ltd. } **REGINALD HIGHLEY**

EVERY EVENING at 8.15

Matinees - Wednesday and Friday at 2.30

TOM WALLS and LESLIE HENSON, Ltd.

present

"A Cuckoo in the Nest"

A Misadventure in Three Acts

By BEN TRAVERS

" The Cuckoo is a bird that lays other bird's eggs in its own nest and viva voce." — Schoolboy's Essay

Characters in the order of their appearance :

Rawlins (*Maid at the Wykeham's Flat*) .. .. ENA MASON
Mrs. Bone .. .. GRACE EDWIN
Major George Bone .. .. TOM WALLS
Barbara Wykeham .. .. MADGE SAUNDERS
Gladys (*Maid at the " Stag & Hunt "*) .. .. RENE VIVIAN
Alfred (*Barman at the " Stag & Hunt "*) .. ..ROGER LIVESEY
Marguerite Hickett .. .. YVONNE ARNAUD
Peter Wykeham .. .. RALPH LYNN
Noony (*a Villager*) .. ..GORDON JAMES
Mrs. Spoker (*Landlady of the " Stag & Hunt "*) .. MARY BROUGH
Rev. Cathcart Sloley-Jones .. .. .. J. ROBERTSON HARE
Claude Hickett, M.P. .. .. HASTINGS LYNN
Chauffeur .. .. JOE GRANDE

OPERA GLASSES MAY BE HIRED FROM THE THEATRE ATTENDANTS 6d. EACH

57

O Weederdee!

Theodore Komisarjevsky (1882–1954), the Russian director, a gentle gnome who came to England first in 1919, could do more than any contemporary with the plays of Chekhov. Elsewhere, one was never sure what might happen. Though a master of lighting and decoration, he could also allow his switchboard to govern him. In English Shakespearian record he is remembered for a small group of revivals, most of them at Stratford-upon-Avon during the 1930s, the opening years of what was then the new Shakespeare Memorial Theatre. Bridges-Adams asked Komisarjevsky, as guest-director, to stage a *Merchant of Venice* in 1932: an exuberant fantastication that used all the available machinery. Later his work varied between a magnificent *King Lear* in 1936 (a variant of his Oxford production in 1927), set upon a steep flight of variously angled narrow steps; and a *Macbeth* among scrolled aluminium screens. Macbeth himself, during a long tossing nightmare, spoke most of the dialogue in the visit to the Weird Sisters (IV. i) at the pit of Acheron. A near-Viennese *Merry Wives of Windsor* (1935), with Falstaff looking like the Emperor Franz Josef, Komisarjevsky described charmingly as 'faithful in word and gesture to Shakespeare'.

There were other productions, but none so capricious as *Antony and Cleopatra* in London; it achieved four performances at the New Theatre in October 1936, six months after the Stratford *Lear*. Komisarjevsky cast as Cleopatra the engaging Russian comedienne, Eugenie Leontovich, admired for her Grand Duchess-into-parlour-maid in *Tovarich*; her English, a pleasant flicker across a tight-rope, was hardly matched to Cleopatra. Mark Antony was the rising

Shakespearian, Donald Wolfit. Round them Komisarjevsky had a fine cast that included, as the Soothsayer (a part surprisingly padded) and the Clown, a subtle classical actor, George Hayes, Stratford's Macbeth in 1933.

Though much of its acting was sound, the night proved to be calamitous. Many of the costumes were absurd (Wolfit described one of Cleopatra's as 'the scantiest draperies surmounted by a fireman's helmet adorned with large white plumes'); and there were strange fumblings with the text. I recall that Komisarjevsky deferred Philo's overture and instead opened trivially with Iras, Charmian, and the Soothsayer. The same Soothsayer roamed in from time to time, given such speeches as 'Swallows have built in Cleopatra's sails their nests', and even ' 'Tis the god Hercules, whom Antony lov'd, Now leaves him', spoken in daylight, a dire mishandling of a scene that demands the apparatus of night and mystery. Enobarbus, no grizzled veteran, was a velvety gallant who used the brocaded tones of Leon Quartermaine. Octavius, who apostrophises the absent Antony at 'Leave thy lascivious wassails!' had, absurdly, to address the lines to Antony in person.

Criticism reflected the general stupefaction. The celebrated notice that follows, with its phonetic ingenuities, appeared in *The Times*, of which Charles Morgan was then principal drama critic, on 15 October, the morning after the première.

Soothsayer .... GEORGE HAYES
Charmian .... MARGARET RAWLINGS
Iras .... ROSALIND IDEN
Alexas .... HUBERT HARBEN
Mardian .... GEOFFREY WILKINSON
Cleopatra .... EUGENIE LEONTOVICH
Antony .... DONALD WOLFIT
Eros .... JAMES CRAVEN
Enobarbus .... LEON QUARTERMAINE
Octavius Caesar ...... ELLIS IRVING
Lepidus .... VERNON KELSO
Agrippa .... EDWARD HARBEN
Octavia .... VERA POLIAKOFF
Menas .... LAWRENCE ANDERSON
Pompey .... ION SWINLEY
Captain of Caesar ..... WILLIAM MONK
Dolabella .... BASIL LANGTON
Clown .... GEORGE HAYES

Hospitality and inclination alike suggest that the least said about this travesty of Cleopatra the better; but the interests of the theatre in England must not be allowed to suffer for the susceptibilities of any actress, though she be a guest, and when a performance in a great classical part is dull, pretentious, and for the most part incomprehensible, it is necessary that criticism should say so. The part of Cleopatra was written in English and in verse; Mme Leontovich has neither. A phonetic script would be needed to describe what she makes of the great speeches, but plain lettering may serve to illustrate her difficulties.

O weederdee degarlano devar
Desolderspo lees falln: yong boisenguls
Alefelnow wimen.

Whoever, reading that once in a perpetual tremolo, can interpret it as:

O, wither'd is the garland of the war,
The soldier's pole is fall'n: young boys and girls
Are level now with men

may attend this performance in peace. Those who do not welcome the task of lightning translation will understand that when

Cleopatra was at last dead and Charmian's superb farewell broke in upon the spiritless babble of her mistress, Miss Rawlings, who has verse and voice and a flashing command, fairly swept the stage. And Charmian's is a small part. Mr Quartermaine, with more opportunity, ran away with the play. Why? Partly on his own high merit, his quickness, vitality, and humour, but also because Enobarbus stands much apart from Cleopatra and is not, like this poor Antony, everlastingly beset by her.

The same is true of Caesar, to whom Mr Ellis Irving gave uncommon liveliness and dignity. So, in lesser parts well played, Mr Anderson's Menas, Miss Poliakoff's Octavia, Mr Hayes's Soothsayer. But who plays with this Cleopatra is lost, for she is so occupied by her own vain struggle with a text which, like her fantastic skirts, is for ever getting in her way that she cannot listen to or understand anyone else, and Mr Donald Wolfit, who has the equipment of a good Antony, and proves it on occasions, finds himself, in passionate scenes with the Queen, one of two vocal islands apparently without communication.

Nor are these difficult circumstances Shakespeare's only rival. M. Komisarjevsky, doubtless in his pursuit of a 'synthetic' theatre, has decided to treat *Antony and Cleopatra* as if it were a cross between a ballet, an operetta, and a revue at the Folies Bergères. The dresses have little to recommend them but a tinsel splendour. The set is so designed that, during the opening of the monument scene, none of the players is visible from the advanced stalls. The order of the scenes has been changed—for example, Charmian and Iras open the play, presumably on the music-hall principle that the house must be 'warmed' for the star's entrance. One receives the impression that, in M. Komisarjevsky's view, nothing is so important as his lighting operations. The stage pales and darkens, smiles and gleams, glows and flashes so often and so restlessly that the whole emphasis is on the electricians. Seldom has a play been so tormented and twisted and stifled or a work of genius been so casually scorned.

The Times

58

Bergner and Barrie

Peter Bull (b 1912) is the actor and writer whose endearing autobiographical books, notably *I Know the Face, But* . . . (1959), from which this extract is taken, and *I Say, Look Here* . . . (1965), have added inimitably to the story of the theatre in our time. He acted in the original English production of Samuel Beckett's *Waiting for Godot* and his view of the piece is an amusingly astringent footnote to the current hyperbole. Here he describes the fate of *The Boy David* (His Majesty's, 1936), the last play written by Sir James Barrie and intended expressly for the Austrian actress, Elisabeth Bergner, who had so overpowering a success in Margaret Kennedy's *Escape Me Never* (1933) both in London and New York. Sir James Barrie, born in 1860, died in 1937, a few months after the withdrawal of his play. C. B. (later Sir Charles) Cochran (1873–1951) was the renowned impresario; for Theodore Komisarjevsky, see introduction to *O Weederdee!* (page 320); during most of his life Sir John Martin Harvey (1867–1944; the hyphen crept into his name) was a prominent actor-manager; Godfrey (later Sir Godfrey) Tearle (1884–1953) was an actor of uncommon distinction. Elisabeth Bergner (b 1900) played Saint Joan at Malvern in 1938 and Toinette in *The Gay Invalid* (Garrick, London, 1951). She is now living in London and made a much-applauded return to the theatre in the Hungarian dramatist Istvan Orkeny's *Catsplay* at Greenwich in 1973.

In my quota of flops, pride of place must be yielded to *The Boy David*, which played at what was then His Majesty's Theatre. It was J. M. Barrie's last play and had been written for Elisabeth Bergner, about whom the distinguished playwright was besotted, and I could not understand anything more easily. Quite apart from her enormous talent, she was the reincarnation of many a Barrie character. Her eternal youth and radiant face would have made a wonderful Peter Pan, but the Biblical David was to prove a sad mistake.

We were first scheduled to open in the spring of 1936, and Cochran, who was presenting the play, had arranged an impressive array of talent. Augustus John was to be the designer, and William Walton would compose the incidental music. To support Miss Bergner, he had engaged Godfrey Tearle, Sir John Martin-Harvey, Leon Quartermaine, Ion Swinley, and Jean Cadell. Hangovers from *Escape Me Never* (besides Mr Quartermaine) included John Boxer and myself, and the entire stage management from that piece. H. K. Ayliff, of the Birmingham Repertory Theatre, was to direct. The publicity was fantastic, and Cochran, who never believed in doing things by halves, made us rehearse behind locked doors in the wilds of Walworth in a not very converted Parish Hall. There was a general atmosphere of reverence and mystery about the whole thing that made us all whisper and creep about, which I found a bit spooky. It was all a bit mystifying, as I found on inspection that the play was totally different from the general conception as conveyed by the Press. It was principally a naïve domestic piece with little or no action, apart from the slaying of Goliath. Yet there was a dramatic power in parts of it, particularly scenes between David and Saul which showed a master's touch. But the thing as a whole lacked cohesion and the casting of Bergner as David was little short of a major tragedy. In spite of her improved English, one felt that the portrayal could not be acceptable to the British Public.

After about ten days' rehearsal, we were quite suddenly told that Miss Bergner had appendicitis and the whole production would regrettably have to be postponed indefinitely. So we all said farewell to the dear old Walworth Road and I, for one, thought we'd never meet again; but in the autumn the whole enterprise was resumed, though with a change of director. This time we had Komisarjevsky in whom Bergner had tremendous faith, and quite naturally after their triumphant partnership in *Escape Me Never*. I was pretty keen on him myself, with his wicked smile and great sense of humour. Back in the Parish Hall we found very little changed and there was still rather too much reverence about.

Sir James came down and had a poached egg on toast at the ABC, and we were all pretty frightened of him. It was not without cause, for he did not at first like the opening scene in his play as brought to life by Robert Eddison, Basil C. Langton, Eric Elliott and myself as the brothers of David. It was an almost impossible scene in which we wrangled and I made terrible jokes. My first line was 'I call the world to witness that there is a piece of flesh in Eliab's bowl,' which took the curtain up and really should have made it descend immediately, as the tentative way in which I spoke it was not likely to inspire confidence in the customers. Sir James was deeply displeased by the way we all played it, and at one period I was on the verge of being asked to leave the building, saved once again in my career by the intervention of Miss Bergner. The author's main complaint (he was a bit deaf) was that he couldn't hear his own words, so Komis told us all to speak up, and after bellowing our way through the next rehearsal in terror, it became the author's favourite scene and he made us do it very often. He couldn't quite understand what Komis was aiming at and was not, I think, a very easy author to have around the place, but for the magic and pleasure he has brought to the theatre we must never cease to be grateful.

Before leaving for our try-out in Edinburgh we had another nightmare dress parade. After the whole cast (there were many extras for the Philistine fight sequence) had trailed back and forth across the stage for several weary hours, I heard Mr Komisarjevsky exclaim in a loud voice to Mr Cochran and the author (in the stalls): 'Only one thing is clear. Bull must be clothed'; so another smelly old skin was added to my wardrobe. We were due to open at the King's Theatre, Edinburgh, on Saturday, November 21st, 1936, and we went up two days early for a couple of dress rehearsals, one of which was never finished, though we went on through the night. The advance publicity, to say nothing of the booking, was enormous, and as the Scots capital wished to honour one of its most distinguished sons, the castle was floodlit and seats were put up to twenty-one shillings for the first night. Miss Bergner, as usual, had managed to avoid the Press, and any information the latter received was at the hands of the two boys playing and understudying the part of Jonathan. One was Bobby (now Robert) Rietti and the other Kenneth Connor, now the well-known comedian. I kept quiet as a mouse in some nice digs with John Boxer and viewed the whole thing with gloom. I was not having an easy time with the Prophet Samuel with whom I had rather a lot to do in the play, mainly because Sir John Martin-Harvey would not concede that I had any name at all after six weeks of rehearsals, and though I called him 'Sir John' with great reverence, he would not speak directly to me and would merely ask Komis if 'the stout gentleman' could move a bit farther downstage. This was lowering to the morale. But both Mr Tearle and Mr Quartermaine (with whom I played picquet a good deal) were charming, and after all there was always Miss Bergner at whose feet I was still in hopeless adoration.

The Edinburgh first night was a curious experience. Although the audience was friendly and attentive, it was quite obvious that they were disappointed, and the evening seemed interminable. Barrie had decided at the last moment not to come, and there was a general air of anti-climax about it all, rather like an unsuccessful rocket-experiment. The reception at the end was lukewarm, and Judith Furse (who had assisted Komisarjevsky on the production) and I went and dined rather grandly at the Caledonian Hotel with my brother Anthony, who had turned up on business. The menu included 'Délice de Sole Elisabeth' and 'Biscuit Glacé Bergner', which I fear was a fairly accurate description of the evening. I was flabbergasted the next day to read in a Scottish gossip column that, owing to the reverence of the occasion, the company had been too over-awed to celebrate at the Caledonian except for a minor member of the company, which put me in my place.

The criticisms the next day were respectful but non-committal, and for the next fortnight we played to packed houses who saw a different show every night. We rehearsed continuously and whole scenes were omitted at some performances and then put back the next night. The part of Goliath was sometimes seen but not heard and then not seen but heard. There was an episode where Saul's Little Thoughts came to Life with some young ladies playing the title-roles, and this scene was wisely withdrawn from regular consumption. But I readily confess that there were some unforgettable things in the production and at times Elisabeth was intensely moving, and there was a pictorial piece of magic that I shall never forget. This was when, after David's fight with Goliath and a very noisy general battle scene, there was suddenly dead silence, and from way backstage a tiny figure appeared, dragging an enormous spear behind her. Komis had lit all superbly and Godfrey Tearle was magnificent as Saul. Unfortunately, after his disappearance in Act 2 there was a far too long whimsical scene between David and Jonathan, which had no tension and sent the audience away baffled and disappointed.

I think it was improved by the time we left Edinburgh and we were to open at His Majesty's Theatre on December 14th, 1936. There were reports of an unprecedented library deal and the excitement before the first night was tremendous. But although the donkey on which the Boy David made his (or her) first entrance behaved impeccably on this occasion (at Edinburgh he or she had done the lot on the first night), the waves of dislike and even hate that came wafting over the footlights were unmistakable and very frightening. I know I had never felt it before at a first night, and it was my first taste of the fickleness of public adoration. The idolisation of Elisabeth Bergner had changed overnight for no apparent reason. She was still obviously a great artist in the right setting, she had behaved with great dignity throughout, and yet suddenly the phrase 'she's always the same' became general. The terrifying thing is that she never regained her popularity in this country, and heaven knows what we have missed.

The reviews were very bad indeed and the library deal story must have been a myth, as the audiences were thin, even over the supposedly festive season. After five weeks it was announced that *The Boy David* would be withdrawn the following Saturday. As frequently happens with this sort of disaster, a stampede started at the box-office, and the mounted police were called out on the last day of all. I am sure we could have run through the spring, but Cochran had lost faith and both Bergner and Barrie were heartbroken by the play's failure. Elisabeth was quite wonderful through all this, but I fear Barrie was never the same again and he died not very long after. The play is sometimes revived, but is a sad epitaph to his life in and for the theatre.

Peter Bull

59

Gielgud as Lear

Sir John Gielgud (b 1904), that noble Shakespearian of whom Ivor Brown has said, 'He is the text incarnate', played his third King Lear when he went, for the first time, to the Memorial (later the Royal Shakespeare) Theatre at Stratford-upon-Avon in 1950. It was an extraordinary season: Angelo, Cassius, Benedick (in his own production of *Much Ado About Nothing*) and Lear. He had acted Lear previously at the Old Vic in 1931, and again (rehearsed under the eye of Harley Granville-Barker) in 1940; he would return to it at the Palace, London, in 1955.

T. C. Worsley (b 1907), whose Stratford review appeared in his collected essays, *The Fugitive Art* (1952), is one of his period's most honoured critics, a writer with a fine, independent mind and the gift of re-creation that takes immediate criticism to permanent theatre record. His principal work has been for the *New Statesman* and the *Financial Times*.

A first night is always hazardous. For if the occasion may call out from the actors that extra edge, it may equally with all its different minor accidents be enough just to turn the balance against the highest perfection, and this especially in so tremendous an undertaking as *King Lear* is. It was so at the first night at Stratford last week. In a beautifully staged production, effectively dressed in glowing colours by Mr Leslie Hurry, and well acted all round, Mr Gielgud's own performance trembled all the time on the brink of greatness but, except perhaps at the very end, kept all the time just short of it. Yet a strong conviction that this was an accident of the night rather than a fault inherent in the conception persuaded me to stay for the second performance. And I was rewarded by seeing the perfection come right through.

Oh the little more and how much it is!
And the little less and what worlds away!

The second performance differed from the first in hardly a detail of its actual movement and articulation. But in the first we were conscious of Mr Gielgud acting: we admired the grasp, the range, the subtlety, the sureness, the intellectual force, the largeness of the conception. In the second we were never left at the distance where we could merely admire. We were caught up into the play from the very start. This seemed not acting—something conscious and willed—but the actual enacting itself of events seen for the first (and only) time, into the heart of which we ourselves are led, stumbling with the old King down the steep descent.

If Mr Gielgud is the great tragic actor *par excellence* of our generation, is it not by virtue of his ability to exhibit the particular kind of simplicity that lies at the heart of passion in highly conscious, complicated personalities? Both Mr Wolfit and Sir Laurence Olivier strike harder, clearer, louder at the note of the majestic or the terrible. But they both over-simplify—for us. An actor, like any other artist, must be 'absolutely modern'. It is in the contrast with the consciousness of complication that the simplicity of pathos stabs us. It is the weight Mr Gielgud gives to the ironies, the irresolutions, the subtleties, that gives the still moments when they come their extra turn. The razed vacant ruin that his Lear holds up to us at the height of his madness is only quite deserted for a few fleeting terrible seconds. Mostly it is thronged and peopled with the shuttled echoes and images from a whole long complex human history.

Mr Gielgud's performance is such as might convert those, if there still are any, who prefer reading *Lear* to seeing it. Two scenes in particular might change their opinion since both depend primarily on the acting. The first, the little scene after he has delivered the curse on Goneril and before he moves on to Regan, when the fool is pathetically trying to distract him with his poor little jokes and Lear no less pathetically tries to play up to him. It is the shortest of scenes, in which Lear has only a few half sentences to speak. But it foreshadows all that is to follow. The first storm has come and gone; and with it has gone the look of wilful pettish arrogance—caught beautifully at the beginning in a series of apt touches like the childish nod of gratification at Regan's boast of love, or the sulky refusal even to look at Cordelia when France accepts her, and carried over to the hectic, boisterous, over-attended entrance to Goneril's palace. This look—expressing the whims that unbridled authority indulges in—has given place to an amazed and frightened half-realisation of how far he has exposed himself. A projected self-pity makes him gentle with his fool as with a dog. But in between these indulgent caresses, the follies of the last few days flash up one after the other, and are held there, each in a half-broken sentence, the last, a premonition of the future:

> *O let me not be mad, not mad, sweet heaven.*
> *Keep me in temper, I would not be mad.*

The weight that is put into this short scene carries its echoes right through the play. And to mark it deeper there is a charming little piece of business at the end (Granville Barker's, too, like so much of the rest?). When Lear for the second time asks impatiently if the horses are ready, and at last they are, the fool—to distract him out of his melancholy mood—gently nods out the chucking noise that ostlers make with their tongues, and leads him off to that. And here I should like to congratulate Mr Alan Badel on his haunted, haunting fool, the very embodiment of pathos, loyal as a mongrel, frightened as a lost child.

I have never seen the recognition scene, when Lear wakes from his long sleep and finds Cordelia at his side, so movingly played. The bewildered waking, the ghost of a voice speaking as if from some other dimension, the fall on to his knees that is half a fall from the bed, and then the stumbled pleading recognition—I should not believe that anyone, however visually imaginative, could in his study bring the tears to his own eyes as Mr Gielgud does to ours here. And beside him there is Miss Peggy Ashcroft to shed the tears for us. She has, more than any other actress, the power of touching us simply by her posture and the atmosphere she distils. The change from anxiety to a flooding relief here is beautifully done. Her 'No cause, no cause' is marvellously dropped like two reassuring tears of forgiveness and then again a shift into the feigned courtliness of her 'Will't please your highness walk?'

The acting of the whole cast, though not perfect, is worthy of the fine central performance. Miss Maxine Audley and Miss Gwen Ffrangcon-Davies are admirably contrasted as the two sisters, Miss Audley's icy whiteness freezing the air at the beginning with her 'Not only, sir, this your all licensed fool', and Miss Ffrangcon-Davies' following up with a red ferocity, at its best at the moments of violence, her own death and the putting out of Gloster's eyes. Mr Leon Quartermaine, the Gloster, was at his best here, too: elsewhere he is in the greatest danger of self-parody. I liked Mr Cruickshank's slide into the Doric for Kent, but I wish he could moderate the pace and loudness of his speaking; phlegm is the keynote of Kent. Mr Harry Andrews, perhaps a little large in proportion as poor Tom in the cave, is otherwise a telling Edgar. And others in the large cast who effectively contributed were Mr Paul Hardwick, Mr Michael Gwynn and Mr Robert Hardy.

The play is particularly well staged by Mr Gielgud and Mr

Quayle, if we make one major exception. At the beginning of the storm scene canned music disastrously competes in our ears with Lear's speeches. Let me implore them to moderate this, if they cannot bring themselves to suppress it entirely. It is a dreadful and unnecessary blot. And then the drenching rain that comes over the loud-speakers is not a good realistic touch, in view of the all too dry and altogether too unruffled appearance of the figures on the stage. (Gloster enters through the storm as if he were taking a stroll through Padua's Burlington Arcade.) This apart, the direction is strikingly sure and effective. And let me pay a tribute to the small-part players and to the skilful handling of all the varied detail of pageantry, and to the stage management generally, which is at Stratford now on a very high level.

T. C. Worsley

JOHN GIELGUD

and

GWEN FFRANGCON-DAVIES

in

RICHARD OF BORDEAUX

By GORDON DAVIOT

Produced by JOHN GIELGUD

NEW THEATRE

Licensee, HOWARD WYNDHAM   Lessees, THE WYNDHAM THEATRES, LTD.

Under the Management of HOWARD WYNDHAM and BRONSON ALBERY

Evenings, 8.15   Mats. Thur. & Sat., 2.30

Bill of John Gielgud

60

Olivier as Othello

We find Robert Speaight here, in another of his capacities, as a wise and potent drama critic. Sir Laurence Olivier's Othello became a part of theatre history at the Old Vic (then the home of the National company) on the night of 12 April 1964: very close to the four-hundredth anniversary of Shakespeare's birth. (Before this I had seen the first public performance, on 6 April, at the Alexandra Theatre, Birmingham.) Everyone will have a special memory of this Othello. I think of the third-act farewell which sounded every clarion, billowed out at 'Jove's great clamour counterfeits', and ended, as Kean's did, on a 'Farewell' lengthened and lingering, from a stricken heart. Even finer was the 'Pontic sea' where the icy current and compulsive course ne'er felt retiring ebb but raged in growing flood as the lines—unpunctuated and superbly vowelled—swelled to the Propontic and the Hellespont. Then the isolation, the yearning, the agonised recollection on those two words, 'humble love'. Again the flood beat down everything before it: 'Till that a capable and wide revenge swallow them up.'

Robert Speaight's review appeared in *The Tablet* of 30 May 1964.

For the English actor Othello is the Everest among Shakespearian parts, and until yesterday it had been scaled only by Edmund Kean. There have been interesting and honourable failures—a Czech who could not speak English and a Negro who could not speak verse—and in general we have had to look to Italy for the voltage of temperament and range of voice that the part requires. Salvini and Grasso are each a certified legend. Nevertheless Sir Laurence Olivier's triumph was always predictable, if he could deepen his lower register. He may have taken comfort in the fact that Verdi scored the part for a tenor, and in any case there is never an instant of vocal insufficiency. Voice and face alike are carefully characterised, but never to the obscuring of personality; and temperament can look after itself. I never doubted that Sir Laurence would electrify: I was less certain—from what I had read of the performance—that he would convince. I am, in theory, opposed to a negroid Othello, but it matters little whether he comes from West Africa or the West Indies provided he drew his 'life and being from men of royal siege'. Sir Laurence combines sovereignty of mien with simplicity of character—and the sovereignty is also simple. Taking a hint from Dr Leavis, he presents at the National Theatre an Othello of noble but self-deluding egotism, the seeds of whose undoing are within. The tragic grandeur of the part is in no way impaired by this conception; only Iago is reduced by it. But Iago is a small character, although the mischief he works is monstrous. Playing lucidly within the context of a sinister practical joker (a hint, here, from W. H. Auden) Mr Frank Finlay unselfishly serves the general design.

Sir Laurence has sometimes been reproached for his neglect of Shakespearian verse. I found his speaking of it—or, better, his acting of it—personal without being in the least perverse. The words are chiselled as they spring, new minted, from his mind and heart. None of the great things are lost, or even blurred, in the kind of iambic scurry to which actors who want 'to get a move on' are occasionally prone. The pace is deliberate, but never drags; and every pause has meaning. Some of these are inspired, as when Othello, in the first throes of jealousy, stumbles before the word 'love'—matching the pathos of 'Cassio hath my place' and 'O the pity of it' when he effaces himself against the wall. The earlier scenes have a leisurely and even humorous self-confidence, and the sensuality, though it is evident, is never over-stressed. (The National Theatre programmes are most intelligently composed, but we really did not need Miss Mary McCarthy to inform us that the 'final scene of *Othello* is patently sexual'.) For all its realism—the fit of epilepsy rightly appals—Sir Laurence's Othello has a refinement, a kind of spiritual lightness, a romantic gallantry, which come easily to an English actor; and if, as James Agate used to insist, an actor's quality must be judged by his success in the highest reaches of his art, then this is great acting indeed. In the years to come it will be matter for a fireside story.

There is an excellent, womanising Cassio from Mr Jacobi; Miss Joyce Redman's indignation as Emilia flames nobly in the fifth act; and Miss Maggie Smith's Desdemona, though it is cast a little against the grain, comes into its own during the later scenes. Mr Dexter's production is inventive without fussiness; but surely in Lodovico's last speech 'the object poisons sight' refers to the 'tragic loading of this bed'—not to Iago, who by then should anyway be pinioned. Miss Jocelyn Herbert's décor has a sombre spaciousness, although the Senate scene was a little cluttered; and her costumes a dusky Tintoretto magnificence.

Robert Speaight

61

'The Woman Plays'

Some of the references in this essay, which appeared in *Window on the World: the Illustrated London News Review* (1968), are to:

Plays

Caste by T. W. Robertson (1867); *The Elder Miss Blossom* by Ernest Hendrie and Metcalfe Wood (1897); *Diplomacy* by B. C. Stephenson and Clement Scott from Sardou's *Dora* (1878); *A Scrap of Paper* by J. Palgrave Simpson from the French of Sardou (1861); *The Likeness of the Night* by Mrs W. K. Clifford (1900); *The Man from Toronto* by Douglas Murray (1918); *Tilly of Bloomsbury* by 'Ian Hay' (1919); *Lord Richard in the Pantry* by Sydney Blow and Douglas Hoare (1919); *The Conquering Hero* by Allan Monkhouse (1924); *The Right to Strike* by Ernest Hutchinson (1920); *Bella Donna* by J. B. Fagan from Robert Hichens's novel (1911); *The Dark is Light Enough* by Christopher Fry (1954); *The Aspern Papers* by Michael Redgrave from Henry James's novel (1959); *The Heiress* by Ruth and Augustus Goetz from Henry James's novel (1949); *A Bill of Divorcement* by Clemence Dane (1921).

Personages

Peg (Margaret) Woffington (*c*1718–60), actress; Kitty (Catherine) Clive (1711–85), actress with Garrick; George Anne Bellamy (*c*1727–88), actress; Eliza O'Neill (1791–1872), actress (retired 1819; later Lady Becher); Marie Lloyd (1870–1922), music-hall artist; Marie

Tempest (1864–1942), actress notable for her technique in comedy; Mrs (Mary Ann) Yates (1728–87), tragic actress; Adelaide Ristori (1822–1906), Italian tragedienne; Sarah Bernhardt (1845–1923), French actress; Eleonora Duse (1858–1924), Italian tragedienne; Gabrielle-Charlotte Réjane (1857–1920), French comedienne; Mrs Warner (Mary Amelia Huddart; 1804–54), actress, notably with Macready; Adelaide Neilson (Lizzie Ann Bland, 1846–80), actress; Aphra Behn (1640–89), dramatist; Mrs Elizabeth Inchbald (1753–1821), dramatist; Shelagh Delaney (b 1939), dramatist; Sir Barry Jackson (1879–1961), theatre manager, dramatist, and founder of Birmingham Repertory Theatre; Whitford Kane (1882–1956), actor; Nance (Anne) Oldfield (1683–1730), fine actress in comedy and tragedy; Joan Littlewood (b 1914), director of Theatre Workshop; Maria Sulyok, one of the leading Hungarian actresses; Meggie Albanesi, (1899–1923) actress.

Characters

Mrs Arbuthnot in Oscar Wilde's *A Woman of No Importance* (1893); Mrs Erlynne in Wilde's *Lady Windermere's Fan* (1892); Mrs Tanqueray in Arthur Pinero's *The Second Mrs Tanqueray* (1893); Mrs Dane in Henry Arthur Jones's *Mrs Dane's Defence* (1900); Miss Moffat in Emlyn Williams's *The Corn is Green* (1938).

'Say what the theme treats on . . . and so grow to a point.' Following Bottom's advice, I see myself again in a dressing-room at a remote English repertory theatre in the 1920s. A girl is speaking. Twelve months out of school, she hovers still between assistant stage management and the weekly ingénue; she is very earnest, and she is in the theatre as a career. 'But what will it all mean in the end? Actors have the best of everything.' Probably, in discouragement, she married—among actresses there is a steady annual 'wastage'—and the curtain fell. Her question, I am sure, had been asked through the years; it is heard even now in a world apparently overflowing with entertainment and bristling with parts for actresses.

Actresses have been with us for rather more than three centuries: Anne Bracegirdle, let us say, speaking Congreve's epilogue:

> To poison plays I see some where they sit,
> Scattered, like ratsbane, up and down the pit;

Nell Gwyn, woman first, player far behind; a huddle of eighteenth century names, Peg Woffington, Kitty Clive, George Anne Bellamy; a heroine stark mad in white satin, her confidante stark mad in white linen; Mrs Jordan, with the laugh like 'sparkles of bubbling water'; Sarah Siddons, the midnight bell, who began to think in iambics, 'Beef cannot be too salt for me, my lord.' Then the nineteenth century and after: Eliza O'Neill rapt on a marble balcony; somebody else crying 'O wretched woman! lost, wreck'd, swallow'd, accursed, blasted'; Helen Faucit, infatuated ingénue into *grande dame*; Ellen Terry, born under a dancing star, but a year earlier than she knew; Madge Kendal, as stern as Ellen was mercurial; Geneviève Ward, Roman matriarch, Volumnia Victrix; Gaiety girls and champagne in the slipper; women with a past, Arbuthnot and Erlynne, Tanqueray and Dane; the Cockney voice of the Halls, Marie Lloyd following the van; Marie Tempest, steel under porcelain, at the tea-table: the progress, tragical-comical-historical, towards the modern theatre, its group of Noble Dames, and an age where at last actor and actress seem to be more fairly matched.

But are they? The record of First Actors since the Restoration runs from the tongue as easily as the names of the Five Members of the Cabal: Betterton, Garrick, John Philip Kemble, Edmund Kean, Macready, Irving, Forbes-Robertson—with our personal choice from today's stage. It is harder to name offhand the indisputable First Actresses. Bracegirdle certainly; Siddons, Ellen Terry, but how are the crevices filled, and in what order? And the major woman dramatists—where are these? Plainly it has been a man's stage. We look up 'actress' in the most celebrated choice of quotations and find Samuel Johnson's words to Garrick, 'I'll come no more behind your scenes, David; for the silk stockings and white bosoms of your actresses excite my amorous propensities.' We consult an anthology of drama criticism. Peg Woffington 'touches the tender Passions very feelingly'; Oliver Goldsmith observes that 'beauty seems a requisite qualification in an actress'; Mrs Yates grows 'rather too plump and *majestic*, for the delicate Jane Shore'. There are notes on Rachel, Ristori, Bernhardt, Duse, and Réjane; nothing for the British actress but the usual full-scale recognition of Siddons and Terry, with a word on Mrs Patrick Campbell, who was both witty in herself and the cause of wit in her critics.

'The woman plays today' said the prologue to an *Othello* version during December 1660 when presumably the first English actress appeared as Desdemona in London. But until now, relatively few legitimate actresses have been the primary attraction. 'The woman plays today.' Yes; but who is the man? 'Actors have the best of everything.'

Just after I had begun this, Lady Olivier—who is professionally Joan Plowright—regretted the lack of good parts for actresses on the modern stage. Encouraged by the National Theatre, which had cause to be conscience-pricked, she asked a group of women novelists to write one-act plays entirely for women: the best sort of feminism in an appropriate year. (None, alas, was very good.) Reviewers at the same time were debating a life of Ellen Terry, some of them saying—in the common form—

that they distrusted books on actresses, but all ready to be lured back to the lamp. We know of Ellen's charm, something that means more to an actress than Barrie's 'bloom on a woman'. She never lost it. Her author gives only a line to the night when, at 72, she played in *Romeo and Juliet*, the West End revival of 1919: 'Her memory sadly astray, she appeared as the Nurse.' Nothing else; but a critic who was there, Archibald Haddon, wrote: 'The Nurse dominated the play . . . After a memorable scene when the curtain fell on her teasing of Juliet over Romeo's message, the enchanted audience called the actress again and again, and would not be content until she had answered the call alone.'

For many historians she takes her call alone. She conquered at an hour when the actress had to be an alchemist. So had an actor; but most women were left with scenes that affect us, on reading them, as red-currant jam affected Polly in Robertson's *Caste*: 'At the first taste, sweet; and afterwards, shuddery.' T. W. Robertson, during the 1860s, tried to restore naturalism, and his actresses appreciated it.

Women, towards the end of last century, needed all the help they could get. There were selected classical parts, mainly Elizabethan and Jacobean, and some from Sheridan's day. In the 1880s and 1890s Ibsen would come, and later Shaw, each originally for the few. Between these limits players had to grab from two centuries of the hollower invention, costume romps, minor tushery. Pinero and Henry Arthur Jones did help in the 1890s. Though they repeated themselves in a set of emotional women—'The future is only the past again, entered through another gate'—the lines at least were speakable; more so than during the rest of the century when the theatre had been a home of platitude, the large, vague romantic gesture. Much of the more lavish rhetorical stuff, of a type that I heard a Cornishman call 'barnicum-bailey', went to the men; it could be an actress's task to listen. True, there were splendid names of all kinds: Eliza O'Neill, the great might-have-been, who retired so young; Vestris, the comedienne; Louisa Nisbett, Helen Faucit, Mrs Warner, Julia Glover, Ellen Tree, Adelaide Neilson (born

Lizzie Ann Bland), Marie Wilton (Bancroft). Good names, yet expressly for the specialist. It was a century of actors: Edmund Kean and Macready; the comedians, Mathews senior and junior; Charles Kean, Phelps of Sadler's Wells, Henry Irving. Outside London the stock companies and the strollers battled on. Such young men as Thackeray's Pendennis, their 'amorous propensities excited', as Johnson put it, might go again and again to see the local 'Fotheringay' as Ophelia or Mrs Haller. No doubt, wherever the Dickensian Crummles troupe went, Miss Snevellicci was admired. Still to the wider public it was a man's world. 'The woman plays today.' But what is Mr Macready giving us? . . . What is there for Mr Irving? Did not Lord Beaufoy say in Robertson's *School*: 'Some women would kill gallantry and chivalry by something called equality with men'?

Dramatists, however gallant and chivalrous, have had a way of letting men govern. Lady Olivier, anxious today for her colleagues—it is hardly coincidental that she speaks in the jubilee year of the Vote—has no help from history with its Aphra Behns, Cowleys, Inchbalds, and Centlivres. Even if they have fared a trifle better in this century, few women are natural playwrights. (What has happened to Shelagh Delaney from Salford?) The first to turn dramatist, surprisingly, was a nun, Hrotsvitha, of the Benedictine abbey of Gandersheim in Saxony during the tenth century. Though collectors have tried her work, she has not stirred the catholic repertory of the National Theatre. Even Sir Barry Jackson, who in performance enjoyed the least probable texts ('Might be sound?' he would say, flicking over the pages), seems to have forgotten Hrotsvitha and the six plays she based in technique on the pagan works of Terence, but with a purpose highly moral. One merit would please Lady Olivier. In her first play, glorifying the 'laudable chastity of Christian virgins', Hrotsvitha had plenty of women's parts, and loyally she kept this up.

Good; but whatever happened within the walls of Gandersheim, or in the mid-sixteenth century *commedia dell'arte*, or later in France, there were no actresses in England: no one comparable to, say, Flaminia or Isabella Andreini or Madeleine

Béjart, not even when a Mrs Coleman sang daringly, in recitative behind a gauze veil, the part of 'Ianthe, the Sicilian flower', from Davenant's *The Siege of Rhodes*. That was in an all-but-clandestine production during September 1656 in Rutland House, Aldersgate Street, London.

Until the closing of the theatres in 1642 for an interval of eighteen years, the boy players had ruled. They had created the women parts of Shakespeare, devised for them with so much tact; now the women themselves could take over. A male *As You Like It* at the National Theatre in 1967 was not intended to reproduce Elizabethan methods. Somebody quoted an essay by the Polish mage, Jan Kott; there was a hullabaloo in the name of experiment. But Lady Olivier may have asked, as many actresses did, why the National, having then done so few Shakespearian plays, had allowed actors to seize a comedy with one of the greatest women's parts. Why not, it was said, retaliate with a female Lear: 'Let not woman's weapons, water-drops, stain my man's cheeks!'

Minor events omitted, it is over three hundred years now since an English actress first took her proper place. The Desdemona on 8 December, 1660, in Vere Street, Clare Market, could have been Margaret Hughes. It was certainly Thomas Killigrew's company in a free version of *Othello*. The prologue announced: 'No man in gown, or page in petticoat/A woman to my knowledge . . .' Today, when the line is spoken, 'Here comes the lady; let her witness it,' we can remember that this ushered in not Desdemona alone, but all the English actresses. It was the cue for Mrs Barry, Mrs Bracegirdle ('Is't tragedy or comedy you want, Melting Almeria, flashing Millamant . . . ?'), for Nance Oldfield and Peg Woffington, everyone to the senior Dames who lead our British stage, Sybil Thorndike and Edith Evans; the future stars in their courses at RADA or the Central School; the workers backstage at the provincial Reps.

As a very young playgoer, I never thought my earliest experiences were odd: a pantomime with the principal boy a girl; a farce in which the leading man impersonated his friend's aunt;

and a classical comedy where the heroine was a boy. Sometime, indeed, any actress must be a 'boy in white silk hose', though, unlike Dickens's Miss Belvawney, she does more than stand with one leg bent and contemplate the audience. The first great actress I met was strictly feminine and off stage. For some reason Dame Madge Kendal, then well over seventy, opened a bazaar in the West Country town where I had been for three months on a local newspaper. It was a dullish suburb, tar-macadam, railway track, and doll's house architecture in equal parts; the bazaar occupied a tin hut by a tidal estuary, the tide out and the mud in. But Dame Madge, brown-furred that day and wearing an august bonnet, transformed it all, making of the hut a stage set, and using a voice that must have carried over the water to the woods beyond. She said nothing in particular, but while she was speaking, it sounded like eloquence. It was, I realise, a redoubtable study of a famous player opening a bazaar (not in any irrelevant Ruth Draper context) and glorifying a very poor part.

She had done this all her working life. I knew that nearly fifty years earlier, she had created Dora in *Diplomacy*, still not uncommon at our local Repertory Theatre, but nothing else she had played, Shakespeare apart, meant anything to 1926. *The Elder Miss Blossom*, *A Scrap of Paper*, *The Likeness of the Night*—what were these? It was enough that, though her career had ended 18 years before, she had been able to illuminate any part, lift any play. Among the theatre's few women dictators—you did not ask who would act with Madge Kendal—she was proud of her profession: a rigorous woman, bred among the provincial pomping folk, the 22nd child of her parents, and keeping to the last an uncompromising Victorianism. Madge Kendal, I feel, rarely 'captivated'; no one wrote about her as Wilde did so rapturously of Ellen Terry, a year older and also of players' stock:

> No woman Veronese looked upon
> Was half so fair as thou whom I behold . . .

Both would have had much to say to that young actress who

talked to me in her repertory dressing room, her first interview and shyly proud of it, the words tumbling out: 'But what will it all mean in the end? Actors have the best of everything . . . What am I to do if I keep off Shakespeare? Ingénues only simper, and I'm tired of parlourmaids . . . We want a really big dramatist who'll write for actresses—a woman dramatist.' To this both Dame Madge and Dame Ellen would have replied with varying degrees of emphasis, 'Take what you're given, and be glad.' Ellen would have added 'My dear'; Dame Madge, 'My girl.' That dressing-room grumble is repeated through the decades, the actress's eternal plaint. Ellen said of one of her own butter-muslin parts: 'I'm angry at having to do it—but patience!'

Like Madge Kendal, Ellen Terry had long ceased to act when I went to the play. My theatres were in a city on the extreme edge of the British stage. Beyond it was territory that, even if it had nurtured the young Irving, had been the province of the fit-up, the minor pomping folk. In my town we had a weekly-change repertory theatre, among the gallantries of the period; a resolute music-hall, an old city theatre, opened during the Regency, that took plays in a chain from 200 companies on the road; and a pair of rough-and-ready houses that used between them the melodramas of seventy years. At the big central theatre, with its Ionic portico, four levels, and deep stage, I saw the Shakespearians, the musical-comedy companies—actresses in an enclosed and demonstrative world—and carbon copies of the most recent London plays: middle period Maughams, young Cowards, earl-and-the-girl Lonsdales.

Here were the careless sophisticates, tropical sirens, sentimental hoydens, that the 1920s loved. Out at the melodrama houses, heroines would be dewy, wives suffering. One leading lady, about sixty, five feet tall, with eyes rimmed in lamp-black and a despairing seagull-voice, was indefatigable in *Mademoiselle from Armentières*, *No Mother to Guide Her*, *The Heart of a Shopgirl*, *A Woman Beyond Redemption*, *The Price She Paid*, and *Saturday Night in London*. I recognised the method on reading Whitford Kane upon a Northern actress, innocently surprised when night by night the same artificial flowers were handed up to her. These melodramas were a similar artificial bouquet. I enjoyed every preposterous occasion, especially when the company strode to the footlights, banging its speeches over to us like killers at a lawn-tennis net.

These troupers scorned our repertory theatre: it was 'highbrow', they said in inverted commas. As a rule it used about five actresses, playing in between forty and fifty productions a year, mainly from the last four decades, with *Caste* and *London Assurance* thrown in, and an eighteenth-century group—two Sheridans, one Goldsmith—islanded as 'Old Comedy'. It did a lot of Shaw, so the 'new women' parts offered some relief. Otherwise, much of the work had the now derided big-house setting, with the mistress of the house, the daughter, a guest to thicken the plot or decorate it—even Maugham must have a Mrs Shenstone in the first act of *The Circle*—and probably a maidservant or two: the young ASM was always searching for a new cap and apron. Drawing-room dramas were built to a third act climax, with a rapid fourth act to put things right. Whimsical comedy and farce came in three acts. French windows abounded; but the line, 'Anybody on for a game of tennis?' can be traced to Shaw's *Misalliance*, 1910.

Upon the tea-tray stage we had the dramas of Pinero, Jones, and Sutro, the comedies of Wilde and Hankin, R. C. Carton and Hubert Henry Davies, a Northern blast from Houghton or Brighouse, the light luggage of Milne. Now and then there would be clothes-and-the-woman comedies, a first act sparrow the peacock of the second; and the company was prepared for such amiable snobbishness as *The Man from Toronto*, *Tilly of Bloomsbury*, and *Lord Richard in the Pantry*. Pollyanna figures were intermittent. A contralto leading lady disposed of the desperately emotional parts. Some of the routine plays seemed difficult enough, though once a repertory actress had learned her words not much could trouble her.

The company did better things: the best of Shaw, capable Maugham (women were not despised there), Galsworthy's dramas shaped to 'a spire of meaning', Ernest Hutchinson's now forgotten *The Right to Strike*. Dialogue as a rule was formed and literate; actresses could not toss it away. It was on this stage that the young American, Molly Tompkins, whom Shaw admired, had her testing in repertory. I can see and hear her struggling with Lady Teazle. Her baffled director found her humourless and cold, but Shaw encouraged her: 'People who have any positive character always begin in that cold way; they go farthest in the end.' Peter Godfrey was there with Molly Veness, his wife; they went from *Beauty and the Barge* and *Oliver Twist* to the top floor of a Covent Garden warehouse to lead the day's *avant-garde* rebellion. And I recall an old actress who would wander in, dress, make up, and go on in ten minutes; she could play a ragingly comic cook, or Wilde's ghastly Mrs Arbuthnot—'A woman who wears a mask, like a thing that is a leper'—besides having a shot at all, such as it was, that lay between. Such as it was. 'Actors have the best of everything.'

That theatre has been demolished for nearly forty years. The kind of drama it fostered has been shredded in a whirlwind. Actresses—more of them than ever—have a wider range of major parts; Ibsen, Chekhov, Strindberg, Pirandello, are familiar, and the ignored classical plays are in circulation again. Consider the records, Shakespeare aside, of four famous Dames. Sybil Thorndike, among so much else, has acted Hecuba, Mrs Alving, Medea, Aase in *Peer Gynt*, Jocasta in *Oedipus Rex*; Edith Evans, Rebecca in *Rosmersholm*, the Witch of Edmonton, Arkadina, Ranevsky; Flora Robson, the Stepdaughter (*Six Characters*), Mrs Alving, Gunhild Borkman; Peggy Ashcroft, Electra, Hedda Gabler, the Duchess of Malfi, Ranevsky. These were bounties not extended to the Terrys and the Kendals. And from their contemporary theatre the old actresses had no parts so rewarding as Saint Joan, Emlyn Williams's Miss Moffat, Bridie's Lady Pitts, Fry's Countess (*The Dark Is Light Enough*), Catherine (*The Heiress*), or even Brecht's woman of Setzuan.

Women certainly have more to act, even if the avant-garde stage, as repetitive in its fashion as the tea-time plays of the Edwardians, has not been very helpful to them. Several actresses do draw the public in their own right: to *Saint Joan*, for example, which returns regularly as a show-piece: Celia Johnson, Siobhan McKenna, Barbara Jefford, Joan Plowright, Judi Dench, have all played in it since the war. Actresses generally have far more choice—of a sort. Television, the cinema, radio, have enlarged the scope of a world the Siddonses never knew. In one sense, my repertory actress was born too soon, though I doubt whether she would find the routine parts more exciting now than then—it is just another form of routine, no cap-and-apron but plenty of kitchen work. Sacrificing middle-class mothers are mum, adventuresses silent. No one remembers *Bella Donna* or *The Man from Toronto* or *The Price She Paid.* Silver teapots are tarnished, and the period's favourite tea party is in the labourer's cottage of *Roots.*

Events recur: the single part that creates a reputation. The discipline of polite West End comedy is a loss. Joan Littlewood, toughest of women directors, offers another type of rigour, the less polite discipline of improvisation. New dramatists, crying for freedom, have so far written little for an actress that will be permanent. Outside the classics, our players must still transform for themselves—just as Dame Sybil, at an early Edinburgh Festival, ennobled the tinsel of Home's ancient *Douglas.*

Given the parts, old or new, we have actresses to match them. Selection may be injustice; but we think of Dame Edith's Lady Bracknell, an animated Himalayan peak voluble in its utterances; Irene Worth, Joan Plowright, Judi Dench, Celia Johnson, Margaret Leighton, Eileen Atkins, Janet Suzman, Wendy Hiller, Elizabeth Spriggs, Pauline Jameson: names stream on. Maggie Smith (who has been a Desdemona) turned a hitherto unmarked line in *Hay Fever*, 'This haddock's disgusting!' into a catch-phrase of the period. It goes with Dame Edith's crescendo on 'A *hand*-BAG!' There we can leave our contemporaries. The best actress I know who has never had her London due is Doreen Aris, once of the Birmingham Repertory; and if I am to make a suggestion for the future, the name is Gemma Jones.

We began with a procession and we end with another. Granted the power, where in stage history would I choose to go, today's actresses and all foreign travel disallowed. (If it were permitted, I would look again for Maria Sulyok, of Budapest, as the Nurse in *Romeo and Juliet*.) No première at Gandersheim—apologies to Hrotsvitha. No flamboyant Bernhardt; no haunted Duse; no Rachel of whom Charlotte Brontë wrote in *Villette*, 'She could shine with pale grandeur and steady might; but that star verged already on its judgment day.' I must avoid, too, the mayflies of a moment; any lesser 'personality' player whose symbol is one of those very small clocks lost in a gaudy gilt sunburst.

Where then? I would ask to see Sara Allgood when she first played O'Casey's Juno; Meggie Albanesi, genius untimely dead, as the daughter in *A Bill of Divorcement* by a woman dramatist; Madge Kendal in *The Elder Miss Blossom*, a play hopelessly forgotten; Mrs Campbell, nonpareil of personality players, while she acted Paula Tanqueray's first scene, 'I love fruit when it's expensive'; Ellen Terry as Henrietta Maria; Helen Faucit preferably in *The Lady of Lyons*, with Macready as her Claude; Eliza O'Neill, myth in her own right, as Juliet. Further back, I would want to see Sarah Siddons: 'She conjures up the ghost of the character she personates, beholds it with the piercing eye of strong imagination, and embodies the phantom.'

Little else now: the sound of Dorothy Jordan's laughter; Mrs Bracegirdle's entry as Millamant, fan spread, streamers out; a word with Pepys at *The Mayden Queen* for the sake of Nell Gwyn, its Florimell. Finally, a seat among the audience that waits for Desdemona in that winter of 1660. 'This only,' says Othello, 'is the witchcraft I have used. Here comes the lady.' And upon the stage, the theatre silent and attentive, comes the first woman to use the witchcraft of the English actress, the centuries already stretching out before her, and actors (do they?) having the best of everything.

J. C. Trewin

62

Epilogue

Valeria, daughter to Maximin, having killed herself for the love of Porphyrius in *Tyrannic Love* [Dryden], when she is to be carried off by the bearers, strikes one of them a box on the ear and speaks to him thus:

> Hold! are you mad? you damned confounded dog,
> I am to rise and speak the epilogue.

W. Clark Russell